FINDING MY
FOREVER

THE BEAUMONT SERIES

THE BEAUMONT SERIES

Forever My Girl – Beaumont Series #1

My Everything – Beaumont Series #1.5

My Unexpected Forever – Beaumont Series #2

Finding My Forever – Beaumont Series #3

Finding My Way – Beaumont Series #4

12 Days of Forever – Beaumont Series #4.5

My Kind of Forever – Beaumont Series #5

Forever Our Boys - Beaumont Series #5.5

The Beaumont Boxed Set - #1

THE BEAUMONT SERIES: NEXT GENERATION

Holding Onto Forever

My Unexpected Love

Chasing My Forever

Peyton & Noah

Fighting For Our Forever

Tobacco Sunburst by Eric Heatherly

© 2012 ERIC HEATHERLY/PSYCHOBILLY MUSIC/ASCAP

MATT COOPER/DB COOPER ENT/ASCAP

Cover Designed by: Sarah Hansen at © OkayCreations.net

Photography by: Scott Hoover at ScottHooverPhotography.com

Model: Brandyn Farrell

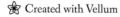 Created with Vellum

For Emily

1

JIMMY

Jimmy Davis is a womanizer #stayaway
Hung out with JD tonight #epicfail
I hate Jimmy "JD" Davis #lifelesson
4225 West's JD is so freaking hot #inlove
Call me, Jimmy #cantwaitfornextime

I hate Twitter. It's the worst thing ever invented. It's an avenue for women to slag me off every chance they get, and believe me, they're relentless. I can't quite figure out why they like to air their dirty laundry all over the Internet. Don't they realise that millions of people see what they tweet and judge them on those one hundred and forty characters? Probably not, is my guess. They're just adding fuel to the fire for the next girl who wants a bit of Jimmy "JD" Davis so she can brag to her friends.

Right now, there's only one girl I want a taste of, but she's not here, nor is she tweeting about our night together. I should take that as a sign that she's not interested, but I don't. It makes me want to have my wicked way with her again, show her exactly what I'm all about. If I didn't leave her begging for more, then my game wasn't up to par.

Sighing heavily, I turn away from the door back to the bar. The girl serving my drink winks at me, obviously thinking I'm interested because I'm looking in her direction. Sadly for her, she couldn't be further from the truth. I don't piss where I eat. The reason I've sworn off relationships has just walked into the bar. I can ignore her, but she won't ignore me. She likes to tease me, tempt me. She plays her game to remind me that she left me when I thought things were perfect.

I put my phone away and study my beer bottle. It's fascinating that the dark brown glass holding the amber liquid numbs my problems. I pick at the label in a failed attempt to look busy. I'm the prey right now, being hunted by the feminine wiles of two women. One, I'd take in a heartbeat, just to show her what she's been missing. With the other one, I'd have to be really drunk. I like this bar. A lot. I don't want to make the mistake of shitting on my own doorstep.

"Hello, Jimmy."

I close my eyes at the sound of her voice. She finds me every year on this date without fail. I know it well; it's our anniversary. So many things happened on this day. I thought I was smooth, always doing something special on the date we started going out. For the first year, I proposed. I slipped a three-carat diamond on her ring finger. The second year, after I signed my contract with 4225 West and we became famous, I bought her a house. On the third year,

I caught her in our bed with another man. Well, actually it was two men, but the shock and hurt wasn't any different. She destroyed me. Coincidentally, each event happened on the same day, our anniversary. Each year, for three years she gave me a memory I'll never forget, no matter how hard I try. God I *love* that day.

Chelsea Spencer sits down next to me. Her name alone screams money. I give her the once over, starting at her shoes—which are no doubt by some new designer I've never heard of—and work my way up her long, toned legs. I have every inch of them memorised, even when I've repeatedly tried to forget what they feel like wrapped around me. She's wearing a black and white dress and her hair is styled to perfection. She's a real life Barbie doll. Everything about her is refined. That should've been my first warning sign when we started seeing each other. Her parents hated me, but she wanted to show them she could make her own decisions and started dating the wannabe rock star. Even with my famous father and grandfather I wasn't good enough for her.

"Well, if it isn't my beautiful ex. Tell me, sweetheart, to what do I owe the pleasure? I'm guessing it's no coincidence that you're here on our anniversary? Time flies when I'm not thinking about how you tore my heart out and trampled on it repeatedly."

"Dramatic much, Jimmy?"

I shrug. "Just keeping it real, love."

Chelsea never shows emotion, at least not anymore. When we were together I made her laugh every day. Her mum told her that laughing would cause wrinkles and I told her I'd kiss each one away. Now she's some straight-laced

piece of totty who only smiles when she's paid a compliment. It's a pity really because she's so beautiful when she laughs.

She orders a white wine spritzer. I try not to laugh at how stuck-up she's become since we broke up. When we were together she was a beer drinker. It's funny how things change people.

"How's your business doing?"

"What business would that be, Jimmy?"

I knock back my beer, then slam the bottle down hard on the bar. When I signal for another, I gain a wink in return. Too bad she's barking up the wrong tree.

"The escort service." I try to stifle my laugh, but to no avail. Chelsea slaps me across my arm. It stings, but I don't show it. I can't let her know that she still affects me in any way.

"You're such an imbecile, you know that?"

"Yet, here you sit next to me trying to catch my attention with your legs. Is this your way of showing me what's on offer, because I have news for you, Chelsea, I ain't buying it. So what do you want?"

Chelsea turns in the stool and faces the bar. "I saw that the band filed a restraining order against Moreno Entertainment."

"Yeah, we did. We've been having some issues with Sam. Do you remember her?"

"I do. She was an evil little thing, wasn't she?"

"Still is," I answer before taking a swig of my beer.

"Was," Chelsea states.

"What do you mean, was?"

She takes out a newspaper clipping and puts it down in front of me. My eyes widen as I read the article

Samantha Moreno was found dead in her apartment after an apparent drug overdose. She is the daughter of ...

I reread the first line multiple times so that I can recite it word for word. I need to tell Liam.

"When did this happen?"

"Right after Christmas," Chelsea says.

The wedding was after Christmas. It makes me wonder whether this was a reaction to Liam getting hitched.

"Look, Jimmy, that's not why I'm here. Obviously I had this in my purse for a bit, waiting to find you."

Cocking my head, I glare at her. She always has an ulterior motive. "What do you want?"

"I miss you, Jimmy. I was thinking we should try again."

"Pardon me? I think I misheard you. I'm pretty sure you said you wanted us to start over, but I know that can't be the case since mummy dearest would have a fit and daddy would cut you off. Surely you prefer spending your dosh more than you like having me hanging around."

"That's not true, Jimmy. I made a mistake." And she's making one now. I flinch when she touches me, but that doesn't register with her. She keeps her hand on my shoulder, her perfectly manicured nails tracing circles on my shirt.

"A mistake? Is that what you call shagging two blokes in my bed?" Finishing my beer, I signal for the tab. "Listen, Chels, I need to get going. You can call me or whatever, but I'm not sure how the whole dating thing will work out." I kiss her on the cheek as I get up, throwing some cash on the table for my bill. Thing is, if she's serious, I'd probably let my heart take a kicking and take her back.

As the girl behind the bar takes my tab, I have second thoughts about not pissing where I eat. I'm frustrated and I have needs, and right now I need to get Chelsea out of my brain. I signal to the girl with the 'fuck me eyes' and she knows exactly what I want. Chelsea's mouth drops open. She knows what I'm about to do and right now, I don't give a flying fuck.

I SHOULDER my guitar while I wait for my suitcases to show up on the baggage reclaim. Thoughts of leaving Chelsea at the bar play over and over in my mind. Most would call me an idiot for leaving her behind last night when she's pretty much an easy shag for me, but the heartache that comes from loving her is too much to bear, even if it's for one night or two. Her incessant text messages clogged up my phone as soon as I disappeared with the bargirl. She even had the nerve to ask me what I was doing. I have no doubts that she listened outside the bathroom door. The bargirl was definitely the safer option last night for sure.

Chelsea's parents don't approve of me and she always listens to them. They have the money that lets her live a lavish lifestyle, and while I know I could make sure she is well looked after, it would never be what she's used to.

I haven't called Liam or Harrison to let them know I'd be back a week early. Liam is still in his honeymoon period and Harrison is shacking up with his honey, playing house and all that crap. They don't need to open their doors to me when they're busy like this.

I stand patiently at the car-hire desk. I didn't make a reservation because, to be honest, I didn't think I needed one in such a small town. Yet here I am, tapping my fingers lightly on the desk while the clerk bites her lower lip and flips her hair every so often while staring at a computer screen. Subtlety is obviously not her forté. I have no doubt that on the screen is her frigging Twitter profile and she's tweeting something about me. Maybe I should search for my name while I stand here and tweet her back.

Looking at my watch, I exhale loudly. By the time she gets around to finding me a car, I could be knocking on Liam's door and sitting down for breakfast.

"Sweetheart, would it be easier if I found a different car-hire place to provide my transport while I'm in Beaumont?"

"Oh no, Mr. Davis, I was just communicating with our fleet manager. I'm printing the paperwork now." And just like that the printer starts spitting out my hire contract. Amazing how that happens.

She puts the contract down on the desk and shows me where to sign my name. When she hands me my copies, her business card is attached at the top.

"Call me if you have any problems. I've even included my cell number in the event that we're closed."

"Aren't you open twenty-four hours?" The expression on her face is priceless. I've never seen someone blush so quickly before. Okay, that's a lie. There's that girl that I'm itching to see again. I had her blushing in a matter of seconds, which I think was a record, even for me. Usually I have to sweet talk and romance them first, but not her.

I look around for a hidden camera. This is a moment I want to document. I wink at her as I pick up my keys. Her face turns even redder. She tries to smile, but it looks more like a frown. I hope she doesn't do anything stupid now that her attempt at being sexy has failed miserably.

I find my car easily enough in their enormous fleet of fifteen vehicles. I don't know why people—women, in particular—just don't come out and say what's on their minds. Hell, maybe she could've paid me a compliment. That would've made my day. But no, they um and ah around the topic and the only thing they succeed in is wasting my time.

When I pull up at Liam's, I'm happy to see Harrison is here. Now that I'm here it will give us more time to finalise what will be on the CD before Tyler arrives to start on the production. As much as I wish we were in L.A. doing this crap, I like coming out to Beaumont to escape reality. There are no paparazzi to bug us. I can chill out with family without people hiding in the bushes or analysing everything I'm buying at the supermarket. Liam was right when he moved back. The way of life here is total serenity.

The only thing missing is the eye candy. I need them. They entertain me and remind me that I'm nothing better than what my father said I would be. I won't be stupid though. I won't get any of my girls up the duff, and I'll definitely never get married. Kids and marriage complicate things. My dad was married to my mum for a long time, but had so many flings on the side that he lost track, same with my grandfather. I guess it's in the Davis' blood to not be tied down.

I walk down the stairs to the studio. Both of them turn and look at me. Their stupid big grins tell me that they're up to no good. Good thing I'm here to burst their happy little bubble.

"Sam's offed herself."

Liam and Harrison freeze like statues and their mouths fall open.

"What did you say?" Liam asks.

"Chelsea came by looking for a shag and showed me a newspaper article reporting that Sam died of an apparent drug overdose just after Christmas."

"She's dead?" Liam asks again.

I nod and watch for another reaction from him. I'm not gonna lie, Sam being gone gives us more opportunities. We've been thinking for a while now that she's been influencing venues and blocking them from working with us and we know for a fact that she sabotaged our tour. I never want to wish bad luck onto people, but Sam not being in the picture anymore is a blessing in disguise.

"That's sort of messed up," Harrison says. He's right, it is.

"I never wanted her to die. I just wanted to be free. We're free," Liam says.

Harrison and I nod. We're free.

2

JENNA

I've managed to survive a vicious three-year marriage to the most vile man I've ever known. For years he tried to get me pregnant and each time I did what I had to do to prevent it. I feared the day that he would find out about my methods, but it was a risk I was willing to take. There was no way I could bring an innocent child into the world with him as the father. Yet, here I sit, surrounded by dozens of pregnancy tests all telling me what I already know. The swollen breasts, tight fitting clothes, and protruding stomach are signs I've been trying to ignore, but I can't anymore. I'm about to be a mother. One slightly drunken moment and I'm pregnant and all I can think is, *Thank God this child doesn't belong to my ex-husband.*

You never know someone well enough. I thought I knew Damien Mahoney. I loved him and thought he loved me, but I was sadly mistaken. Our courtship lasted two years until we were married in a fairytale ceremony. My Cinderella wedding dress still hangs in my parents' closet. I never wanted to part with it, even after I left him. My tiara sits atop my childhood dresser, collecting dust, no doubt. Our marriage was anything but a fairytale. I didn't get my happily ever after. I got abused, physically and mentally.

No one ever prepares you for the abuse, whether it's by the hands of the man your father gave you to in front of all your family and friends; or by the hateful and hurtful words that come out of the mouth from the one who vowed to love you, who stood up in front of everyone and said he'd always protect you. When the first slap comes, when you feel the sting resonate across your cheek, you forget those vows. You forget that the man standing in front of you is your husband and you ask yourself why.

The first hit came one night after we had been out with some friends. We started fooling around when we got home and I accidentally hit him between the legs. It was a knee jerk reaction to something he did. I jumped and caught him. I apologized and kept trying to touch him, only to have him bat my hands away each time. That should've been my sign to leave him alone, but I kept at it, attempting to comfort him. His hand came across my face so fast I didn't have time to register what was happening until I was holding my cheek and tears were flowing down my face.

He held me tight. Promised me it would never happen again. I believed him.

Until he lied.

After each incident he would beg me to forgive him. He'd tend to my cuts and bruises. He'd berate and belittle himself. He promised me it was the last time.

Until it wasn't.

I learned how to hide my bruises from my friends and

family. I became a klutz every time I'd break my arm or collarbone. I pretended I loved him.

Until I couldn't.

I stayed because I had taken my vows seriously. I stayed because he sought help and for a while it worked.

Until it didn't.

Some would think that leaving was the hard part, but that's not the case. The hardest part was calling my dad to tell him that I needed help. I had to wait until Damien went on a business trip. When I knew he was gone, I finally found the courage to call my dad and tell him everything. He came that night, packed my belongings, and took me home. My dad never said anything. He moved fluidly through my house while I stood there with tears streaming down my face. The car ride to my parents was the longest ride ever. He didn't speak until we pulled into the driveway.

He sat there, staring straight ahead with his hands holding onto the steering wheel. He said, "Jenna, you're my daughter, and if I didn't raise my hand to you, then no man will."

The next night I left and ended up in Beaumont. I left my parents behind. I added my signature on divorce papers that my father prepared for me and promised to file. I left for a place where I had no ties and was far enough away from the main road that I could blend in and get to know everyone. I've been here for four years and love it. It took me the first two until I could finally walk around without always looking over my shoulder. I know Damien will find me. He'll come for me. It's only a matter of time.

And now here I am, happy and sad that I'm pregnant. I don't know what I'll tell my parents. They'll want to meet the man responsible and that's just not possible. He has a life away from me and it was a one-time thing. It's not like I can call him up and ask if he remembers me and drop the bomb mid conversation, "Oh, by the way ..."

I'm trying not to freak out. I know I can do this, but I'll need more hours at the store or I'll have to find a new job. I don't want to quit on Josie though. I'll have to talk to her. I pick up all the applicators and throw them away, saving one. I'm not sure why, but it feels right.

The clock shows just after five; I need to get to Whimsicality for open mic night. This is a night where I'll make decent tips. Now that Josie can serve alcohol, nights like these have been a hit. People sign-up weeks in advance just for the small hope that they'll be playing in front of someone from 4225 West. The guys are usually in the back and rarely make an appearance. Liam doesn't want to take away from what Josie is doing for these artists.

I live on the same block on which the shop is located. Living on Main Street has its perks. I don't need to drive and the only time I take out my beat up Corolla is when I babysit the kids. Everything is within walking distance, too —the bank, grocery store, and doctor's office. I've waited almost two months; it's time that I make my appointment. I can't put it off any longer.

I wrap my scarf around my neck as I step out into the cold, crisp air. I'm counting the days until spring. Not that it's overly cold in Beaumont, but I'm looking forward to some sun. I want to watch the flowers bloom as they line the street with every color imaginable. The trees in the park will turn nice and pink with the cherry blossoms. I want to sit on the bench and rest my hand on my swollen belly and feel my baby kick.

I want to enjoy these things with a partner, but that's not possible. It would figure that when I finally have enough courage to be with someone, it's a one-night stand and there's no hope for us to get together. It's just my luck that I'm attracted to the one guy who doesn't really know I exist except for in some hidden room away from everyone. I hate thinking that he doesn't know my name. I'm telling myself that he does. I'm writing my own story from that night, one filled with unadulterated passion and lust. A night where we watched each other from the other side of the room and when we met in the hallway, alone, we knew.

It was the first time I had felt safe with a man in a long time. Even though it was just sex, he held me. He kissed me like he was never going to see me again. At least that was true. He moved his hands over my body like he had been there a hundred times before.

I know I can make a happy story for my child, one in which the night he was created was full of love and laughter, that he was loved from the moment I found out.

Taking a deep breath, I enter the shop. I'm pleasantly surprised to find the guys here.

"What's going on?" I ask no one in particular.

"We're playing tonight. JD arrived early and we're bored. The kids will be down to help you bus tables, and Ralph is coming in to help you bartend." Liam kisses me on the cheek after he finishes rambling.

"Are you expecting a big crowd?"

"I tweeted about it and put the word on the street,"

Jimmy answers as he walks by with a big box in his hand. He sets it down and starts plugging cords into the back.

"You tweeted?" I question.

"*Twitter*, social networking, innit?"

"I know what *Twitter* is, Jimmy."

Jimmy smiles devilishly. This guy is bad news through and through. "Stay off *Twitter*, sweet lips. It's full of celebrity wannabe's and wanna-don't-be's."

He starts whistling some tune that I'm sure is one of their hits. I suppose if Jimmy 'tweeted' all his loyal harems will be out in droves tonight. That means shitty tips and rude women. Yay, fun times for Jenna.

I go out back, take off my coat, and store it in my locker. I think it's funny that we have lockers, but Josie is all about safety. I admire her for that. We aren't allowed to leave the shop at night without someone walking us to our cars and, in my case, my apartment. She usually has Liam or Harrison do it, but if they're not around she calls her friend and local police officer, Paul Baker, to come down.

Josie walks in, followed by Noah. He looks bored and is probably wishing he were at home playing video games.

"Jimmy tweeted," I say. "I think that means we'll be busy."

Josie starts to laugh, covering her face instantly when she snorts. "Oh God, how embarrassing. I can't believe I just did that."

"I can," Noah says with a roll of his eyes. "You do it all the time. It annoys Dad, by the way."

"Oh hush, you," Josie pushes him away slightly. "Are you over the flu?"

I nod. I hate lying to her, but she'll have so many questions that I'm not ready to answer. Truth is I'm not over it. Certain foods make my stomach turn and I'm thankful none of those foods are served here.

I walk out to the front and start making the coffee. We serve wine and beer mostly. For food, we have pastries and sandwiches. I busy myself setting up. As soon as the doors open, people file in. I ready myself for our first customer, except it's not a customer who steps up. I give him a half smile, the only thing I can muster. I don't want people to know, and for the life of me can't understand why he's standing here looking at me. We aren't friends. It was one moment, a moment that I'll remember for a lifetime and one that he can forget about.

3

JIMMY

Sitting in Josie's café and people watching is entertaining. At the table opposite me is a couple. The girl is dressed in jeans and a jumper while her companion is wearing boat-shoes and a tweed coat. It's laughable really, the differences between the two. I can already tell you, without even knowing her, that if she had the opportunity she'd go home with a band member. Not because of who we are, but because of what we represent. Danger. Excitement. Her friend, on the other hand, would rather be in front of a fire, smoking his cigar and watching some boring documentary on TV. My bet is that the only shagging style in his vocabulary is missionary. His bird, though, I can tell she likes it rough. I bet she likes to have her hair pulled and her arse spanked, maybe. Their relationship is in its early days. They're testing the water and it's about to get rocky. I should offer the poor bloke a dinghy to save his slowly sinking ego.

The café part of Josie's business is small, but has a homey feel. I like that I can come in here whenever I want and play an acoustic set or just sit in the corner and have a coffee. She always has fresh chocolate chip cookies, too, and I really like those.

Jenna walks past with a tray of drinks. She's usually wearing a skirt or dress, but tonight she's sporting a pair of black trousers that accentuate all of her curves. Her dark red hair is longer than normal. I remember she was wearing it up for Liam and Josie's wedding because I couldn't stop staring at her neck. But I didn't stop at her neck. I took in every inch of her body. I've never been a parts man, but looking at Jenna makes me want to be one, although I'd never be able to stop at just one place as far as she's concerned.

I have trouble talking to her and I don't know why. Our earlier conversation, albeit short, was stupid. I felt like a complete numpty when I was trying to explain what Twitter was. I think everyone, except maybe Aubrey, knows what it is. I've known Jenna for about a year and don't know anything about her. Maybe if I spend more time in Beaumont we can become friends, although I'm kidding myself thinking someone like her would want to be friends with someone like me. She reminds me of Chelsea with all her little foibles. Jenna's always laughing when she's with Josie and Katelyn, and it hasn't escaped my notice that she's never with a man.

Sitting in the corner, I watch her as she waits on the customers. She takes them their food and drinks and does it all with a smile that lights up her face. I look around and watch the tables fill up with customers. A few of these people I've seen when I've performed here before. It's nice to recognise some friendly faces, and I've partied with them a couple of times, but all too soon they start taking liberties and telling people they know the band. No one "knows" the band unless they're family.

A blonde girl waves her fingers at me, and I wink back, letting her think that she's caught my eye. I can't honestly say that she has, but she'll flutter her eyes at me all night and I'll flirt back until I see something better come along. Or maybe I won't. Maybe she'll be my next conquest for a couple of hours, although I'd hate it if Josie lost a customer because I definitely won't be calling this one the next day.

Liam says I should change, but I take great pleasure in reminding him that he was, in fact, exactly the same way. As is my dad and granddad. It's in my blood to never settle down. My mum would like me to. She'd like me to find a nice girl who's going to love me and take care of me, one that will give her grandchildren. The thought makes me shudder. No kids for me, not now, not ever. I saw what my father's cheating did to my mum, so no thank you very much. He learned his pathetic habit from his father and I'm not willing to hurt anyone like that. The amount of tears my mum shed over my father is ridiculous, he didn't deserve them. I don't want a girl crying over me like that.

Jenna carries her tray past me again, paying no attention to me. What if I need another drink? Shouldn't she wait on me? No, she knows better and so do I. Liam made it clear that we're more than capable of helping ourselves here. I look around once more and catch the blonde staring again. Maybe we should get better acquainted.

I walk over to her and lean down to whisper, "Come outside with me." I don't wait for an answer and make my way out of the front door. I don't care if she follows me or not, she's one of many as far as I'm concerned.

I lean against the wall, take out a cigarette, and light it. As soon as I take a drag the door opens and the blonde steps out. She looks left then right, and smiles when she spots me. I want to roll my eyes at the way she's walking. She thinks she's a supermodel on a catwalk, the way she's strutting her stuff and pouting. If she's trying to impress me, it's not working. I only want her for one thing.

"Hi, Jimmy."

"Are you a fan?"

"Of yours, I am."

Putty in my hands is what she is. I take another drag and exhale away from her. I'm a dickhead, but at least I have manners. Pulling her closer, I run my nose along the underside of her jaw, inhaling her perfume. It smells sweet and sugary, not feminine at all. It's a warning sign for me. It's always the young ones who smell like candy. I can't be too careful and definitely can't afford any bad press.

"How old are you?" I ask, pulling back.

"Tonight's my twenty-first birthday. We had plans until we saw your tweet. We drove an hour to get here."

Maybe I like *Twitter* after all.

I pick up a few strands of her blonde ponytail and twist them around my finger. She steps closer and puts her hand on my chest. She's shy. Her hand shakes. She's expectant even though I can tell she's never done something like this before.

"Do you want a birthday kiss?" I ask, fully aware of what her answer will be. She nods, biting her lower lip. Her eyes go from mine to my lips and back again. I lean in, taking my time. I want to put her on the edge with just a little kiss, because that's the game I like to play with the fangirls.

"Jimmy?"

I turn my head sharply. The girl's head bounces on my shoulder.

"Sorry, love," I say without looking at her because I'm focused on a very pissed off Jenna. "What's up, sweet lips?"

"Liam is looking for you ... I saw ... never mind." Jenna walks back into the café before I can say anything.

I move away from the birthday girl only for her to grab my hand. Freezing, I look down at our joined fingers. I bring hers to my lips and place a kiss there before letting go.

"Don't you want to know my name?"

I shake my head. "Sorry, love, it ain't gonna work like that." I leave her standing there with what I'm guessing is a hurt and annoyed expression on her face. It's a face I've seen many times before, but I can't be arsed to care.

Stubbing out my cigarette, I throw it in the bin before running up the stairs to enter the café. Jenna's behind the counter. She looks up, as if she heard me walk in, but I know that's not possible because of the old guy sitting in the corner playing his banjo. I walk past her and head into the back. I stop before I'm out of sight and turn. She's watching me, but looks back at her customer. I don't know what I can say to her without sounding like a total knob.

"Jenna said you were looking for me?"

"Yeah we're about to go on."

"Okay, cool." I walk back to where I was sitting and pick up my guitar. The crooner is just taking a bow. *Who does that?* The clapping is so minimal that I almost feel sorry for him. He was here in the hope of gaining a fan. Sucks for him that his performance is about to become instantly forgettable.

A man sits down next to my table. I can tell straight away that he's not from here. Thoughts of a potential agent slip through my mind. It would be nice to have a full-time agent again. This bloke is trying to hide. He keeps his hat on —the brim covering his eyes—and doesn't take off his coat.

Harrison and Liam walk past me and I follow, stepping onto the makeshift stage. We are going with a toned down, acoustic version of our songs tonight. We can't really perform like we're in a normal venue. We'd bust the windows and I think Liam would be in the dog house if he did that. Putting my guitar down, I sit at the piano. We are starting with "Guaranteed Tears," which seems to be a favourite with the radio DJs these days.

Liam starts singing the lyrics and Harrison adds a soft drumbeat, enough to keep the tempo of the song. Jenna stops near the stage and puts down three bottles of water. I watch as she walks to her newest customer. He doesn't look at her when he orders. I can't take my eyes off her or shake the sudden bad feeling I'm getting from this guy. If he's an agent, he's not watching us and it doesn't look like he's listening.

Jenna returns to his table with a tray full of drinks; she's making her rounds. She puts his glass down, but he looks up and she screams, dropping the tray all over him, the table next to him, and the floor. Glass shatters, getting Liam's attention.

The man stands up, grabbing Jenna's arm.

I stand, frozen. Liam jumps off the stage, quickly followed by Harrison.

"What the fuck are you doing?" I hear Liam shout loudly. Other customers are moving away from the scene, some of them leave. I step off the stage and stand with my band mates.

The man looks at Liam with menacing eyes. "Nothing," he says through gritted teeth. "I'll be back," he says to Jenna. He doesn't just let go of her arm; he tears his hand away, causing her to scream out in pain. She falls into Harrison's chest.

Liam steps in front of the man. "If you need someone to pick on, I'm right here, big boy."

The man side-steps Liam and walks out of the café.

"We're closing," Josie shouts out to the remaining clientele. "Don't worry about your tabs. It's on the house tonight."

Katelyn and Josie usher everyone out while Harrison holds a now crying Jenna. I feel like a total shit for not reacting sooner.

"Who was that?" I ask, no longer willing to be a spectator here.

"My ex-husband," she says through her sobs. She's the only one breathing right now because we are all standing here, not knowing what to say and, judging by the expressions on Josie and Katelyn's faces, the ex being here is not a good thing.

4

JENNA

"I'm sorry. I'm so sorry, princess. I didn't mean to. Look at me." He pulls up my face. His eyes are full of tears as his thumb lightly caresses my cheekbone. I want to think those tears are for me, but how can I be sure? My husband, the man who vowed to love and protect me, did the unimaginable. I flinch and try to pull away, but his fingers dig into my neck. "Forgive me," he whispers as his lips touch mine.

I nod, fearful of my voice betraying me. I've never been hit in my life, not even when I was a child. But my husband of three months just backhanded me. His hand flew across my face. His knuckles crashed into my cheek as his arm extended. It's my fault, I know. I should feel lucky that he's still sitting here with me since I accidentally kneed him.

He pulls me into his arms and onto his lap. He rocks me back and forth, holding me tighter and tighter. I wrap my arms around him, afraid to let go. I cry into his shoulder as I try to figure out what just happened. I know he didn't mean it, but that doesn't lessen the fact that it happened.

"I love you, princess." He says this over and over again in between placing kisses on my face. "You need ice. I'll go get you some." He moves me off his lap and onto the bed. I'm scared to look at my face. I don't want to know what I look like. If the pain that I feel is substantial, I'm sure the evidence is going to be horrifying. I lie down, careful not to bump my cheek. I'm trying not to cry, but the tears come regardless. My heart is breaking.

Damien returns with a bag of ice and a towel. He is gentle when he touches my face. I hiss at the pressure being applied, but know I need it, even if I don't want it. He crawls in the bed and sits behind me, cradling me to his body. He fits against me because we are made for each other. This is how I love to sleep, with his chest against my back, but right now I want to curl up into a ball and hide away from him and everyone else.

I jump slightly when I hear the door lock. Harrison has one arm wrapped around me. His body is tense though. I can feel the strain in his muscles.

"Who was that?" Jimmy asks again.

Closing my eyes, I wait for the room to stop spinning. I knew he'd find me, but after being gone for so long I hoped he'd stop caring. I shouldn't have stayed here for so long.

"That, apparently, is her ex-husband," Josie says from behind me. She puts her hand on my back, reassuring me. It's not going to work. I need to leave Beaumont. I can't stay here and let them be in danger.

As I move away from Harrison he takes my arm and guides me to the nearest chair. Everything moves slowly, in a blur. Josie and Katelyn sit down, one on each side of me. Each places a hand on my back. They hover because they don't know what else to do. Me? I just want to scream and head to the bus station with no destination in mind and start over.

Liam and Harrison pull out a couple of chairs and sit down. Jimmy stands off to the side, staring. I try to offer him a smile, a weak one at that, but that doesn't change his expression. His eyes are cold.

"Jenna?" Liam says my name so quietly that I can barely hear him over the sounds in my head. I feel like my head is submerged in water. All I can hear is Damien warning me that he'll be back in his cold, menacing voice. Everything echoes around me. I jump when the coffee machine clicks, alerting us that it's gone into sleep mode from lack of use.

My hands are clammy. I'm sweating. My teeth hurt from grinding them together, the learned response before another blow comes to my face.

"Jenna?" Liam says again. I look at him and wish I hadn't. The rage mixed with pity is the same look my father gave me the night he picked me up from my marital home. Somehow I think if I give him the okay, he'll hunt down Damien and make sure he can't bother me again. I'll have to tell him the same thing I told my dad: I can take care of it, which is a lie.

I close my eyes and cry into my palms. Josie and Katelyn both hug me as I sob. I don't mean to be like this, but I can't help it. I don't want to leave them but I have no choice. I won't put them in harm's way. They've all been so good to me, but this is the only option I have.

"I didn't even know she was married." I hear Harrison say.

"This is bullshit," Jimmy says. I feel the table shift. "Jenna, who the fuck was that guy?"

"Her ex, JD, she's already said," Harrison answers.

"Yeah, I understand that, but what the fuck just happened? He was angry and he hurt her."

"Jenna, you need to tell them before Jimmy goes crazy," Josie whispers in my ear. I nod, wiping my tears. When I look up the guys are watching me, intently. Each one of them looks confused, but also angry.

Taking a deep breath, I close my eyes. "I was married to him for three years. I left one night when he went on a business trip."

"Why?" Liam asks.

I open my eyes and look around the room. Josie and Katelyn nod, showing me that I need to tell them about my marriage.

"He uh ..." I swallow the lump in my throat. "About three months after we got married, he hit me. It was a reaction to what I did to him and I believed it was an accident, except he did it again a few months later. Each time he did it, he'd hold me and tend to me and promised he'd never do it again."

A bottle of water appears in front of me. I don't know who put it there, but I say thanks to all of them. I take a long drink before I continue. "The night before he left for this week-long business trip, he beat me. Usually it was one or two punches, but this time he kept hitting and hitting. He said he was making sure I didn't leave him for another man while he was gone, said that no one would want me if I were bruised.

"I waited half the night to make sure he wasn't coming

back and I called my dad. He took me to the hospital and to the police station, but all they did was take pictures. Damien's best friend is one of the sergeants on the force and he kept asking me who did this to me, and when I told him, he just shook his head. The next morning my dad had all the necessary divorce papers drawn up. I signed and emptied our bank account and bought a one-way bus ticket across the country. We stopped in Beaumont and I didn't get back on the bus. I thought I was far enough off the beaten path that he'd never find me."

"Where are you from?" Jimmy asks.

I sigh. "Blaine, Washington. It's a small town near the Canadian border."

"Come on, let's go home," Liam says softly as he stands. Harrison follows and comes to stand behind Katelyn. Wrapping his arms around her, he kisses her cheek. Josie stays with me, her hand rubbing my back.

"Can someone walk me home?" I ask. As much as I want to say good-bye to everyone and I think it will be best if I just leave, I want to make it home first and pack a few things.

"Yeah, I'll walk you back." All eyes turn to Jimmy who stands there like what he just said is no big deal.

"She's not going home, she's coming to our house," Liam announces. I open my mouth to protest, but he holds his hand up. "For all we know he's been following you around and knows where you live. We aren't taking any chances until we can get Paul to check him out."

"Paul's too busy with—"

"With what, doing police business? It's his job and I

know he doesn't take too kindly to men who raise their hands to women. Come on, let's go."

Josie stands and takes my hand. Lights are switched off as we walk out as a group. I try not to look around and see if Damien is standing there, watching. I know he is. I can sense him crawling around on my skin. I huddle closer to Josie, trying to hide. It will be no use though. He's found me now. He'll find me again.

I climb into the backseat, followed not by Josie, but by Jimmy. Once the car doors shut and the dome light goes off, he slides his hand into mine. I know not to think anything of this. He's just being kind, but it's nice to feel his hand in mine. It's almost like it's the reassurance I need to leave my new family behind.

I lean my head on his shoulder. He doesn't tense like I thought he would. He shifts so that I'm leaning on his chest. He holds me, stroking my hair. He kisses the top of my head. But as soon as I clutch his T-shirt he pulls away. I sit up and stare out the window, turning away from him. Someday when he decides to settle down, I have no doubt he'll be a good husband to someone, although that someone will have to be at least ten to fifteen years younger to keep up with him. He won't have a problem finding someone. The women flock to him, they desire him.

Resting my hand on my stomach, I rub my thumb back and forth. This is the reason I need to leave. I need to protect my baby and I know its dad won't be around so leaving won't a big deal. Damien can't know I'm pregnant. It will surely set him off. His face, full of rage, flashes before my eyes. He'll kill me. I know this in my heart.

Jimmy reaches for my hand again, but I pull away. I don't need his sympathy. I don't want it. I was stupid to stay here for so long. It's time to leave.

5

JIMMY

We sit around. No one's talking. Each one of us is on eggshells. Harrison is convinced we were followed. I didn't pay attention. I was too busy being selfish and wondering why it's okay for Harrison and Liam to comfort her, but I can't. I pulled away from her hesitantly when she grabbed my shirt. I freaked out. But now she's pulled away and I'm left scratching my head. She doesn't know what that does to a man's ego. Or maybe she does. By her I mean Jenna. I wanted to hold her hand, to let her know that I'm here, but she doesn't want that.

I take one look around the room and walk to the front door. I need a break, a breather. The tension in the air is so thick a knife wouldn't be able to cut it. I get that everyone is worried, but I'm a firm believer in letting the police do their jobs. Liam called his friend as soon as we got here and now we just wait for him to show up. Or for Jenna's ex to show up, whichever happens first.

I'm hoping it's the latter. I may have had my fair share

of girls, but I would never hit them. That's just something you never do. This bloke needs his motherfucking arse kicked. He needs to know what it's like to get beaten up over and over again. I know I could do some damage. Harrison too. But if Liam ever gets hold of the little twat, he better fear for his life. Liam may be a former high school football player, but that doesn't mean he didn't keep up his physique this whole time. He's always in the gym if he's not in the studio. Makes a guy like me look like a toothpick.

Lights flash in the drive as I step outside. Sitting down, I wait for whoever to walk up to the front door. I swear to God, it better be their policeman friend because if it's that loser I'm going to knock the ever-living crap out of the bastard.

The mysterious driver gets out of the car and heads toward me with his hand on his gun. Seriously? Does he think that I'm the idiot who just threatened his ex and am sitting on the step having a cigarette before I go in? Idiot. Maybe it's true what they say about small time coppers.

"What's your name?"

I stub out my cigarette and hold my hand out. "Jimmy Davis at your service. I'm not the guy you're looking for, but I'd be more than happy to help you track him down."

He shakes my hand, but keeps his other on his gun. He makes me want to roll my eyes at the stupidity. "Paul Baker. Liam called about a possible assault."

"They're inside. It's a long story." I point toward the house. Officer Paul Baker leans sideways to look inside the front window. He won't be able to see anything, though; Liam is pretty strict about privacy. "Come on, I'll take you in."

Rising, I put the cigarette butt back in my pocket so I can throw it away in the house. When I open the door I expect their talking to stop, but it's still as quiet as it was when I came outside. Paul follows me into the living room. Liam and Harrison stand when we walk in.

"Come with me, Paul," Liam says. Harrison follows. I don't know what I'm supposed to do. I'm an outsider regardless of my status in the band. I don't live here. I'm not with them every day. I stand on the in between, teetering back and forth. I want to be here for Jenna because I think she's a top lass, but shit, what the hell am I going to do? Up and leave Los Angeles because this is where my band mates want to live? I live a life there, my mates are there. My dad and granddad are there.

I look around the room and see Josie and Katelyn, but not Jenna. "Where's Jenna?" I ask for reasons I keep to myself.

"She's not feeling well, so she went to lie down," Josie answers.

Glancing at the stairs, I wonder what room she's in. Could she be in the one I use when I stay here? She could be, especially since I told Liam I would stay in a hotel this time so he and Josie can have some privacy.

I nod and walk away. If she's not sitting down here it's not like I can go up and see her. I could pretend that I'm tired and that I forgot I was staying somewhere else. I could go and sing to her like my mum sang to me when I was sick. I don't think she'd go for it though. I'm pretty sure she wants nothing to do with me. It's easier this way.

I find the guys sitting around the kitchen table. They're telling Paul what the dickhead looks like. I didn't get a good look. All I saw was the black hat and long coat. Christ, I thought he was an agent. Instead he was biding his time until he could pounce on Jenna.

I pull out an empty chair and sit down. I guess this is probably the best place for me to be right now. I can't offer support to Jenna without raising suspicion and right now neither of us need that.

"Did you get a good look at him?" Paul asks me.

"No, I didn't. I saw him sitting there before we went on. I thought he was an agent. It wasn't until I saw Jenna drop her tray that I knew something was up. But I froze. I should've beaten the crap out of him when I had the chance."

"Me too," Liam adds. "We didn't know there was an ex until today or the extent of their relationship. If we had, you'd have him sitting in the back of your police car."

"He has police connections, too," Harrison adds. Liam and I nod. "A friend on the force in Blaine, Washington, that's where they're from."

"And you just learned all this tonight?"

"My wife's known for a long time. She and Katelyn weren't shocked at all when Jenna muttered the word ex."

Liam looks like he's deep in thought and it makes me wonder if he is thinking about how long it's taken him to finally make Josie his wife. Once he got her back, he didn't shut up about her. Not that we minded, we love her—it's as if she's always been a part of this adventure.

"I should probably talk to Jenna."

"I'll go get her," I volunteer, probably too quickly. Liam and Harrison look at me like I have two heads. I try to play it off. "I have to use the bathroom anyway." I excuse myself and take the steps two at a time until I'm on the landing. The door to the room that I usually stay in is closed. My steps are quiet, in case she's sleeping. I knock softly.

"Come in."

I twist the handle slowly and push the door open. The bedside lamp is on and Jenna's lying on her side, holding her stomach. I can't imagine what's going through her mind right now. Is she holding herself because the memories are so vivid?

"Hey, sweet lips."

She smiles softly. I like that I can make her smile with her nickname.

"I should ask why you call me that, but not tonight."

"No, not tonight. Let's save that question for another time, like when you can really appreciate my answer." I sit down next to her and pull her legs onto my lap. I can be a good friend to her, maybe her best guy mate if that's what she needs. "Josie says you're sick, what's wrong?"

"Flu," she answers quickly.

"My mum used to give me tea and then she'd sing to me."

"Did it work?"

"God, no. My mum can't bloody sing and I can't stand tea so it would make me feel worse. She liked to sing though because it would make me smile. Want me to sing to you?"

Jenna curls her arm underneath her head and looks at me. "You never take the lead on stage, how come?"

I shrug. "It's Liam's band. I joined after he and Harrison had already signed a record deal. I just do what I'm asked. It's easier that way. Besides, I'm more talented. I can play the guitar, piano, and harmonica. I could probably bang out a decent beat on the drums, too, if I tried."

"You want to sing to me?"

"Yeah, if it will make you smile, I'll do it."

"Okay then, let's hear it."

I clear my throat and try to say something, but nothing comes out. She laughs and although that was the reaction I was going for, I didn't want it to be at my expense. "Give me a minute to think of something." I act like I'm thinking. Tapping my finger to my temple, I think of some words I can throw together that will sound almost decent.

"Okay, ready?"

She nods.

"I've never felt like this before. I see our ship comin' from the shore and that horizon in your eyes is like tobacco sunburst. After we set sail, there's gonna be storms. Just don't lose faith in me 'cause I'll keep us on course. Remember this day, it's written in the stars. We're on our way to forever, girl, it's not that far ..." I trail off and have to look away from her. I don't know where those words came from; they've not only shocked me, but her as well.

She pulls her legs out of my lap and sits up. "Who wrote that?"

I shrug. I can lie and say I've heard it on the radio or say that my dad did or I can tell her the truth. "My dad," I say. It's the easy way out. "He used to sing it to my mum a lot that's why I remember it."

I get up and walk to the window, looking out to survey the area. Can someone climb up to the roof to get in? Chances are yes he could, if he's determined, but Liam has a state of the art security system in place. No one is getting into this house if he doesn't want them to.

"Anyway, the policeman is downstairs. I was supposed to come and tell you." I don't look at her before I leave the room. She doesn't ask me to wait for her, even though I'm not expecting her to.

Opening the door, I head back into the hall. I walk down the stairs as quickly as I can. I need to separate myself from this situation. I just did something I've never done before and I'd rather forget about it.

I smell her perfume before I hear her coming down the stairs. I mistakenly turn to watch her walk down. The memories are there, but I fight them. I don't need a reminder. I shake my head and walk to the front door, needing the fresh air to get my mind straight.

As soon as I sit down and light my cigarette the front door opens. I know it's her. Closing my eyes, I will her away. I don't understand why she's hell-bent on torturing me.

She sits down next to me and wraps her arms around her legs. "You shouldn't do that."

"Do what?"

"Smoke."

I stub out my cigarette and blow my smoke away from her. If she doesn't want me smoking in front of her, I won't.

"Sorry, it's a bad habit."

"A lot of musicians smoke," she says. She's right, it makes our voices raspy and the girls love that shit.

"You're supposed to talk to that guy in there."

She looks back at the house. "He's going to ask me out. He has in the past, and I've always told him no, but I have a feeling he'll say it's for protection or something. I haven't dated anyone since ..."

"Tell him you have a boyfriend."

"But I don't."

"So tell him I'm your boyfriend." I don't know where those words come from, but the look in her eyes tells me that she likes the idea. I want to take them back, but that would be an idiot move to make. "Just because you tell him we are, doesn't mean we have to act like it unless he's around," I add, just to set the record straight so she doesn't get the wrong idea.

"Okay."

"Okay," I say, knowing I'm totally fucked.

6

JENNA

The summer before my tenth grade year, I met Damien Mahoney. I was instantly in love. He was older and sexier, way sexier, than the guys at my school. That summer he asked me to be his girlfriend. I said no. I wasn't allowed to have a boyfriend until I was seventeen, so that was the only answer I could give. He'd meet me after he was done with his classes and walk me home. Each day he asked again and the answer would always be the same until he finally asked me why. When I told him, he sat on my front porch and waited for my dad to come home. I watched out the window, peeking through the curtains every few minutes wondering when he'd give up and go home. He didn't.

I never asked my dad what he said to Damien. I was too embarrassed. The next day at school I found a note in my locker, *"We can't be boyfriend and girlfriend, but we can pretend."*

Hearing Jimmy say we can pretend means something else though. Damien wanted me. Jimmy doesn't. He's just doing it to be nice so Paul will back off. If I was smart I'd latch onto Paul and hope that maybe he'd be okay dating a pregnant woman. Maybe he wants to be a dad and wouldn't mind taking on someone else's child. I know in my heart that the baby's dad won't care. He doesn't want kids. He doesn't even want a wife. Josie has mentioned it in passing one time too many. As far as unplanned pregnancies go, this takes the cake.

I could tell him, but I'm not sure I could deal with the expression on his face. I don't know how I'd take his retreating backside as he runs for the hills. I don't need his money and maybe he won't realize the timing. I know giving him the option is the right thing to do, but I don't want him around out of obligation. We both screwed up that night. We both don't need to pay. I'm perfectly happy taking on the motherhood role while he lives his playboy life.

Jimmy doesn't look at me, and five minutes into our pretend relationship I'm already getting the cold shoulder. "I guess I should probably go in."

"Yeah, he's waiting to ask you some questions about your ex." Jimmy looks at me over his shoulder. "You know he'll never touch you again, right?"

My lips form a thin line. "I know, but honestly that scares me. I don't want you guys to get hurt because of me."

"You're family, Jenna. Liam and Harrison won't let anything happen to you."

I nod. It doesn't escape me that he said Liam and Harrison. What about him? He's probably not counting himself because he won't be here next week. Mister "blow into town, break some hearts and leave again," just when we're used to him coming around. I get up and walk back into the house, leaving him on the porch. He confuses me. If he's supposed to be my pretend boyfriend, don't you think he'd walk me in and act like it in front of my suitor? Not Jimmy. I have the most obtuse pretend boyfriend in the history of pretend boyfriends.

"Jenna," Paul says when I enter the room. I want to turn back around and head outside and sit in silence with Jimmy, but I step forward with a fake smile on my face. I sit down next to Liam and Harrison even though there's a seat next to Paul. He glances at the empty seat and shrugs. "Had a scare tonight, I hear?"

"Yeah," I reply, because what else can I say? No, I wasn't scared that my psycho ex who beat the ever-loving shit out of me showed up in the town where I've been hiding for the past four years?

"What's his name?"

I look down at my slightly protruding belly. I know no one suspects anything—you can't tell unless I lift my shirt up and I won't be doing that until I can figure out a way to tell Josie.

"Jenna?"

"Um ... sorry. His name is Damien Mahoney."

Paul writes down his name on his notepad. "I have to ask this, but is Jenna Palmer your real name?"

I shake my head slowly. I feel all eyes on me, but I can't look at them. "Jenna's my first name, but Palmer is something my dad came up with. He had some documents made up with the name before I left town."

"How do you think he found you?"

"I don't know. I call my parents once a week from a disposal cell phone."

"You've taken a lot of steps so he can't find you."

I nod. It seems like it as I tell them, but it didn't work. "I guess not enough since he found me. I should've left Beaumont a year after I got here. That was the plan. That I'd move around to keep the trail cold, but I met Josie and ... well, it'll be almost five years here and I couldn't bear to leave. But I'll be gone soon."

"What do you mean?"

I look up to see Josie and Katelyn standing in the entryway. I bite my lip to keep myself from crying. "I need to move on."

"No you don't, you can stay here. We'll protect you from this sicko," Josie says.

I shake my head. "I can't put you and the kids in harm's way. I don't know what he'll do and I couldn't live with myself if he hurt one of you or the kids. It'd kill me."

"Leaving might be a bit drastic. Let me look for him and see what I can do to diffuse the situation," Paul offers. "I think you'll have enough protection here. Liam has his normal crew and he's already spoken to them about adding staff around everyone. If we can keep the paparazzi out of Beaumont, surely we'll get an abusive ex-husband out."

"Okay," I say, but have no intention of staying. It will also be best for the father of my baby if I just leave. My luck, my baby would look just like him and everyone in town would know. I know how Josie felt, especially when Liam came back. Everyone suspected that he was Noah's father, but she never let on. But when Liam showed up in town, everyone's suspicions were confirmed. They're getting their happy ending though. I won't be so lucky.

"For now, I hear you'll be staying here."

"Oh no—"

"Yes she is," both Liam and Josie say at the same time. I don't know who to look at first. I choose Josie. She's standing next to the table with her hands on her hips. She's challenging me to defy her. Liam has his arm resting on the back of my chair. He cocks his head to look at me. He's waiting, too. No wonder those two make such a great pair.

"I have an apartment."

"And he probably knows about it," Liam says in his fatherly tone.

"My things are there."

"We're going over there tonight with Paul to get your things. You can come, but I'd prefer it if you stay behind."

"Liam, there are things women like to pack themselves."

"Then you go with us, Josie. I don't think it's a good idea for Jenna to be out there tonight. He's out there waiting for her. He probably knows where she lives and is just waiting for her to come home and that's not happening on my watch."

"Or mine," Harrison adds.

"Mine either," Paul says. The only one missing is my pretend boyfriend who hasn't come back in. I don't know what he's thinking, but if he's serious, no one is going to believe that he's my boyfriend.

"Mine either. I was walking around outside and noticed a car down the road. Whoever is in the car has a torch because when I started walking toward them, it was switched off. If it's him, he's looking for an opportunity. Josie and I can go and get Jenna's stuff, but I think Liam and Harrison should stay here with Jenna. Paul, you should leave and circle back around and maybe check those license plates unless he follows us out of here."

The room goes quiet as Jimmy stands in front of us. We hadn't heard him come in, but the room falls silent when he speaks. Mouths open and close again. No one's sure what to say in response to his outburst. He must've been thinking about this for some time to come and assert himself.

"Sounds like a good plan," Paul says, standing up and leaving the table. Everyone starts shuffling around me. My need to move on, to leave Beaumont, has fallen on deaf ears. If I'm to do this, I'll have to do it in the dark of night.

"What do you need from your apartment?" Josie asks when she sits down next to me. She has a piece of paper and a pen in her hand. Her paper says 'Mommy Notes' and I realize that the kids are nowhere to be seen.

"Where are the kids?"

"Mr. Powell has them. We thought it would be better if they stayed away tonight."

"That's not fair."

Josie looks up and smiles. She rests her hand on top of mine. "You're family, Jenna. You're important to me ... to us. Please let us help."

"He's dangerous."

"Yeah, well, my husband is big and likes to hit things so he can be dangerous, too."

I know she's trying to make light of the situation and I do smile at her comment, but I don't want them to bend over backwards more than they already have.

"One night," I say with no conviction. Josie rolls her eyes and nods, but I have a feeling she doesn't believe me, not that I believe myself. I tell her what I need and where she can find everything. She kisses me on the cheek and yells for Jimmy. I jump when the front door shuts and anxiety builds knowing that Damien is out there and he could be watching this house, waiting to pounce on my friends.

"Everything will be fine." Katelyn sits next to me and holds my hand. I hate feeling like this. I worked hard to get over the things that happened to me, but in the blink of an eye he's back and I feel on edge and afraid.

"I wish it were that easy."

"It can be, if you think positive. Maybe he just wants to talk, or maybe after Paul gets a hold of him he'll realize that Beaumont isn't safe for him. Harrison and Liam aren't going to let anything happen to you, and neither is Paul. You have friends here, Jenna, friends that care and love you. Liam thinks of you as his sister. So do I."

"Yeah," I say, my voice breaking. She's going to make me cry and there isn't a thing I can do about it. "I don't want anyone to get hurt."

"We'll be more hurt if you leave us or if we don't beat this psycho at his own game. You're one of us whether you like it or not."

Thing is, I like it. I'm just afraid of what they'll think when they find out I'm pregnant. I don't even want to know what they'll do if they find out who the father is. That's a secret I'll take to the grave.

As soon as we drive onto the road, the car I spotted earlier turns its lights on. He thinks he's being a sly little shit, hiding in the dark like the big bad wolf. What he doesn't know is that Paul is lurking behind Liam's gate waiting to see if the car moves. I watch out of the rearview mirror as Paul's lights flash. Josie turns around and watches while I drive her car away from the scene that's taking place behind us.

"Should we stop?"

"No, we'll get in the way," I say even though I want to turn around and get a good look at this dickhead so I can try and protect Jenna. "We need to get her stuff and get out of there while Paul is talking to this guy. We don't know if he knows where she lives, just where she works and we have to make sure she's never alone."

"That's really nice, Jimmy."

"What?"

"You wanting to take care of Jenna. I know you're not

around much so it's usually just the five of us. I'm really hoping to set Jenna up with Paul."

"Why?" I ask.

"He likes her and he'd be good for her. We've known him for a long time. He'd make a good husband."

For some unknown reason my jaw clenches together. My teeth grind at the thought of Jenna being with Paul. I shouldn't give a shit. She's just a friend. A friend that I care about a little more than I should.

I remain silent until we arrive at Jenna's apartment. I look around as I get out of the car. There's no sign of the car or Paul and I'm hoping they're still talking. Josie and I run up the stairs and down the hall to the apartment. I look around, mentally taking a note of her neighbours. It's very quiet up here so if she were to scream I'd like to think someone would hear her. But then again, if this was L.A. and someone screamed they'd ignore it, so who knows?

Josie lets us in and gets to work. I tell her we should keep the lights off if at all possible so we don't draw attention to her ex in case he's outside.

"Where did you learn all of this?"

"What?" I ask, picking up a photo of Jenna and Josie from the wedding.

"Well, you were pretty impressive at the house, directing everyone, and now with the lights."

"Oh ... my ex-girlfriend's uncle is a detective and in her dad's attempt to change me he got me to go on the beat with his brother for a few nights. The guy talked a lot, and I listened."

"Was that Chelsea?"

Looking up, I find Josie standing in front of me. I put the picture of Jenna down. "Yeah, how'd you know that?"

"Liam told me, said you weren't always a womanizer."

I can't help but laugh. He's one to talk. "I'm not a womanizer. I just like women."

"Same thing, Jimmy. You need yourself a good girl to keep you happy."

I smirk at the thought. There's one woman I'd like to keep me happy, if she was willing, but I have no doubt she wants nothing to do with me. Unfortunately, that's something I need to accept and move on.

My phone vibrates. I take it out of my pocket and shake my head at the irony of the situation.

"Speak of the devil," I say aloud.

I've been thinking a lot. I want to see you.

I don't even know if I should respond or ignore Chelsea. She puts my head into a mind-fuck. I wanted to marry that girl and have gorgeous babies with her, but she ruined me. She made me feel like I was worthless. She made me think that everything we had shared meant nothing to her.

"You okay?"

Clearing my throat, I put my phone back in my pocket without replying to Chelsea. "Yeah, you ready?" I reach for the bag she's carrying and put in on my shoulder. I follow her out. I look around Jenna's apartment and try to picture her in it, curled up on the sofa reading a book. In my mind she seems happy, content.

I walk down the stairs first and tell Josie to wait when I step out onto the path. It's late and there isn't much traffic. The wrought iron lamppost casts a soft haze over the street. I look left and right, trying to decide if anything is out of place. I nod at Josie. She walks out and heads toward her car, climbing into the passenger seat. I walk around to the driver side. As I step onto the road, a car whizzes past and slams on their brakes. They stay in the middle of the road with their lights shining.

"Get in the car, Jimmy," Josie yells.

I scramble, opening the door and sliding in just as they reverse past us. Turning on the ignition, I quickly put it into gear.

"Call Liam and tell him that we're being followed. We can't go home right now."

"He knows where we live."

"I know he does. He also knows where Jenna lives, and he doesn't need to know we are heading back to your place. Find out where Paul is."

Josie speaks to Liam as I drive around. I'm watching my mirrors, waiting for this arsehole to come up behind me.

"Liam says go to the house."

"He does?"

"Yeah, he says security is there and the gate will be locked tonight."

"Okay." I do as Liam suggests and drive back to the house. We aren't followed, which is suspicious to me. What is this guy playing at?

We get stopped at the driveway and the car is checked. I know it's a precaution and I'd be doing the same thing, but for God's sake, I have the owner of the house in the car with me. As soon as we're given the okay, the gate shuts. It's a fortress here. Liam had walls and massive fencing put up when he bought the house. He didn't want anyone watching his son. I don't blame him. If I had one, I'd never take him out in public.

Josie and I rush into the house. She runs straight into Liam's arms.

"What the fucking hell is going on?"

"We don't know," Liam replies. "Paul called from the station to say he had the driver of the car in custody, but wouldn't say if it was Jenna's ex, just said that you were right. I called him about this other car and he thinks it's a bunch of teens just screwing around."

"You've got to be kidding me?"

Liam shrugs. "I did that shit when I was a kid so why not?"

"That's such bullshit. Those fuckwads scared the crap out of your wife."

"I'm fine, Jimmy."

I throw my hands up in exasperation at this whole mess. I see Jenna sitting down and carry the bag in my hand over to her.

"Thanks, Jimmy."

I kneel down in front of her and watch as she hides her face from me. She doesn't want me to see her crying.

"You don't have to hide from me." She sees all the ugly that I am; I should be able to see hers, too.

"You give me whiplash, Jimmy."

"What does that mean?"

Sighing, Jenna wipes her face with the back of her hands. "It means that one moment you're this untouchable rocker who doesn't care, and then the next you're this sweet guy who does."

I sit back on my heels, directing my gaze down at the

floor. Is that how others see me, too? I look at her. Her green eyes glisten from her tears. "I'm sorry. I don't mean to confuse you. I'm just being me."

"Yeah I know," she says so sadly that it makes my heart ache. What did I do to her to cause her pain? It's stupid, I know what I did and that's exactly why it won't happen again. "We're friends, right?"

"Of course, we are." I get up from the floor and sit down next to her on the sofa. I'd pull her toward me, but I don't want her to feel awkward. It's hard to stay friends with someone like her, but I'm going to try even if she doesn't want to be my friend. "Do you know what you need?"

"What's that?"

"A holiday."

Jenna laughs. "That'd be nice, but I make just enough money for me to pay rent and live. I don't save for things like a vacation."

"I'll pay."

She shakes her head. "No, I'm not borrowing money from you."

Sitting up so I'm in her eyesight, I pull her chin up so she's looking at me. "I think we should go somewhere for a week or two. Let things settle down and just relax. Besides, I think we have some things to discuss."

"I don't know, Jimmy. It feels wrong and I don't want to be a third wheel."

"Third wheel?"

Jenna sighs and fiddles with her fingers. "I don't want to watch you hit on women."

Does she actually think I'd take her on a holiday and go

on the pull for other women? This girl is crazy. Her ex messed her up good and proper, that's for sure.

"Sweet lips, I want to take you on a holiday so we can relax. We can lie on the beach, drink some girly fruity crap, have fun in the sea, and eat overly expensive food. I want to do this because you're my friend."

She blanches at the word friend. I don't blame her, but I need to keep the lines defined. I'm not boyfriend material for her and I don't want her thinking I'm going to settle down like Liam and Harrison have.

"It's just a holiday, Jenna, nothing more."

"I'll have to ask Josie for the time off."

"Do you really think she's going to say no?" I ask, trying to stifle a laugh.

"No about what?"

We both turn to find Josie walking toward us. She's carrying a tray of food, and right on cue my stomach growls.

"I figured as much, Jimmy. So what am I not saying no to?"

Taking a sandwich off the tray, I offer a smile in thanks. "I'm taking Jenna on a holiday to take her mind off things."

"Really, you two on a vacation together?"

"Yeah, why not?"

"Oh I don't know. You're not exactly each other's type."

I shrug. "So, I'll change for a week."

Josie and Jenna both look at me. The room is silent. I can't help that I like my ladies' man persona. Chelsea made me this way. Loving someone who does that much damage totally fucks with your mind and your sense of being.

"Have fun on vacation," Josie says, leaving us to plan.

"So, sweet lips, where do you fancy going?"

Her eyes light up and her lips turn into a huge smile spreading from ear to ear. I know I said I'd keep it in my pants where other women are concerned, but if I'm going to get to stare at Jenna and her fit body in a bikini for a week, she and I may need to come to a friends with benefits understanding.

No, that can't happen.

8

JENNA

I look out the window and sigh. It's been raining for three days straight with no sign of letting up. I suppose if we were going to have a weather element, I'd take rain over a hurricane or tornado. Not sure how I'd deal with a tornado warning.

I'm depressed. Not in the *I'm going to go do something drastic to myself* sense, but more in the *I'm bored out of my mind from being locked up*. I'm supposed to be sitting on a warm beach someplace in the south, but Officer Paul Baker had to burst my fantasy bubble. When Jimmy announced that he was taking me on a holiday, Paul put his foot down ... literally. He said that I couldn't leave, not in the middle of an active investigation, which confused me because I hadn't pressed charges. But he said I need to stay and Liam agreed.

Jimmy didn't say anything. In fact, he left that night and hasn't been around since. That was almost two weeks ago. I don't know what I was expecting, but I thought that maybe we'd be friends. I know that is far-fetched considering his history and his need to be free all the time. I mean, why would he want to babysit me, when he can be out doing who knows what and not suffer the consequences?

I did that. I took that step and look where it got me. My palm finds my stomach and rubs along the outside of my sweatshirt. I'm lucky that the cold weather is allowing me to wear layers because right now my oversized sweatshirt is hiding an even bigger bump. I'm not going to be able to hide it much longer. The truth is going to come out sooner or later. I just hope that they don't freak out on me. I know Josie is going to want to know who the father is, but I need to keep that to myself out of respect for him. I keep thinking I'm going to tell him, but then I imagine the expression on his face when I tell him that our one moment produced a child and I can't bring myself to say those words. Watching him walk out on me will break my heart.

Liam's car pulls into the driveway, shaking me from my reverie. I focus harder through the rain sheeted window when I hear four car doors slam individually. From the time that it takes me to leave the living room and walk into the foyer the door is open. Liam walks in first, his arms and hair dripping with water. Josie's next, but under the cover of Liam's jacket. My heart aches, knowing I won't have that kind of love. The next person to walk in is my mom, but the fact that she's standing there, staring at me, is not registering. I look at her hard, questioningly. She smiles, her eyes sad. My dad steps in and shuts the door. He looks at me, smiling widely.

I run the five or so steps it takes me to get to my parents. I collapse into them, one on each side of me, and don't even try to stop the tears from coming. My parents are here in Beaumont. I haven't seen them in so long and they're here, standing in Liam's house, dripping water all over the floor, but that doesn't matter because I'm holding them now.

"Let me take your coats," Liam says, moving around us, trying not to bother our reunion.

I pull back and look at my parents. My mom, she's aged, but is just as beautiful as the last time I saw her. My dad, he's graying more and has earned himself a bit of a belly.

"I must be dreaming," I say.

"You're not dreaming. Your friend, Liam, arranged this for us."

I glance over their shoulders at Liam, who is acting shy, as if he doesn't like to be the center of attention. If he weren't the lead singer of a successful band, I'd almost believe that he's shy. Liam looks at me and offers me a half smile and a shrug.

"He's pretty great," I say, downplaying the situation for him. "Come on, you must be so cold in those wet clothes. I'll take you upstairs and you can change."

"I'll go get their things," Liam says, slipping into his coat.

"I'll go with you, son," my dad says.

Liam freezes, his hand on the doorknob. I see Liam's jaw clench, but he nods, accepting my dad's help. I'll have to find a time, privately, to tell my dad that Liam and his father have a rough relationship.

"I'm so happy to see you, Jenna." My mom takes my hands in hers. Her eyes water as do mine. The last time she saw me I had a bruised cheek that even make-up couldn't hide.

"I can't believe you're here." Pulling her into my arms, I hug her tightly. I mouth 'thank you' to Josie, who is standing there watching us. She looks like she's about to cry. She shakes her head, telling me everything I need to know. Liam set this up. He did this for me.

The men walk back in with luggage in their hands. Liam nods to the stairs and my dad follows. I'll gladly take the couch if it means my parents are going to be here for a while.

"How long are you here for?"

"Well, dear, you and your father need to figure out what to do about Damien, and I'm going to take care of you."

I fight the urge to roll my eyes. "I'm fine, Mom. Ever since that night, Damien hasn't been around."

"I know, but that doesn't mean he isn't waiting for you. Lurking out there like the sick man that he is." She closes her eyes, clearly remembering the night that I came home battered. I will never forget the expression on her face when I walked into the house or when she sat with me in the emergency room while the police took pictures—pictures that they never did anything with.

"I wouldn't know. I'm being held captive."

Josie scoffs in the background.

"It's true. This is the Westbury jail. I'm not even working and I hate that."

"With more people watching now, you can go back to work." Liam's voice startles me. I turn away from my mom to find him and my dad behind me.

"Is that why you called my parents, to babysit me?" I ask, trying not to laugh. He shrugs. "Well, thank you." I give him a hug. "I really needed them here," I mumble into his shirt.

"I know." He rubs his hands up and down my back. "We just want you safe."

I nod, biting my lip to keep from crying. I can't keep crying at the drop of a hat. I know I'm emotional, but it's getting to be too much. I'm going to dehydrate myself if I'm not careful.

"We need to talk, Jenna," my dad says, motioning toward the table. I follow him, pulling out the chair across from him. He slides papers over to me. Everything moves in slow motion. The last time we did this, I ended my marriage. What will I be doing this time?

I flip through the pages. Each page detailing previously told incidents from the diary I kept. I can't read them. I don't want to relive those nights in my life. When I married Damien, I was happy, I was in love.

"Sign on the back there."

"What am I signing?"

"It's a restraining order. It's a long shot, but we're going to try it. I can't practice here, but Liam says he already has someone that I can work with to get this squared away."

"What does this mean, Dad?"

He folds his hands on the table and leans toward me. "It means, if the judge accepts this order, Damien won't be able to come within two thousand feet. It's far-fetched, but we're hoping to pull some strings."

"And what happens if the judge doesn't go for this?"

My dad leans back and scratches his belly. I stifle a laugh. He won't like it if I'm not taking this seriously. "The worst case scenario is we get thrown out, but I'm hoping it doesn't come to that."

"We don't even know where he is."

Dad flips though the papers sitting in front of him. "Officer Baker has been keeping tabs on him. He placed a GPS beacon under his car. It's illegal, but it allows Baker to track Damien's whereabouts."

"Is he waiting for me to leave the house?"

"Yes," Liam says, coming into the room. "This is why Paul was adamant you stay in the house. He's waiting to bust him and was hoping he'd trespass, but he hasn't. So now Paul wants you to return to work."

"I'm the bait."

Liam shrugs. "Or the solution. Your dad will file the restraining order tomorrow, asking for an emergency hearing. Your ex doesn't have to be at the hearing, but Paul will serve him when he sees him."

It sounds too complicated. I do want to go back to work, but seeing Damien is not something I want to do. I sign my name and leave the table. I have to trust that my dad, Liam, and Paul know what they're doing.

I take the stairs to my room. I need to lie down and try to sleep off this headache I'm developing. My mom is in my room—well, now her room—putting away her clothes. She smiles when I walk in. I sit on the bed and watch her for a minute.

"Have you been sleeping well?"

I shake my head. "A lot of thoughts run through my head when I'm alone."

"That happens when you have so much on your plate."

She sits down next to me, putting her arm around me.

"I have something to tell you, but you can't tell Dad."

"Okay."

"You have to promise." I know once she does, she'll never tell.

"I promise, sweetheart. Tell me what's going on." She runs her hand through my hair, like she did when I was younger. Just like she did the night before I married Damien.

"I'm pregnant." I lift my sweatshirt and show her my little bump, a bump that I'm very proud of.

"Oh, Jenna." She covers her mouth. I can't look at her for fear of seeing the disappointment in her face. "Who's the father? Have you been together long?"

I shake my head, biting my lip. "We're just friends, but he doesn't know. I don't know if I'll tell him. He's not really the commitment type."

"Do you think he'll change his mind when you tell him?"

I look at her and see myself years from now. "It's better if I do this by myself."

9

JIMMY

Everything is white and sterile. This is a new side of Chelsea. When we lived together it was girly pink with posters of boy bands, tiaras, and pompoms in the corner. The virginal Chelsea was sweet, innocent, and ready to rebel against her straight-laced corporate American father and her beauty contest winning mother.

I was her salvation.

She was my destruction.

"You're new here."

I look at the leggy blonde lying on the sunbed next to me. I don't remember seeing her when I sat down, but I can't say I was paying much attention.

"Yeah, I am. My dad lives here. I'm only staying here until I find my own place."

She turns to face me, putting her sunglasses on top of her head. "Where are you from?"

"London."

She sits up and swings her tanned, toned legs around.

She's posh, upper-class. Right up my father's street. He'd call her arm candy.

"What's your name?"

"Jimmy. Jimmy Davis," I say, as I hold my hand out to her. She takes it and I shake it firmly.

"Can I call you James?"

Shaking my head slowly, I smile at her. "Nope, my name's Jimmy, not James. You'd have to ask my mum why she didn't call me James."

She laughs and for the first time since I've been in Los Angeles, I'm laughing, too. When my mum suggested I should come out there to live with my dad I was against the idea. She told me this is where I should pursue my dream of making music and if I didn't like it, I could come back and try and be successful in London as a famous musician. She wanted the best for me.

I didn't want to come. I can't stand my father. I think I'm the only child to ever celebrate when my mum finally kicked him out, but she says I need him in my life. I beg to differ, but I'm here and enjoying the luxury that his apartment has to offer.

"What's your name?"

"Chelsea Spencer."

"Do you live here?" I point to the towering apartment block in front of me. My dad lives on the seventeenth floor. It's a penthouse, bigger than our flat in London, and it pisses me off that he isn't looking after my mum, given that he clearly has the funds to do so.

"Sometimes I stay here or at our country house."

I give her a once over and decide that she's from money. I should've known. I wanted to avoid everything that was the typical L.A. cliché, otherwise known as 'the rich-list' in Los Angeles, and the first woman I talk to is just that. Chances are, daddy dearest is probably some high-powered politician.

I look back at the pool and watch the other women. They flirt with the waiters and other men passing by. No wonder my dad thinks the way he's treated my mum is okay. He lives it on a daily basis.

"Did I say something wrong?"

Pressing my lips together, I shake my head. "No."

"How old are you, Jimmy?"

I try to avoid eye contact with her, but to no avail. She's sexy and I'd be stupid to ignore her. I'm lucky she's even talking to a bloke like me. I'm sure she has some man waiting for her once he finishes work. She adjusts the straps on her bikini, giving me an eyeful.

"I'm nineteen," I say, moving my legs around so I can face her. I reach over and adjust the fabric of her top to cover her nipple. "You're showing."

"Oh shit, thank you." Her hand covers mine and she holds it over her tit longer than should be normal seeing as I just met her. My fingers squeeze on their own accord. I try to remove my hand, but she's holding it there firmly.

"Um ..."

"Sorry," she says, letting go. "I think you're really hot."

"I think you're fucking sexy," I blurt out.

"Want to see my room?"

When we lived together we had vibrant art, mixed lines, and warmth. Her apartment now lacks colour and life. This is what I think as I lie in her bed, staring at the ceiling. Her tanorexic arm is lying across my stomach. One of her bare breasts rests on my chest. Her head is snuggled into my neck. I used to enjoy this. I used to beg for this.

But now I want to run.

I turn my head a little to look at Chelsea. Her dark blonde roots are starting to show over her bottled hair colour. If I tell her that her roots need doing, she'd go running to the hairdresser to have them taken care of. She's superficial like that, and right now I'm in that frame of mind. I know everything there is to know about her and that's still not enough for me to stay. Yet, the moment I touched back down in Los Angeles, I called her because I knew she'd come running and now I lie here, regretting it.

This isn't where I want to be. I've never been able to say no to her, but I never imagined that I'd be back in her bed. She knows how to wear me down and does it with perfect precision. I'm the way I am because she's my first love and I haven't even tried to love anyone since her. Maybe that's my problem. Maybe I need to put my heart on the line again to get Chelsea out of my system.

I know who can do that for me. She's already creeping in. I just don't know if I can be enough for her. If I tried and she rejected me, then I'd be no better off than I am now. All I know is this isn't where I want to be.

I could just go to her and make myself available. If she turns me down I'll act like it's not a big deal. Typical Jimmy Davis.

"What are you thinking so hard about?"

I close my eyes the moment her lips touch my chest. I should push her away, but I won't. I should tell her that we won't work, but she already knows that and here she is, still willing to keep me as her dirty little secret.

"Life," I say, not wanting to look at her. She doesn't delve any deeper. I know she doesn't care. She's a good pretender, but in reality I'm just something she's using to pass the time until the next daddy-approved boyfriend comes along.

Her mouth starts sucking on my dick and he springs to life in no time. I bite on my lower lip to stop from hissing. I don't want her to know that I'm enjoying her attention, but I'm a fucking bloke and this shit feels fucking fabulous. I keep my hands behind my head, close my eyes, and enjoy the moment. I imagine the girl I want sucking me off instead of the one that is. Her nails roam over my stomach, down my thighs, and back up again. I shift, lifting my hips up to increase her speed to ease the pressure that's building. She slows down and it's not exactly what I had in mind. She lets go and moves. I know what she wants, but I don't think I can bring myself to be with her anymore.

She holds my cock. My eyes spring open when I feel myself slide into her. I sit up and grab her hips. She moves to kiss me but I throw her off me.

"What the fuck, Jimmy?"

I sit up and put my feet on her wooden floor. She moves behind me and starts kissing my back.

"Stop, Chelsea."

She does and sighs heavily. "What's wrong?"

"You know I don't shag without wearing protection."

"Jimmy, baby, we've been together for three years. We've done it before, I just wanted to feel you," she coos in my ear as she puts her arms around me. Her lips find my ear and tug lightly on my lobe.

"No, Chelsea, we haven't been together for three years. Regardless of that fact, I don't want kids. You know that."

"So put a condom on and make love to me."

I shake my head and stand up. I walk over to the chair where she put my folded clothes at some point during the night.

"I've gotta go."

"I just got you back and you're leaving me?"

"I'm not back, Chels. This was a mistake."

I put on my jeans, pull on my boots, and slide my T-shirt over my head. I walk over to the girl I once loved knowing that I'm never coming back here. Cupping her cheek, I pull her to me.

"You know it's for the best. Your dad doesn't approve of me and he'll make your life a living hell." I kiss her once on the lips and back away from her.

"Don't leave me. I need you, Jimmy. You have no idea how bad I need you." Tears follow her words, but they aren't enough for me.

"Good-bye, Chelsea."

"HOW WAS LOS ANGELES?" Liam asks while he tunes his guitar.

"For the first time since I moved there, I couldn't wait to get out. I have some news though." I hand Liam the papers that were delivered to my apartment from Mr. Moreno. He flips through them, his eyebrow moving up and down each time he gets to an interesting part.

"She wasn't ever pregnant?"

"What?" Harrison exclaims as he stands up from this stool. Taking the papers from Liam's hand, he reads them. He looks at me, then at Liam, and back at the papers.

"What a bitch," Harrison spits out.

"She was sick," Liam says. Why he's defending her, I have no idea.

"Sick or not, she tried to ruin your life. If you keep reading, it lists out all of the other shit she did. She kept a diary and Mr. Moreno has included some of her entries," I add.

"She rigged the tour last year," Harrison says as he reads. "The dressing room, the weird phone call I received after I met that chick in the bar, it's all here, Liam. She kept notes on everything." Harrison continues to turn the pages, flipping them rapidly. "Nothing about Alicia though."

Harrison throws the papers on the table and runs his hands through his hair.

"Liam?" He's staring off, not really listening to what Harrison just said. "Yo, man, you okay?" I push him slightly on the shoulder.

He looks at me and shakes his head. "What?"

"You're off in cloud cuckoo land."

"She lied," he says. "I didn't get her pregnant."

"She lied about everything. Everything that's happened to us since we've met her has been because of her evil mind. She's fucking twisted," Harrison says. I know he's upset that the information he's after isn't in there. He'll never know why Alicia did what she did, but at least with the rest of the information, we can move on.

Liam picks up the papers again and reads through them before putting them aside. "We need to get serious about hiring a manager or hang it up."

"You want to quit?" I ask. The band splitting up is the last thing I want, but if he's ready to call it a day I'm not going to stop him. He's got a kid now. Christ, Harrison has three. I'm the odd man out. No wife, no kids. Nothing keeping me at home.

"No, I don't, but we need a manager. We need to release a CD and get the airplay. I'll make some calls," he says.

"I can make some, too," I volunteer. With me still living in LA, I'm around the scene more. I'm sure there's someone looking to add to their client list and won't mind if the talent doesn't live anywhere near them. It shouldn't be a problem at all. "What's going on with Jenna's ex?" I ask, needing to know the latest.

Harrison sighs. "It's not good."

"No, it's not. Her parents are here and her dad tried to get a restraining order against him, but the judge wasn't buying our reasoning. He's not a threat just because he showed up at the café."

"He's beaten her up before—"

"As she said, there's no record aside from the one hospital visit and those pictures apparently never got logged," Harrison explains.

Picking my guitar up, I put the strap over my head. I plug the lead into the amp and start tuning. I don't know if there's anything I can do for her, but I'm going to give it a try. No one should have to fear for their lives, and if it means I have to be a permanent fixture at Whimsicality then so be it.

10

JENNA

I'm happy to be back at work even if it means I'm looking over my shoulder. Damien is gone, at least that's what Paul says, but I know he'll be back. Nothing about him goes quietly into the night. He doesn't like to lose, and I know him well enough to know that he's pissed off and will seek revenge. Sadly, I'm his target.

My mom is currently yapping it up with Jimmy. He's been sitting at the same table since we opened. The first few days I found it odd, until Harrison spilled the beans that Jimmy is currently seeking a full-time job as my babysitter. The guys are overprotective, but it's nice to know that when Damien does return, they'll be around to protect me. I'm just afraid they'll get hurt. Liam assures me that they can and will take care of themselves and the people that they love.

Each time the door chimes, my body turns cold. I hate living with fear. I've grown so accustomed to being free that this constant sense of dread washing over me is getting to be too much. I could be free if I left Beaumont, but something tells me I wouldn't get very far.

I smile at Nick when he walks in. He's dressed in his usual dark slacks and white button-down shirt. He's here to see Aubrey for lunch. He does this every day that she works. It's sickeningly sweet, but gives me the tiniest bit of hope that someday I'll find my Prince Charming.

Nick always chooses to come into the flower shop before going to the café, and each time it's because he's buying his wife a single flower. Today he's buying a red sunflower. I like how he's still supporting Josie after everything that went down. I know what happened was for the best though. Nick never smiled like this until he came home with Aubrey.

"Busy today?"

"Not really. The sun is out so I think most everyone is enjoying it before it rains. How's the office?" I ask, wrapping Aubrey's flower in paper and tying it with a ribbon.

"Same ole skinned knees, bumps, and the perpetual cough," Nick says, handing me his payment.

"But you treat them all the same and with a smile, right?"

"Of course," he replies, smiling. "Aubrey and I want to have you over for dinner soon."

"Thank you, I'd like that."

"Have you told everyone yet?"

I shake my head.

Nick caught me going into the obstetrician's office. I couldn't hide my elation and he guessed. He and Aubrey both know, but haven't said anything, and they both know I appreciate them keeping my confidence. Nick will be the baby's doctor, if I decide to stay in Beaumont.

"I'm telling Josie and Liam tonight."

"And the baby's dad?"

"No, not yet. I just don't think it's a good idea."

Nick leans forward and lowers his voice. "Please rethink not telling him, Jenna. Even if he's not around, it's important that he know he has a child out there. Besides, he might surprise you and want to be around."

"I don't think so. Having a baby would ruin his life. It's best that I just keep his identity a secret."

He nods, even though I know he doesn't agree with me.

Nick picks up Aubrey's flower and gives me a small wave before turning toward the café. I watch as she meets him on the side, squealing in delight because he brought her a flower. She does this every time. I can't imagine how happy she'd be if he brought her a bouquet or jewelry. Aubrey loves Nick dearly. You can see it in the way she looks at him.

I used to love Damien that way, even after the abuse started. I believed that if I loved him harder, that if I loved him more, he'd stop. I thought that he'd see how much he was hurting me and realize my pain was because of his fist, but it never stopped. I realized, albeit too late, that he loved hitting me more than I loved taking it.

I PULL out the chair across from Josie and Liam. Tonight's the night. The truth, well most of it, will come out. They look at me expectantly and I want to laugh at how absurd this has all been, but I needed to wait, at least for me, before telling them.

I fold my hands in front of me and take a deep breath. I smile, hoping to convey that, yes everything is okay, even if it might not be.

"What's up?" Liam asks, breaking the ice. I know he's busy and I'm probably keeping him from something important.

I look away, down at my hands, and say, "I'm pregnant."

The audible gasp is from Josie. I'm picturing her with her hand over her mouth. I hear nothing from Liam. I chance a look and am met with indifference. I can't tell what he's thinking. Even though we've only known each other a short time, it's been enough for us to form a bond.

"How far are you?" Josie asks, her voice wavering.

I bite the inside of my cheek and straighten out the tablecloth. "I'm past my first trimester. I'm starting to show. My clothes are tighter and my mom knows. But she can't really keep a secret and is dying to tell you. I know she's excited." I chance a look at Josie. She's smiling widely and that makes me feel relieved.

"Who's the father? I haven't seen you with anyone, ever." Liam's words remind me that I've been alone and will continue to be that way.

"Liam," Josie scolds.

"What?" He shrugs. "I'm just asking. She's family, right?" Josie nods. "Well, if she has someone in her life, I'd like to know him."

"You can't," I blurt out.

"Why not?" he asks.

"Because he's not around."

"What do you mean 'he's not around'?" Liam's tone is hard and to the point.

I swallow and square myself for battle. "I've decided not to tell him. We're not together and he doesn't live here. It's for the best."

Josie's face goes pale just as Liam's turns red.

"Are you kidding me?"

I shake my head and bite the inside of my cheek.

"You know what, that's some very selfish bullshit. Josie tried to tell me that she was pregnant and it kills me every day knowing that I wasn't there for her and Noah. I wasn't given a fucking choice on whether or not I was going to be a douche or not. It was made for me. What makes you think the father doesn't want to be involved?"

"He's younger and not in the right frame of mind to be in this situation."

"So why sleep with him?"

"Liam," Josie scolds again.

"No, I want to know. You have to know the risk when you decide to sleep with someone. Hell, I knew and the biggest bitch burned me. Men don't think of these things when we're having sex, but women do. Your clocks tick and all that shit. So if he's not father material, why do it?"

Tears stream down my cheeks while Liam rants. I know he's right, but it's not like we planned this. It just happened.

"It wasn't planned, Liam. It was a one-night stand." I take a deep breath. "It's not ideal, but it's my decision. I can do this by myself."

"Until your ex comes around. I'm sure once he finds out that you're pregnant with another man's baby that will set him off."

I nod because he's right. Damien always wanted a baby and I did everything I could to prevent us from conceiving.

"I'll deal with him then."

"No, we'll deal with it. You have to tell the father, Jenna."

"I can't."

"Why not? He has a right to know," Liam pleads.

"I'm pretty sure he regrets sleeping with me. I don't need to see the expression on his face when I remind him of the night we spent together and how we're now having a child. That sort of stuff ruins lives, Liam. I don't want to ruin his life."

"He has a right to know, and if he doesn't want to be a part of your baby's life, then he's the one missing out, but you have to give him the opportunity whether you think he's father material or not.

"Don't take the opportunity away from him. It was taken away from me and I live with a gap in my heart. He deserves to know."

Liam gets up and leaves us. Josie and I jump when the basement door slams. She moves over next to me, pulling me into her arms. I try not to cry, but it's to no avail. It should've been easier to tell Josie and Liam over my mother, but it wasn't. My mom has always known that I want to be a mother. She knows this is my chance.

"Congratulations. Are you happy?" she asks.

I nod. Pulling away, I wipe away my tears. "I am. I really am." I set my hand on my stomach, smiling. "This is a good thing."

"It is, babies are wonderful, believe me I want another one, but it's not in the cards. But do me a favor and really think about telling the dad. I wish Liam were there for Noah. I know that things with him and I may not have worked, but I have no doubt he would've been there for his son. Every dad needs to be able to make that choice himself."

When I made the decision not to tell, I hadn't thought about what Liam and Noah have gone through. Or even Nick. But this man, he doesn't want this. He wants his life the way it is and this isn't a bump in the road, it's a sinkhole, and I'm not sure if me being pregnant is enough to make him change his life.

11

JIMMY

"What are you doing here?"

I look up from my piece of sheet music and find Liam at the door. The studio has a private entrance and we've always been told it's okay to come whenever we want, but judging by the expression on his face, he doesn't want me here right now.

"It's late."

I take a quick look at my phone and notice the time. "I'll go."

"No, stay," he says, moving farther into the room. He picks up his guitar only to put it back down. He walks toward Harrison's drums, hitting the cymbal with his fingers a few times before walking back in my direction. The studio isn't that big with all our equipment in here and his wandering around makes the room feel much smaller.

"Do you ever feel like your head is going to explode?"

"All the time. Why, are you and Josie having problems?"

Liam shakes his head. "Her and I are solid. Every day I have with her is the happiest day of my life."

"If this is about a manager, I have a mate who's in a band. I can ask him and see if his manager is interested in helping us out. We might even be able to do a tour with them this summer if we need to."

"It's not about the band. We'll figure that shit out. It's about life."

I have no idea where he's going with this, but if he says he's happy with Josie then I don't have a clue what's weighing so heavily on his mind. This is the notable difference we've all seen in Liam since he moved back to Beaumont. It's like he's more human. Before, he wouldn't give a shit about anything, but now everything matters. I like this Liam, but I'm not gonna lie, the emo crap gets on my nerves.

"Is it Noah?"

"No, it's Jenna."

Jenna? What the hell could be going on with Jenna that Liam would be so depressed about? I don't want to be nosey, but I'm curious. I know I'm not as close to her as he and Harrison are, but I still consider us to be family and if she's in trouble I'd like to be able to help. I don't know if there's anything I could do, but I'd damn well try.

"What's wrong with Jenna? I thought the ex was gone."

"He is, at least according to Paul."

Liam stops talking and sits down on his stool. Picking up his acoustic guitar, he strums a few chords.

"Do you know how I found out about Noah?"

"No," I say. Liam kept Noah a secret from us for a while after he found out about him. Harrison and I never understood why, but I think it's because he was afraid that Josie was going to take him away.

"I was having a meltdown over Mason's death and

everything was closing in. I was minutes away from saying 'fuck it'. Instead, I got on my bike and started driving and ended up at this sports museum we have in the next town. Walking in was a mistake because there I was, staring back at myself. I was being mocked by the cocky teenager that I was and there wasn't shit I could do about it.

"I could hear the crowds cheering in my head. I could remember every pass I had thrown to Mason and every touchdown I had. All these memories came flooding back and it was the sound of laughter that broke me. I ran to the bathroom to hide because I didn't want to be recognized.

"When I came out, this boy ... this shaggy-haired boy was crying and I thought he was being bullied and remembered that Mason and I beat the crap out of some kid in high school for bullying someone who was weaker than us. I felt rage boiling inside of me. Do you know what I did?"

I shake my head.

"I spoke to him and he told me that he wasn't allowed to speak to strangers and I thought 'wow, what a smart kid'. It was when he said he'd seen me kissing his mom that I knew. I tried to play it off, but one look and it was obvious. One look into his eyes and I saw her, the one I left behind. I knew I had fucked up so badly that I'd never be forgiven. I knew that I was never leaving Beaumont again because I had a son whether this boy knew I was his dad or not. I would've stayed in the background just to watch him grow up, but I would've been there."

"Josie loves you, Liam."

"I promised her the world when we were in high school. I knew she was my girl, but when I went to college, shit was bad and I freaked out. If Mason hadn't died I wouldn't know my son."

"You shouldn't think like that, man. I'm sure she would've found you." I know he said that he and Josie are fine, but I'm starting to think otherwise. Why is he going on about him and Noah like this when they're a family? When they seem to have everything going for them?

"Jenna's pregnant and doesn't want to tell the baby's father even though I think she's making a mistake. I told her that the dad has a right to know."

I play a few chords, working out a melody. "I didn't know she had a boyfriend. Why doesn't she want to tell him?"

"I don't know, something about him not being father material and they're not together."

Taking my guitar off, I put it on its stand. I rub my hands down my legs. "I'm sure she'll come around."

"I don't think she will. She won't even tell us who the dad is."

"How many weeks is she?" I don't know why I'm asking, but I need to know.

"She's past her first trimester. I didn't know what that meant so I looked it up before I came down here. She got pregnant sometime around the wedding. A one-night stand with a lasting memory."

I swallow hard and stand up. I don't have anything else to add to the conversation. I have no idea why women make the decisions they do, but I do understand why Liam is upset. He missed out on a lot where his son is concerned. No one should have to experience what he did, unless it's by choice.

I SIT OUTSIDE, replaying Liam's words over and over in my head. Jenna's pregnant. The way he opened up about him and Noah really struck a chord with me. Liam always wanted to be a father. I know my mum wanted me, but my dad ... he couldn't have cared less.

I light a cigarette, blowing the smoke into the cool night air. I make smoke rings to entertain myself while I try to work out how to get Jenna outside. I should just go to her room and kidnap her. That would be exciting and slightly stalkerish, but she'd forgive me. Her father may shoot me though.

"You shouldn't smoke."

I turn sharply at the sound of her voice. She's wearing a long white pyjama top and I'm unable to see her belly, not that I'm looking, but I'm definitely curious.

"Jesus, you put the shits right up me, sweet lips." I stub my cigarette out. The last thing she needs is me blowing smoke in her direction and hurting her baby.

"I did what?"

"Ah sorry. I mean, you scared me."

"You have an interesting way with words, Jimmy. What are you doing out here?" she asks, sitting down next to me. Her gown covers her legs, still making it impossible for me to see any evidence of a bump. I don't know what my infatuation is with her, but I think she's beautiful and this baby is going to be lucky if he's staring at her all the time. She could be having a girl with the same dark red hair and green eyes.

"What are you looking at?"

"You," I reply, smiling.

"Why?" She brushes her hair with her hand and looks away.

I reach over and pull her chin toward me. Her muscles are tense. Her eyes are downcast. I hate that she's afraid of affection.

"I'm just counting your freckles."

"Sprinkles," she says. I look at her questioningly. "I called them sprinkles when I was younger and never stopped."

I drop my hand, but let it rest on her leg. She doesn't push it off or shift away. "Will you call them sprinkles for your baby, too?"

She looks at me in surprise. I shrug in response, not wanting to give up the source of my information. I try to smile at her, but it turns more into a flirty gesture. I rub my hand over my face, still unable to move my other hand from her leg.

"You know what, I promised you a holiday. What do you say we leave right now, get a flight to some tropical island and sit on hammocks for a week while waves crash onto the beach around us? You can go to the spa and get pampered and I'll treat you to moonlight walks and dinner under the stars."

"I don't know, Jimmy, what will all your girls think of this treatment?"

I shake my head. "Only you get this side of me. I want to give you a week of pure bliss. It's the least I can do seeing as you never look down on me."

"Okay," she says, not hesitating in the slightest. I thought she'd definitely put up a fight.

"D'you want to leave now?" I know I do. I want to get

out of Beaumont as quickly as we can and go where no one will know us, where no one will bother us unless we request their attention.

"What about arrangements?"

"Go and change and don't pack anything. We'll buy everything we need when we get there." I stand and reach out for her hand. "Come on, you go change and I'll leave a note to let everyone know. I want to sneak out before someone tells us you can't go or it's no good for the baby. It'll be good for the baby's mum and that's what's important right now."

Jenna hesitates, she doesn't move when I pull on her arm.

"What?"

"Who are you and what have you done with the Jimmy Davis I know?"

I shrug. "My friend needs a week of rest and relaxation and I'm going to provide it. Come on, sweet lips." I move forward without thinking and place my lips on hers. She doesn't pull away, she freezes. I try not to let my disappointment show. I'm not sorry that I kissed her, but I am sorry that she didn't kiss me back.

12

JENNA

I should've said no. That one syllable word with two letters mocks me. But I said yes and now I regret it.

Jimmy helps me off the flight. His arm is cinched tightly around my waist, holding me up. I spent a majority of the flight in the small, overly cramped bathroom throwing up. It was the food. That's what I told Jimmy. But in all honesty, the moment I smelled the processed chicken in First Class I knew it was going to be a long flight. He tried to comfort me. He even held me while I tried to sleep.

Now he's holding me as we walk through the terminal to our waiting car. He helps me in and gives the driver the address to our hotel. The *Four Seasons*, of course. Closing my eyes, I lean my head against the back of the seat. Nothing about this trip is going smoothly. I'm betting Jimmy is going to drop me off at the room and hit the bar to find some entertainment for the night. I can't really blame him, even though he said he wouldn't. I might have to encourage him just so he'll relax.

Jimmy wakes me up when we arrive at the hotel. The

valet opens my door and helps me out. Jimmy's right, the sun does feel good. He gets out of the car behind me, puts his hand on my back, and guides me to the door. It's odd arriving with no luggage, but I know why we did when we walk in. There are stores lining the walls with everything that we'll need.

Jimmy gives a name, not his, but someone called Edward Windsor. I stifle a laugh and make a mental note to ask Josie and Katelyn what the guys use for aliases. I think it's fitting that Jimmy's given himself the last name of Windsor. The desk clerk taps his figures over the keys. The clickety-clack gives me a headache. I don't want to depend on Jimmy, but right now I need him. I need the comfort he's willing to give me. I lean to the side and rest my head on his shoulder. He wraps his arm around me, holding me to him. I can't resist and rest my arm along his waist. It feels good to be in his arms. If I wasn't pregnant I think I'd be willing to see how far I can go with Jimmy while we're on vacation. What's Bora Bora without sun, sand, and a bit of sex?

"Just a few more minutes, sweet lips." He's so sincere in the way he's talking to me and the way he's been since we left Beaumont. No one, at least those of us in town, ever see this side of him. I'm sure all his girlfriends see him like this. It's probably why he has so many women flocking to him.

"Mr. and Mrs. Windsor, congratulations." The desk clerk beams with excitement as he hands Jimmy—aka Edward Windsor—his credit card. I'm trying to play along, but the congratulatory greeting is confusing. "I hope your honeymoon is everything you've ever dreamed of. When you're in your room and need assistance, just dial one and the operator will help you."

I look up and stare at the clerk. He's smiling so bright I have to wonder if his cheeks hurt.

"What's he talking about?" I ask, quietly, not wanting to draw attention to the clerk's screw up.

Jimmy shakes his head slightly and turns us toward the waiting bellhop. We follow him down the path toward our suite. Calm waters surround us on each side. The turquoise blue water looks so inviting. Leave it to my pretend boyfriend to bring me on vacation to the one of the most romantic destinations in the world. I feel like an idiot.

The bellhop stops and points to our villa. Jimmy pulls me behind him, slapping some money into the man's hand before closing the bamboo door. I walk in and fight back a laugh.

"Something funny?"

I shake my head, wrapping my arms my stomach. "We're in the most beautiful place in the world, apparently on our honeymoon, and I'm betting all you're thinking about are the single women in the bar."

"What makes you think something like that?" He sounds offended.

I turn and look at him. His face is solemn. Sad, even. He looks down at the wooden floor and at not at me.

"I'm sorry, that was rude. Thank you for bringing me here, Jimmy." I step forward and put my arms around him, giving him a hug. I don't know what our boundaries are, but I'm not willing to make him uncomfortable.

Jimmy pulls me tighter to his body and kisses the top of my head. I sigh, melting into him. I like that he isn't afraid to touch me even though my belly is starting to make me look bigger. Most guys would be turned off, but not Jimmy.

Jimmy walks us to the edge of the room. The wall is missing, of course, giving us access to the water. We stand here, looking out at the water while in our suite. There's nothing stopping us from running through the room and out to the water. I can't imagine how we stay safe at night and maybe I'm missing some sliding doors, but this is beautiful and I think I'm in love. I know I'm definitely in good company and thankful that he thought enough to bring us here.

"Want to swim?"

I laugh. "No suit, remember?"

"I haven't forgotten. I'll be right back. Don't go anywhere."

I look at him with confusion. "Where would I go?"

"I don't know. Go have a shower. I won't be long."

Jimmy's out of the room before I have a chance to say anything. I try not to look at the clock, to memorize the time he left. I don't want to set myself up for the heartbreak when his 'be right back' turns into hours and hours of being gone while I sit here in my dirty clothes.

I do as he suggests and take a shower. The water feels good. I don't know how long I stand under the spray, but it's long enough for my body to feel watered down. I pull on the cotton bathrobe and rub the collar on my cheek. It's so soft and inviting. I run my fingers through my wet hair. I'll need to pick up a brush while I'm here. I can go without make-up. Well, maybe I'll get some mascara.

When I open the door, Jimmy is standing by the bed, staring out into the lagoon. My heart beats rapidly. I didn't think he'd come back, yet here he is. He's changed and is now wearing dark slacks. He turns and smiles. I have to stop in my tracks. His white button-down is open, exposing the light smattering of dark hair on his torso. He has one tattoo, a Chinese symbol resting precariously near his hip bone. I want to touch him. I want to run my fingers along his abs, tracing each one until I know every curve by heart. His usual crazy hair is styled nicely, making me miss his Mohawk.

He has a date.

I try not to let the thought ruin my mood, but I can't help it. I offer him a sad smile and sit on the edge of the bed.

"What's wrong, sweet lips?" he asks, kneeling in front of me.

"You're dressed up."

He looks at himself and nods. "So?"

"You have a date, Jimmy. You said no other women." I know I'm complaining. It's childish and stupid. I should just go to the lobby and buy a nice book to read while he's out gallivanting with the female population.

"I do have a date, silly girl, with you."

"What?"

Jimmy puts his hand on my knee, moving the bathrobe out of the way. "I want you to listen to me. Over these past few months I've grown to know you pretty well, and if I'm being honest, you're one of my best friends. I can be myself when I'm around you and not the performer or the guy those other groupies look for. You let me be an idiot and you still don't look down at me. When I found out about your ex, I wanted to kill him and I haven't had those kind of thoughts in years. I thought 'how could a man hit someone as beautiful and sweet as you?' When Liam told me about the baby, I realised that you don't need to do this alone."

"What are you talking about?"

"You said you'd listen."

"No, I didn't, you just started talking," I say, smiling.

"See, that's what I'm talking about. You could be serious right now, but you're joking around and I really like that about you. Can you at least please hear me out?"

I nod, earning a smile from him.

"Will you marry me?"

My mouth drops open when he pulls out a ring. I cover my mouth, shaking my head. Why is he doing this?

"Are you crazy?"

"Yes," he says matter of fact.

"Jimmy, be serious here. We can't get married."

"Why not?" He looks hurt.

Shaking my head, I stand and walk toward the water. Jimmy follows, standing behind me. He places his hands on the back of my arms, rubbing up and down. It feels like I can reach out and touch the water. The view is indescribable. The water is blue now with the way the sun is shining, and moving so effortlessly, unencumbered, against the pillars.

"I'm being serious, Jenna." He turns me into his arms. "I want to take care of you. I know we aren't a couple, but we could be if we tried. We can learn to be a couple."

I shake my head, fighting back tears. "You live a lifestyle that I could never agree to be a part of. I'd want my husband home with me at night and not in some other bed."

"I'd be faithful."

I throw my arms up and wipe my tears. "Oh, Jimmy, how can you say that?"

"Because it's true." He steps in front of me, pulling my

hands into his. "I want this. I want to take care of you. I want to live with you. I even want to fight with you so that we can make-up with each other."

"I've been married before and swore I'd never do it again. Why would I want to put myself through that again, especially knowing what I know about you?"

Jimmy glances down at the ring in his hand. He sighs before looking at me. "I understand what you're saying, and if I were you, I'd feel the same way. I know I'm not the best man out there, but I look at you and you make me want to be better. I know what people think of me. I know you and everyone else thinks I'm a man-whore or I'm too young to be tied down. Maybe this will be temporary or maybe it will be for life, I don't know, but it feels right. I don't do commitments, but when I look at you, I see a future. I see my future."

He sees his future, but does he see me? I want to say no. I want to run screaming away from here. That would be the logical thing to do. To say thanks, but no thanks. Jimmy has a lifestyle that he's used to and that doesn't really mesh with me. I'd be a wreck waiting for him to come home at night. I'd be anxious that he'd find someone else after a lonely night. Am I enough to get him to stay?

What if I am? What if I'm enough to help him change his ways? What if he's what I need?

"Yes," I say, without any more hesitation. "Yes, Jimmy, I'll marry you."

WE WALK, hand in hand, back to our villa. I never thought someone like Jimmy could be this romantic, especially in the spur of the moment. I don't think this was planned, but if it was, I'm impressed.

I squeal when he picks me up bridal style. He carries me over the threshold and into our room that has been mysteriously decorated with rose petals. I don't know if he wants a traditional marriage. I'm not even sure if I can do a traditional marriage with him. The idea of being with him is enticing, but the images of him with other women keep the shutting the door on those thoughts. Maybe he'll be patient and make me fall in love with him. What happens if I do and he cheats? I don't know if I can do this and keep him happy. Surely, he'll want sex. Any man would in this case, but I'm not sure how long he will wait until he leaves me for someone else.

He sets me down and walks over to the stereo, turning on some light music. I can't stop staring at the bed. A bottle of champagne sits on the table with a bowl of strawberries. Setting my hand on my tummy, I move my thumb back and forth.

I jump slightly when his hands rest on mine. He presses his lips against my bare shoulder. The dress he bought for me—a white strapless, chiffon, full-length gown with a white satin ribbon that tied under my breasts—was perfect. It flowed over my bump, hiding it nicely so no one could tell.

I don't know what my parents are going to say, but I know I did the right thing. I've never done anything spontaneous or in the heat of the moment. I know this may be stupid, but being married to Jimmy feels right. I know he's not going to hurt me with his fist. He might with his body, but never will he lay a finger on me to cause harm. That is something I can trust.

Jimmy unzips my dress, letting it pool at my feet.

"What are you doing, Jimmy?"

His lips move across my back. He places small kisses every few inches. "I'm going to make love to my wife."

"I don't understand."

"What's not to understand, Mrs. Davis? We're married and I plan on making love to you every chance I get. It's a perk, right?"

"Are you moving in with me?"

"Yes, I am. I happen to like your apartment very much." He unclasps my bra, adding it to the pile my dress is already in. He wants to be married, in every aspect of the word. He wants to share a bed, as long as I'll allow him to be next to me. I should try, right? I can make a solid attempt at being his wife. Does he deserve this? He deserves to be loved, cherished and treated with respect just like any other man, right? He stands before me, unbuttoning his shirt. I should do it for him, but he mesmerizes me. This is a new side of him. A side that I'm willing to bet no one has ever seen.

He picks up my hand and holds it out so the moonlight can shine off my diamond. "Gorgeous, but not nearly as gorgeous as the person wearing it," he says. I knew he was being honest with me when he pulled out a band for his finger. He's breaking hearts all over the world tonight now that he's taken himself off the market.

He bends, his hands resting on my stomach. He looks at me, never breaking eye contact as he places a kiss on my skin. Tears pool, making my vision blurry. I reach out and trail my fingers over his cheek. He has tears in his eyes and I don't know why.

"Why didn't you tell me?"

I shake my head.

"I've been thinking about you since that night, Jenna. Every day, I see you when I close my eyes. You're burnt into my skin and I've been fighting my demons every time I'm near you."

"Jimmy," I say, fighting back the tears.

"Sweet lips, we're going to have a baby."

I nod, confirming what he knows. What I know.

He smiles, kissing my stomach again. "We created a little human and you're going to bring our child into the world. I'll be there, by your side, through the whole thing. I promise you."

13

JIMMY

Sitting across the room from her is torture. I've never been attracted to a redhead before, but there's something about Jenna that hits me deep in my core. The way she holds herself, she moves with such confidence. I've seen other women hold all the attention in a room before with their fake personalities, but she doesn't need to do that. She's genuine and elegant. She's all woman and probably more than even I can handle.

Every time I've come to Beaumont I've noticed more and more things about her, but she's out of my league. I'm not smooth like Liam or romantic like Harrison. I can't offer her stability or even a seven-day relationship. I'm damaged and broken. I'm a heartless bastard who only wants one thing and has no problem getting it.

I watch as she works the room. She dances with Liam; their bodies move in sync with each other and the music. When she's finished, she's in the arms of Mr. Powell, Katelyn's father-in-law. I should ask her to dance. The only thing *wrong with me doing that is I want to dance between the sheets with our clothes off and our bodies slick with sweat.*

She catches me staring. It's not the first time and it probably won't be the last. I want carnal knowledge of her body and if I don't get it soon I'm going to spontaneously combust. I want to feel her wrapped around my dick while I grind into her. She'll want me to stay and I'll want to say good-bye.

One night—that's all I need—nothing more, nothing less. There's nothing wrong with two adults giving into heated passion to fulfill their needs and desires. She may not need me, but after a minute with me, she'll be begging for me to take her. I have no doubt she'll satisfy my hunger. She'll quench my thirst. Then I can move on. I can get her out of my system and go about my business. No one needs to know. No one can find out.

She walks to the bar and the barman flirts with her. It's enough to make my blood boil. Is he her type? If so, I'm out of the running. He's tall, lanky, and looks like he plays basketball. The only thing I can play is her body and I know damn well I'll be able to make her sing with the touch of a finger. The barman hands her a napkin and I have no doubts it probably has his number scrawled on it. He wants to take her on a date. I want to fuck her.

I down my whisky and Coke and decide to take my chance. She can turn me down, I'll be okay, but I don't think she will. I've seen her watch me. I know that look. I've seen her undressing me, wondering what I have hiding under my jeans. If I play my cards right, I'll be able to show her.

I sidle up behind her, placing my hands on her hips. My thumbs dig into her arse, hitting her pressure point. "Is he bothering you, love?" I say, loud enough to get the barman's attention. He shakes his head and goes back to his work. Jenna turns around in my arms; my hands don't leave their new favourite place. No one told me that when I touched the fiery redhead that my palms would burn.

"What are you doing, Jimmy?"

"I've come to rescue you."

"Who says I need to be rescued?" Jenna crosses her arms over her chest, accentuating her glorious breasts. They're a fine set of puppies that I need to taste, tickle, and push my face into for the next hour.

"Want to have a little fun?" Usually I just have to nod to the door and women fall over themselves to get to wherever it is we are going, but with her, it's going to be different.

"What do you have in mind?"

I look around, making a note of where Liam and Harrison are. The last thing I need is for either of them to give me shit for fucking around with Jenna, but I need to scratch this itch and I'm fairly certain by the looks she's been giving me that she wants it, too.

"Is there somewhere we can go?"

Jenna looks around. She bites her lower lip, enticing me more. "There's a room down the hall past the bathrooms. I'll meet you there."

She walks out first, leaving me to watch her arse sway. I'm not going to have any qualms about lifting that skirt up and burying myself deep inside of her. I want to hear her scream my name and watch her come undone with my expertise.

I wait a few minutes—probably not long enough, but I can't wait any longer, I need to feel her legs wrapped around me. I walk, faster than normal, down the hall. The sound of

*the wedding celebration becomes muffled the farther I put
the party behind me.*

*The door is cracked open. I shove it open, my eagerness
obvious. She turns, her skirt twirling. If I didn't know better,
I'd think we were filming a scene for a B-rated porn film. The
only thing missing is the cheesy music.*

*I shut the door, locking it behind me. Jenna doesn't move
closer. She stands on the other side of the room, her hands
behind her back. Slipping off my jacket, I place it on the
chair. My tie is next. This is going to be quick, but I want her
to touch me. I want to feel her nails dig into my skin. I
unbutton my shirt and undo my belt. Taking out my wallet, I
grab the condom I put there earlier. I place it on the table, her
eyes watching my every move.*

"Ever done this before?"

*She shakes her head. "I've never had sex outside of a rela-
tionship before."*

*I reach out, placing my hand on her hip, and pull her to
me. "If you don't want to, I'll leave."*

Her eyes bore into mine. "I'm here, aren't I?"

"What are you doing?" Jenna stretches out next to me.
For the first time, in a long time, I made love to a woman.
This time it was different. This time the buildup of a rela-
tionship wasn't there. This time it's my wife.

"Thinking."

"About what?" She rolls to face me. I curl her hair
behind her ear, moving closer. Taking her hand in mine, I
kiss her palm.

"About the night we conceived our baby. Were you ever
going to tell me?" She shakes her head, hiding her face in
the pillow. "Why not?"

Her shoulders shrug. I pull her up, enough so I can see her. She looks so beautiful with the sun shining through the window.

"I didn't want you to think you had to stick around. Even now, if you want out, if you want to move on like nothing has happened, I'll be okay. We'll be okay." She puts her hand on her stomach. The small, round but noticeable bump is barely hiding behind her hand. The same hand I placed a diamond ring on last night, a ring that I meant, with every fibre of my being, to give her.

I know life, for me, is going to be different. No more late nights. No more women. Instead, I'm going to have a wife that I'll come home to each night and lie in bed with on Sunday mornings. I want to be different from my dad. No, I have to be different. My child and wife deserve the world. I won't let Jenna suffer because of the fucked up choices I've made for myself during the past three years.

"I don't want out," I say, putting my hand over hers. "This is where I want to be. When Liam told me you were pregnant, I wanted to hurt the guy who was responsible, but when he said how many months you are and that it happened sometime around the wedding, I knew I was that guy. I'm not going to let you do this by yourself. We're going to be partners in everything. The only way you're going to get rid of me is to tell me that the baby's not mine, but I know in my heart that it is."

"We don't have to be married for you to be a part of the baby's life if that's what you want."

I push her down and hover over the top of her. "I want to be married to you. You're fucking sexy as hell and you rock my world, sweet lips."

Jenna smiles and wiggles underneath me, increasing the problem in my boxers.

"Why do you call me that?"

Leaning down, I kiss her once. "Because the first time I tasted your lips, I thought I had died and gone to heaven. They're so sweet. And now they're all mine."

"You're such a dork."

I fall to the side of her and pretend I'm hurt. She runs her fingers through my hair and kisses me below my ear.

"Traditional marriage?"

Raising my head, I smile. "Yes, that means you have to clean my boxers and cook my dinner."

"And you'll come home every night. No other women?"

"No other women ever, except you." I kiss her hard, hoping to eliminate any thoughts she has about me straying. I've only been willing to settle down one other time in my life and that changed in one fateful night. Since then, I've been doing whoever I please because it's easier than having a relationship. That's until now. Jenna's different. I've known that from the night of the wedding. I was just too stuck in my own world to realise it and work out what to do about it.

"I'm afraid to trust you. I'm scared that you're going to figure out this isn't what you want and that our ideas of a traditional marriage are different."

"I understand that, but I'll do whatever you need me to, to make you feel secure." I kiss my way down her body, lifting up my white T-shirt that she slept in. I place kisses over her belly without breaking eye contact with her. I've always thought Jenna was sexy, but knowing she's having a baby, my baby, makes her the sexiest fucking girl I've ever seen. At the moment, I don't want to be anywhere else.

Being a parent wasn't something I've wanted for a while. When I was with Chelsea we talked about babies with her five- and ten-year plans, but when we split up, I swore off children. I was determined not to find the one to tie me down. It's a good thing we found each other because at the moment, I don't want to be anywhere else. Except in the sea, that is. Right now, I want to see my wife in the bikini I just bought her.

"Let's go swimming," I say, kissing my way up her stomach. She adjusts as I move between her legs. Her hands rest on my shoulders. Her eyes are dark with need. I could give into her, and as much as I'd love to spend all our time in this bed, we need to explore and I want to start with exploring her body in the sea.

"I don't have a swimsuit."

"Hmm, not that you need one, because, trust me, I'd love to sit here and watch your boobs get sun kissed all day, but your bikini is in one of the drawers over there." I point behind me.

She lifts her head slightly, and looks over my shoulder. "How'd it get there?"

"While we were off getting wed, I had a bunch of things delivered. Come on now, up you go, love." I sit back on my knees, straddling her. She starts laughing, covering her face. "What's so funny, sweet lips?"

"You and your accent."

"Mhm, well I have it on good authority that you happen to like my accent." I lean forward and kiss her on her neck, her cheek, and chin until I've moved her hand out of the way so I can kiss her sweet, delectable lips.

She shakes her head, causing me to laugh.

"Are you telling me you don't like my accent?"

She spreads her fingers so she can peek out through the gap. "It's not that, it's just sometimes you say things that I don't understand and other times everything is very American."

I sit back again and pull her up. "That's because I spend all my time with those crazy band mates of mine. Have you heard those two get on? They're like an old married couple, I can tell you. You never know what's going to come out of their mouths."

"Well, I like it."

"That's good. Just think, we'll have to spend a lot of time in England so our bub has an accent, too. Now come on my, wifey, let's go get dirty in the water."

I don't give her time to respond. I stand and scoop her off the bed, carrying her over to the chest of drawers. Putting her down, I leave her to find whatever swimming costume she wants to wear. If I stand there too long I'm bound to take her back to bed.

14

JENNA

I know all this is too good to be true. I should be running away from him, but I can't. I've liked him for so long that when he approached me at the wedding there was no way I was saying no. When I found out I was pregnant, even though I knew I couldn't have him, I'd at least have a part of him.

When Jimmy got on bended knee and asked me to marry him, I should've said no. I should've saved him from the mistake he's going to feel in a week or a month. But I thought, for one brief moment, that when our child is older I could say, "yeah, your parents were married", and that would make everything okay. I never suspected that he knew. Honestly, I haven't given him much credit because he's jumping from bed to bed, but he knew. For that, I have to admire him.

I'm not sure how I'm going to trust him. It's going to be very tough. How can a man who's used to being a certain way suddenly change? It doesn't seem possible. Also, I know nothing about him. I've married a total stranger, but then again, who plans to marry the father of their unborn child months after a one-night stand? Not me, that's for sure. I thought we had our moment and that was it. I'd see him when he was in town and we'd be friendly. Never did I expect this.

I stand on the edge of the deck to our villa. Jimmy swims with his back to me. I can make out the faint coloring of his tattoo. I like that he's not covered like Harrison, not that I've been staring at Harrison, but have seen him enough times mowing his lawn to know. Jimmy's are subtle and along his arm, just enough to add a bit of mystery to him.

"Penny for your thoughts, wifey." He pops out of the water, startling me. I cover my heart and try to regulate my breathing. He laughs and swims over to the ladder. I take in his body as he appears. The water dripping off his already tan skin makes my mouth water. I can have him anytime I want. Right now that sounds like heaven, but I can't shake the feeling that once we're back in reality, I'll just be something he has to take care of. I don't think I'm enough for him to change and I'm thinking that maybe we should get this marriage annulled when we get back. No hard feelings or anything. I just don't want to be the reason he's holding back from who he truly is.

He comes behind me, pressing his wet chest against my back. His hands move around me and rest on my stomach. His thumbs move up and down. He kisses my collarbone, moving to my shoulder.

"You're so fucking sexy."

I roll my eyes even though he can't see me. I'm plain compared to the women I've seen him photographed with. "I'm going to be fat soon."

"Is that what you think?"

I nod. It's what I know. I've looked up the pictures of different stages of pregnancy. I know what I'm going to look like. It won't be long before he stops coming home because I'm a grouchy, oversized bitch.

"Come into the water with me." I have no reason to deny him. We're here, on vacation, and this is what people do, they swim. I nod and turn in his arms. I tell my heart to shut down, to not look into his soft brown eyes. Even if he means well now, I don't want the heartbreak later. His hands move up my back and into my hair. He pulls at the elastic hair band, releasing my ponytail. I've been trying to grow out my hair and it's just above my shoulders. I hope he likes longer hair.

"I like it when you have your hair down," he says, his eyes boring into mine. I wish I could read him. I wish I knew what was going through his mind. His lips touch mine softly and only briefly. Maybe he's regretting this already. If that's the case, he just needs to tell me, I'll let him go. I won't hold him in a marriage that he doesn't want to be in. "Are you ready?" he asks, taking my hand in his. He turns me around to face the water.

"Is it deep enough to jump?"

"Of course. You'll be fine, trust me."

I look at him when he says trust me and feel my heart break a little. I offer a small smile and nod. He holds our hands up and we jump in. I shriek at the temperature of the water and make for the ladder. Jimmy grabs me around the waist and pulls me to him.

"Hey, where are you going?"

"It's cold, Jimmy. I'm going back to the room."

"Just wait a minute, sweet lips, it'll warm up." He swims us out a bit and into the sun. I lean back against his shoulder and let the warmth beat down on my face. He holds us in the water, floating. He's right and I hate to admit it. The water does feel good. Jimmy runs his fingers along my sides, over my bump and back again. The romantic side of me wants to think that he's trying to memorize me, but the practical side tells me that he's doing this so that I'll think he's in this marriage for real.

His fingers graze my breasts. I close my eyes and lean farther back against his shoulder. I'm so sensitive and he knows that. Jimmy sucks my earlobe into his mouth, biting me gently. He slides his hands into the front of my top, his hands massaging my breasts. Moving my bikini cups to the side, he exposes me for all to see. I open my eyes and look around, but see no one. It's as if he's paid everyone to be gone so we could be like this.

He slides his hand down the front of my bottoms, his finger pressing against my aching clit. My back arches on its own accord, welcoming the attention he's showing my body. He bites and kisses everywhere he can reach while the water laps over us.

"Jimmy," I say, sounding like a wanton whore.

"Yeah, sweetheart?"

My hand finds the back of his head. I pull on his hair, cementing him to my shoulder. He chuckles, increasing the pressure of his finger. I don't know how I'm not sinking to the ocean floor, but somehow he's holding us up.

"I want to fuck you, Jenna. I want to hear you screaming my name as I make you come. Do you want that?"

I nod, unable to find my voice. His hand pushes my

bottoms down, giving him more access. I move my legs and kick them off, not bothering to hang on to them. Maybe some fisherman will find them when he reels in his big catch and take them home as a souvenir.

I move my head enough so that I can kiss him. He allows it. Moving so that I'm not stretching too far. I can't get enough and stand, the water coming to my neck. Jimmy holds me close, not letting me go. I pull him down to my lips, my tongue seeking out his. He picks me up, my legs hanging loosely around his waist. His fingers dig into my thighs, inches from where I need him. I work my hand into his swim trunks, loving the way he hisses when my hand grabs his hard cock.

He bites my lower lip, sucking it into his mouth while I work a steady rhythm. His fingers penetrate me, pushing into me. We are creating our own waves in this beautiful ocean and all I can think about is watching this gorgeous man move over the top of me with sweat dripping off his body.

I push down his shorts, freeing him from the confines holding him back. He moves, walking us deeper into the water. I don't know what's he's thinking, but I go with it. I startle when I feel wood hit my back. I pull away and look behind me, confused.

"Climb the ladder, love."

"Why?" To say I'm racked with confusion is an understatement. Moments ago, we were hot and heavy and mostly naked, and now he's telling me to climb the ladder.

"Jenna, I want to fuck you senseless, but not in the water. I don't want to harm the baby, or you for that matter.

Now get your beautiful arse up this ladder before I have to work out a way to carry you up."

I don't hesitate. Turning, I climb each rung as quickly as possible. I squeal when I feel him bite my butt cheek, but secretly love it. This is the type of passion I want in my life, and if it's short lived then so be it. I'll cherish each moment until he takes them away from me.

Jimmy's on me the moment my feet touch the deck. He picks me up, only to kneel on the deck. His shorts are still down, around his thighs. I reach out and stroke him. He closes his eyes before he latches onto my nipple. I squirm, needing more attention from him. Chuckling, he moves to my other breast before moving down my body. His lips blaze a trail hotter than the sun kissing my skin. He stops at my bump, his lips whispering along my skin.

My head pushes hard into the deck when I feel his tongue lap at my folds. He pushes my thighs, holding them apart, taking advantage of my weakened state. He sucks on my clit, bringing me to the brink.

"Jimmy," I cry, grabbing onto his hair, holding him there.

"Scream it out, sweetheart," he says as his lips capture mine. He slides into me, filling me. He sits back on his knees, holding my legs out, giving him more space to move. He rubs my clit, causing me to scream out. I arch my back, my body begging for more. "Fuck, Jenna, your pussy is going to be the death of me. The way you feel against my dick, I can't get enough." He pounds into me, emphasizing each word he says.

Heat pools too quickly for my liking. I want this to last, even though I know we can do it again. I don't want him to stop. The sounds of our wet bodies slapping against each other is turning me on and I can't hold off my impending orgasm.

He moves faster and changes positions, throwing my legs up onto his shoulders. He moves closer, gripping my hips as he moves in me.

"Jimmy," I scream as my orgasm takes over my body. I push into him, needing more friction.

"Fuck, sweet lips, take my dick, own it, it's all yours."

His words are my undoing and his as well. He slams into me repeatedly, moaning. My legs fall to his side as he lies on top of me. He kisses me, deeply, holding my face in his hands. It's too sweet, too caring. I refuse to believe he means it because it'll hurt later when he leaves. Keep him at a distance, that's what I need to do.

"That was fantastic," he murmurs against my lips. All I can do is nod. If anything, we'll have great sex until the day we don't.

"It was."

Rolling onto his side, he cradles me. His bare ass is in plain sight for anyone to see. "People probably saw us. We won't be able to show our faces in the hotel."

Jimmy laughs. "All they're saying is look at that lucky bastard with his gorgeous wife having sex. And you know what?"

"What?" I say, fighting back laughter.

"You know damn well that man went back to his missus and just shagged the crap out of her."

I shake my head. "What if it was a woman?"

"Hmm. If it was a woman, she went back to her bloke and had her wicked way with him."

"Is that so?"

"Mhm, yep, definitely." He presses his lips to mine, trailing his hand down my side. He hitches my leg over his hip and adjusts, pushing into me.

"Again?" I ask, seeing the lust in his eyes.

"Sweetheart, I'm a walking hard-on when it comes to you. Thank Christ, I'll never have blue balls again."

Jimmy makes love to me on the deck. This time it's much different, like he's trying to show my heart that he's here and not going anywhere. I just refuse to believe this will be real once we head back to reality.

S he doesn't initiate sex. I don't know what else to do. I can't get enough of her and yet, when I think she's about to make a move, she shuts down and waits for me. She gets so close and then I see the moment she starts to pull away and don't know what I can do to help guide her over the edge. I've tried everything I can think of. The romantic walks on the beach, shopping, and making love to her under the stars. The only thing I've held back on is telling her that I love her ... I don't know if I'm there yet. I don't know what else I can do. I hold her hand. I introduce her as my wife, and I've even told a few other holiday-makers that we're having a baby.

I just want her to want me the way that I want her. I don't want her to feel like I'm going through the motions of being her husband. I'm in this for life whether she thinks I am or not. I just need her to trust me, to open up to me.

I lie on my stomach, watching her over my shoulder as she walks past the bed. She thinks I'm asleep, but I've been awake for the past few hours watching her sleep. She fell asleep in my arms, but at some point in the middle of the night, she rolled over to the other side, as far away from me as possible. I don't like that. I know she's been hurt in the past, but she has to know I'd never lay a finger on her.

The shower switches on, and I realise I can lie here and think about the ways in which I can show her that I'm her husband in every way possible, or I can go shower with my wife and hope that she starts to realise that I'm here and I want to be with her. I knew what it meant when I asked her to marry me, and I can't lie, it's going to be hard. I'm used to doing whatever and whoever I want without consequence. I need to rein my shit in and honour her the way she needs to be.

Bottom line is, I won't be my father.

I get out of bed and sit on the edge. My hand rests on my knee, the sun shining on my ring causing a prism. I look down at my platinum band and smile. I picked this out quickly, and I'll admit, I like wearing it. It makes me feel like I've accomplished something good in my life. I know Jenna probably should've had a say, but I didn't want to give her the option of saying no. I'm married and I'm proud to be her husband. I just have to find the proper way of showing her that.

I run to the bathroom to catch her in the shower. When I open the door, the glass shower doors are steamed up, limiting my visibility of her naked body. Opening the door, I step into the hot water. She turns and looks at me over her shoulder; she heard me come in, thwarting my attempt at surprising her. I'm rewarded with a killer smile, making me believe that she's happy to see me.

I step closer, my chest touching her back. Taking the loofah from her hands, I drop it on the floor. She turns to face me, but I stop her. My intent was to come in and shower with her because that's what husbands and wives do. But the thought of her being covered in soap turns me on, and as much as I want be with her like that, it'll have to wait until next time. One look at her and I can't not touch her. I need to feel her skin against mine.

I step forward until she's pressed against the glass. Her hands spread out, steadying herself. I wonder if she knows what's coming next.

When I have her like this she looks vulnerable, but I know better. This woman can rock my world with just one look. She's dangerous, and if I'm not careful, she'll break my heart. There's a glint in her eye when I place my hands on either side of her face. The water is cascading down over us, making it almost impossible to see each other. I could turn it off, but I really like the steam it creates.

"Good morning, wifey," I say as my lips meet hers. Her hands tangle in my hair, holding me closer. My hands slide off the wall and cup her arse, pulling her against my aching dick. She breaks free of my mouth, much to my displeasure. Her lips move across my cheek, to my ear, and down my neck. Her fingernails trail over my chest, pinching my nipples in their wake. She licks the water that has pooled below my navel. My dick jumps, begging for attention.

She looks up and winks. Her hand wraps about my erection, moving up and down. I tuck her hair behind her ears, my fingertips caressing her cheek. Her tongue snakes out, touching the tip of my dick. I have to lean against the glass when she takes me fully in her mouth. Her hands grab my thighs, her nails digging into my skin. I want to close my eyes and enjoy the moment, but I can't stop watching her. I want to burn this moment into my memory forever.

My hips move at her instruction. I glance down in time to see her looking up at me. She's so incredibly sexy. I can't stand not being buried inside of her. I pull her up from the shower floor. She releases my dick from her mouth with a smirk. I turn her around, pushing her tits into the glass. I wish I had a camera on the other side so I could take a photograph of what she looks like. I'd stare at it all day knowing she was waiting for me at home. I thrust into her, pulling her hair as I do. The way she screams, the way my name rolls off her tongue spurs me to go faster.

Our skin slaps together. The glass squeaks every time I slam into her. I can't seem to get enough of her. This is something different than when I was with Chelsea. This is so much better.

Grabbing her hips, I slam them into me over and over. She slides down the glass, bending at the waist to give me a better angle. She cries out and I know she's close. I'm beginning to learn how I can work her body. It sings to me, and I'm listening loud and clear.

"Oh, Jimmy." I can barely hear her over the water, but I know what she wants. I reach around, brushing her already swollen clit with my thumb. "Oh, God," she says as her body goes rigid around my dick. I thrust faster, deeper, until she's milking everything out of me.

Pulling her body flush with mine, I stand us under the lukewarm water. We're breathing heavily. I hold her with one arm under our child, the other between her boobs with my hand holding her face. I kiss her cheek, her ear and nuzzle her wet hair.

"My God, Jenna, what did you do to me? I came in here to take a shower with you so I could be close to you. I want to learn every inch of your body. I need to know what turns you on. I need to know all of you. Will you let me?"

She nods against my shoulder and that's all I need. She's willing to let me know her more than just physically. Maybe that's what I need for her to finally open up to me and let me in.

———————

"DO YOU WANT A BOY OR GIRL?" I ask. My hand rests on her stomach while she feeds me some grapes. We've managed to move from the shower to the bed. The day is a lost cause since a thunderstorm has rolled in. Now we're lying here getting to know each other, while listening to the rainfall outside.

"I don't know. I really just want a healthy baby, but either one has perks. With a little girl I can dress her in pink with bows in her hair, but with a little boy I can give him a Mohawk."

"So he takes after his daddy?" I try to hide my smile, but I can't. She reaches out and slaps me, making me laugh. It's the first time she's mentioned something about me that she likes, other than my knob.

"Yes, just like yours." She hides her face from me and I hate it.

"Don't do that, Jenna."

"Do what?"

I hover over her, giving her no choice but to look at me. "Don't hide from me. We're married and I'm your husband. I want to be your husband. There's no right or wrong answer when I ask you a question, and I want you to ask the same of me in return. I want you to know me, Jenna. I told you that the other night. I want to be married to you. Yes, we're here because of what we've created, but that shouldn't matter." I move and sit next to her, taking her hand in mine.

"I was married for three years. I was in love and couldn't wait to start my life with Damien. Shortly after our wedding we were fooling around and I accidently hit him in his ... well, you know and he backhanded me. We were both shocked. We both cried. He promised never to do it again and I believed him. When it happened again, he said it was an accident. But it started happening more and more and the littlest things would set him off. He'd come home with a pregnancy test and when it would show that we weren't pregnant, he'd hit me. Everything was my fault. I did every-thing I could to not get pregnant, and then I sleep with you and bam! I'm pregnant and I'm happy. I'm so happy that I'm having this baby.

"I'm happy that you want to be a part of the baby's life, Jimmy, I am. I'm just scared and confused. I'm scared to open up and find that you don't want me. I'm scared that one day, you'll walk out and not return because you'll realize that I'm not what you want. Everything here seems perfect, but what about when we are out there in the real world? Is this ring enough to keep you loyal? Because if it's not, tell me now and we can part and I'll be okay."

"I'm not leaving, Jenna. I meant every word when I said my vows. I'm taking this seriously," I say to her, hoping she'll hear my words. I don't know what else I can do to convince her.

"You don't love me."

Ah bollocks, she's got me there. I have to look away because I don't want her to see the pain that her words cause me. The fact that she said it hits me with such impact. I pick up her hand, kiss her wedding ring, and roll our bodies so that we're facing each other.

"I want to fall in love with you, sweet lips. Since the night of Liam and Josie's wedding, I've been trying my hardest to make sure that I'm in the same room as you, or that I can have any excuse to talk to you. I came to Beaumont early because I missed you, but I couldn't tell anyone that. I need you and I love the fact that you're my wife. I don't want that to change."

Leaning over, I place my lips to hers. Her hand comes up and tangles in my hair. She holds me to her and I want to tell her that I'm not going anywhere.

"Just so you know, when we get back to Beaumont, I'll be sleeping in your bed."

"It's a queen-size bed, ya know."

"Good. That means you won't be able to get away from me in the middle of the night. I like holding you in my arms, but when I woke up this morning you were on the other side. That's too far away from me."

"I do like it when you hold me."

That makes me smile. "Then come here, sweet lips." She snuggles into my arms, her head resting on my chest. Her fingers dance along my pecs, drawing circles and lines over the ridges from my muscles. I want to make her happy. I want her to accept me for me and not the person the media portrays me to be, although it's pretty damn accurate. I can change that. I will change that image. I'll be the man she needs me to be, even if it kills me. The first thing I need to do is to quit smoking. I think this trip has been good for me in that way, too.

16

JENNA

Jimmy sleeps soundly next to me with his arm lying protectively over my ever-growing belly. The sun is just peeking through my window and the only thing missing is the sound of birds chirping. It's the fairytale part of this whirlwind adventure that I'll never see, but maybe secretly hope for. I hold up my left hand so the sun can hit my ring just right. The light dances, creating a prism of colors and shapes on my ceiling. I used to do this when I was a child, playing with my father's watch while my mother washed dishes. I'd giggle each time she'd bat away the light, acting as if it was some bug bothering her. I hope to create those moments with my child.

We've been home barely twelve hours, coming straight to my ... our apartment from the airport. We both fell, albeit without grace and tact, into bed once we walked in the door. Honestly, I didn't expect Jimmy to stay. I thought the excuses would start tumbling out of his mouth the minute the taxi pulled up in front of my building. But he didn't. He stayed. He asked what side of the bed was his and undressed in front of me. We pulled back the comforter together, turned off the bedside lights at the same time, and burrowed deep next to each other. He held my hands in his, his thumb roaming over the top of my ring until my eyes closed. I felt his lips press against my forehead just as I was drifting off. And I don't know what to think about all of this. It seems to be too much too fast. I know he's not in love with me, nor am I with him. But a small part of me wants us to be even though I know it'll never happen. Someone like Jimmy can never love someone like me.

Jimmy pulls me closer; he's waking up. Even though it's only been two weeks of sharing a bed and each other's bodies, I know him. I know what each look means. I know when he wants to be with me. I know when he's tired, hungry, and even when he wants to be left alone. I know most of his expressions except for one and that one lingers in the back of mind. Is he hiding something? I can't figure that out yet and it kills me. Part of me wants to hate that I know all of this about him and the other part, the part that I shouldn't listen to, wants to hold him in my arms and never let him go. That part wants to build a life, a home, and family with him and trust that everything is going to be okay. Sadly, we're back in the real world and my heart aches knowing that my fantasy is short lived. He has a life in California and he'll be returning there, and as much as I hope it's to just pack his clothes and return, I feel otherwise. What if I'm not enough to keep him interested? I'm going to get fat, bitchy, and hormonal. He's Jimmy. His reputation is less than stellar. The stories from Liam and Josie are enough to write a novel. He's young and probably doesn't realize the mistake we've made by getting married. Or the mistake I've made by giving him my body repeatedly.

My fingers move back and forth along his arm. The action seems natural, like it's something that I should be doing even if I'm thinking my marriage is going to fall apart at a moment's notice. Jimmy's lips press against my temple, my cheek, and then the side of my lips before he snuggles into the crook of my neck. If he acts like this, then why isn't it enough for me to accept that he's here for all the right reasons? His hand spreads out on my bump, his fingers start to tap along my skin. I'm curious as to what song he's playing, but am tongue-tied and not able to ask. It's stupid. I'm stupid. My feelings are stupid, and I'm starting to hate that every image I have of Jimmy is tainted even though he hasn't given me a reason to feel this way. But my head … it's telling me to run and run fast.

Closing my eyes, I mentally sort through everything that has to be done today. First, find my parents and share the good news with them. I can't believe I let Jimmy take me away for two weeks and didn't once call and check in. I know I'm an adult, but under the circumstances, I'm sure my parents are worried. They don't know Jimmy like I do and they're here to see me, to make sure everything is okay, and I just upped and left. What kind of daughter does that make me? At some point we need to share the news with our friends. They'll be happy, right? Of course they will, they're our friends and Jimmy and I are having a baby. Everyone will be happy.

I need to stop thinking so negatively. I'm having a baby and I thought I was going to have to do this alone, but now that's not the case. He's here, by my side, and that's going to have to be enough for now.

"What's going on in that pretty little head of yours, sweet lips?" Jimmy kisses my neck, moving toward my ear. He pulls me closer as if he thinks I'm going somewhere. If he only knew that's the fear I carry with me where he's concerned.

"Life," I say with a shrug.

Rising up on his elbow, Jimmy moves my hair away from my face. He leans forward and kisses my nose. As he pulls back slowly, his hand trails down my side. "Don't frown, beautiful. I love your smile and you should be happy."

"Why's that, Jimmy?"

Jimmy moves over the top of me. He leans on his arms, keeping his weight off of me. I fight the urge to pull him down on top of me, to feel him against me.

"Wifey, I never want to see you sad. It's my job to make you happy, and if I'm not doing my job then I need to kick my own arse. Now tell me, what's with the frown?"

I fight the urge to shrug and roll my eyes. He's trying and I owe it to him to try as well. Taking a deep breath, I look him in his eyes. "I feel like crap for being gone for two weeks while my parents are here ... or were. For all I know they've left because I disappeared. I should've called and checked in or something."

He moves to my side, but keeps his leg in between mine. His hand rests, again, on my stomach. He's doing everything I've always wanted my husband to do, everything I imagined. The caring caress, the eagerness to touch and feel his child. It's what I want, so why do I continue to have doubts?

"You were on your honeymoon. I think your mum and dad will forgive you."

I shake my head. "They didn't know I was getting married, Jimmy. Heck, I didn't even know. I should've called them."

"So why didn't you? You had your phone and there was a phone in the room. You could've called and told them, but you didn't. Are you embarrassed of me?"

His question takes me by surprise. I shake my head, vigorously. "Why would you ask such a question, Jimmy?"

This time he's the one shrugging. "If you're worried about your parents, you could've called them, but you didn't. If you're regretting getting married, just tell me. I'm a big boy, I can handle it, but you should know that I'll be here for you and the baby." He kisses me quickly before extracting himself, leaving me with words caught in my throat.

HE'S SWEET. He's caring. He's good looking. He's sexy. He's my husband and I'm about to introduce him as such to my parents and best friend. My eyes are riveted on him as he walks in front of my car. The jeans he's wearing accentuate his ass and I giggle at myself for even staring. But I can stare and touch because he's allowed me free reign over his body, as I've allowed him. I shouldn't feel nervous about what we're about to do. We're adults and we're pregnant. We're being responsible, albeit sudden and rash.

Jimmy opens the car door and holds out his hand, waiting for me to place mine in his. When I do, he tugs lightly, encouraging me to get out of the car. I take my place beside him and we walk hand in hand to Josie and Liam's house. We don't knock, no one does. When we step in, laughter rings out from the living room.

We step into the living room, our hands linked together. Jimmy's finger moves over my rings, squeezing my hand at the same time. If he's nervous, he's doesn't seem to be. He clears his throat, loudly, causing everyone to turn and look. I smile, but it feels weak.

"You're back and you're ... holding hands?" Josie is the first one to speak. Her eyes scan over us, full of questions.

"Jenna, what's going on?" my dad asks. I swallow hard and glance at Jimmy. He's staring at me. His eyes sparkle with excitement. I look back at my parents, Josie, and Liam, and take a deep breath.

"We got married." Jimmy raises our hands in the air in triumph, like we just won some award. My mom gasps and Josie's mouth drops open. I think we've given new meaning to 'expect the unexpected'. Right now, I think everyone in the room is shocked.

"You did what?" I expect this question from my dad, but not Liam. He pushes past my dad and stands before us. The sleeves of his black T-shirt are rolled over his biceps, showing his physique. "What the fuck did you say?"

"Jenna and I got married." Jimmy says, confidently.

"Why?" Liam looks confused and I try not to let that hurt. Does he think I'm not good enough for Jimmy?

Jimmy looks at me. I can feel his gaze penetrating me. He's waiting for me to look at him and give him the okay. I nod, barely, but enough for him to know it's time.

"She's pregn—"

"We know she's pregnant. That doesn't mean you run off and get married."

"Liam!" Josie says his name loudly. He turns and looks at her before turning back to us. I know he wants to protect his friend, but it's not like I'm after his money or anything.

"You didn't let me finish, Liam. Jenna's pregnant with my baby."

Liam's face turns red as his gaze bounces from Jimmy to me. There are two gasps that I assume come from my mom and Josie, and a string of expletives from my father. But for some reason, the expression on Liam's face is what does me in.

"Are you fucking kidding me, JD? You can't go around claiming her baby because you're bored. This is a life we're talking about. And now you're married? How long until you cheat?"

I jump when Liam says cheat. Jimmy's not going to do that to me. That's what I keep telling myself.

"I'm not bored, Liam. I'm taking responsibility. Jenna and I made this baby together on the night of your wedding, and I'll be there by her side when she brings our child into this world."

"What's this about cheating?" my dad asks as he steps forward. I feel like I'm about two feet tall and invisible right now.

"Oh, JD here has a hankering for women and lots of them."

"Liam, that's not fair," Josie adds. I want to say she's right, but I know the truth. Jimmy's a dirty dog, that's what she called him the night of her bachelorette party.

"I won't cheat, Mr. Hardy. Jenna means too much to me

and I won't hurt her. I'm a married man and I'm about to become a dad. This is what I want."

Jimmy leans forward and kisses me full on my lips. He smiles when he pulls back and I can't help but smile, too.

"I can't fucking believe you, JD." Liam doesn't wait for a response, but pushes Jimmy away from me and out of my sight. My dad follows, leaving me with Josie and my mom. Two sets of arms encase me as I fight tears that I didn't know I had coming.

I walk down the path of the unknown. Unknown because most of our business "meetings" take place downstairs in the studio, but not today. Liam pushes me again, literally shoving me as if I'm walking into a torture chamber. Maybe I am. Maybe I'm being duped and I'm not the baby daddy and she's been tricking me. I want to punch myself in the head, repeatedly, for even thinking that. There's no way she's lying about us. She doesn't need to. I remember the night vividly, like it happened yesterday. It's been on my mind constantly because for the first time in years my body craves her. It cries out for her. She's my water after a long night on stage and the more I drink, the more I need.

I step outside into the back garden. I don't know why Liam doesn't use this space more. He should. It's great for entertaining. I can see Jenna and I in a place like this with our little one playing in a sandbox or something equally as cheesy. I want to give this baby everything that I didn't have when I was growing up. I know I have to start with me first.

I need to get some shit straightened out in Los Angeles before I can be the best husband I can be to Jenna. It's all crap I should've done before, but I've never been one to plan my life out. Spur of the moment works best for me, and while I was thinking with my head when I asked Jenna to marry me, I also pretty much think with my dick and that gets me into trouble.

Liam steps around me and opens the door to his garage. I try not to show any fear, but I'm pretty sure it's pouring out of my pores. Jenna's dad stands behind me. He's a big guy, and could easily break my sorry self in half, but I'm hoping since his daughter is carrying my child he'll take it easy on me. What self-respecting man wants to leave his daughter husbandless and his grandchild fatherless? I tentatively look behind me and am met with an ice-cold glare. Slowly turning back around, I take a deep breath before stepping over the imaginary line that is my doom.

The garage is unwelcoming and sterile. Liam is incredibly anal about his truck and motorbike so I know this room is treated like a sanctuary. If I were a gambling man, I'd bet that you could eat off the floor if you ever felt the need to behave like a dog. I have a feeling I'll be eating in here after today. I follow Liam as he climbs up a set of wooden stairs. He flicks on a switch, lighting the rest of my path. Jenna's father, my now father-in-law, is muttering something incomprehensible behind me. I'm willing to bet my life savings that he's plotting ways to cut off my dick so I can't violate his daughter again.

When I get to the top, I'm suddenly taken back to high school with Liam, even though we didn't attend the same school or even know each other. The walls are covered with posters of him and Josie, and him and Katelyn's former husband. I walk around the room, looking at the memorabilia and it's like a shrine. I'm not about to ask why it's all here because I know this is his history and if I had what he did, I'd fight to keep it all, too.

"What the fuck, Jimmy?" He doesn't tell me to sit down or offer me anything to quench my dry throat, not that I deserve it. I glance at my father-in-law and briefly see hurt spread all over his face. I play Jenna's words from this morning over in my mind; she, no scratch that, we should've called her parents to tell them the good news. And I suppose, right now, good is a relative term.

My answer doesn't come quickly enough. I stare between the two men wondering if this is going to be a good cop/bad cop situation. I've been through this before, with Chelsea and her family. Her father was never afraid to tell her that I'm nothing but a worthless piece of shit, and her uncle tried to help me get a respectable job. It didn't matter how much money I made with the band, it was never good enough to satisfy her father. I was never good enough.

"What do you want me to say?" I ask, and it's clearly the wrong question. Jenna's dad, whose name I don't even know, paces. His hands are shoved deeply in his pockets, and as he walks, he mumbles to himself, shaking his head back and forth.

"How much is it going to take?

"Why would you be so stupid to claim a child that isn't yours?"

Both questions are fired at me at the same time and it makes head spin. I alternate looking at both men; each one clearly has a different agenda and I know that I have to tackle the most important one. I step forward, stopping in his path, and offer my hand.

"I'm Jimmy Davis. My friends call me JD, but your daughter calls me Jimmy and I know I should've asked you for her hand in marriage, but I tend to get carried away and act before I think and apparently I talk a lot when I'm nervous, but it's nice to meet you."

Liam doesn't hide the fact that he's laughing at me. I'm sweating bullets and my best mate is in the corner pissing himself laughing at me like this is some type of hilarious joke. Jenna's dad is bloody huge and I'm a nervous wreck because he could probably kill me with his bare hands. Ironically, I didn't care what Chelsea's parents thought of me, but I do care what this man thinks of me because I'm going to know him for a long time.

I drop my hand when he doesn't offer his back. I look away, not wanting to show him the hurt expression on my face. If I have to spend the next however many years buttering up this man, I'll do it because it will make my wife happy. Her mother I can probably win over with my charm, but I doubt this burly man gives two shits about me.

"How much will take for you to go away, to annul this sham of a marriage?"

I step back at his request, stunned. This marriage isn't a sham. We're having a baby and I'm doing the best thing for Jenna and me. I never wanted children, at least not right now, but knowing that she's having my baby ... it does things to me, and I want to be with her. She's fucking sexy as hell and my body craves her. Not being with her isn't an option for me.

"Mr. Hardy, yes, I know that's my fault for going about

this the wrong way and shit, but I'll make it up to you. Either way, I don't want your money. Jenna and I are having a baby, we're married, and I'm not going anywhere." I stand my ground, whatever that's worth. He can take his money and buy off the police or a judge to keep Jenna safe from her ex, but I'm not going anywhere.

"Don't you think you should know the names of your wife's parents?"

I nod because he's right, but to be honest Jenna and I didn't talk about her parents. We talked about us and my reassurance that we did the right thing. "With all due respect, I've known your daughter for some time now and she's never mentioned you."

This revelation makes him take a step back this time. He cocks his head to one side and pulls out his cheque-book. I shake my head. I'm going to stand my ground that's for sure. He walks over to the table and opens it. I step forward, looking over his shoulder.

"Mr. Hardy," I say with conviction, "please be aware that I won't accept your money. I don't think your daughter or your grandchild will appreciate you trying to buy me off and out of their lives."

I turn to Liam, not for help, but for understanding. He's stone faced and seems caught off guard.

"As for your question, Liam, and as I stated earlier, I'm the father. I'm not claiming a child that isn't mine, but one that is solely mine. Jenna and I got together the night of your wedding. She wasn't going to tell me but you did, and when I saw her that night, I put two and two together and took her to Bora Bora with the intention of marrying her."

Shaking his head, Liam pinches the bridge of nose. I'm

dying to know what's going through his mind, but I'm too chicken to ask.

I turn away from both men, leaving them to make their own assumptions about me.

"Stop," Liam says, halting me in my tracks. "You can't pay him off."

"Excuse me?" Mr. Hardy replies. He steps forward, and if I wasn't watching him like a hawk I wouldn't believe my eyes, but he literally puffs his chest out at Liam.

"I said you can't pay him off."

"And why's that? Clearly you have an issue with him marrying Jenna. This seems to be the easiest way to make it all go away."

Liam moves closer to me, and maybe we're showing some kind of solitary front, although it's more likely that he just wants to be to the one to kick my arse.

"I've known JD for a long time, and the one thing I know for certain is that when he does something, he does so whole-heartedly. The other thing I know is that your daughter is pregnant and JD is the father, and if you think I'm going to stand here and let you pay him off so that your grandchild grows up without his or her father, you've got another thing coming. If you want to write them a congratulatory check, I'm sure they'll take it. If not, put your checkbook away and pat him on the back for taking care of your daughter. I wish someone would've told me my girl was pregnant because I missed ten years with my son. I'm not going to let JD miss one minute."

Liam looks at me and I nod back at him. It's a silent thank you because right now my throat has closed up and I can't speak. I'll never forget his words and there's a great big chance I'll never be able to tell him how grateful I am for what he said.

"And if he screws up?" Mr. Hardy asks.

"I won't. Look, Mr. Hardy, I can't explain it, but since I've known Jenna I always feel good when I'm around her. When I found out she was pregnant I knew the baby was mine. I won't sugar-coat anything and tell you we conceived the bub out of love, it was a one-night stand, but I'm here and I'm not going anywhere."

Mr. Hardy steps forward, placing one hand on my shoulder and taking my hand in his free one. "She's my baby. Someday you'll understand what that means. Someday you'll do something stupid like offer money to make what you think is a problem go away. You'll also be man enough to apologize. I'm sorry and I hope to hell you're the right man for Jenna because the last one was not and I'll never forgive myself for giving her to him. He hurt my baby."

"That is something I can promise I'll never do."

I KISSED my wife long and hard before leaving her on the concourse at the airport. Leaving Jenna was hard, but her mother, Angela, said she'd take care of her. After my run-in with her father, which I'm keeping to myself, Jenna and I took her mum to dinner and explained why we did what we did. Her mum cried, but promised me she'd be okay as long as Jenna was happy. I'm trying to convince myself that Jenna is happy, but she's hard to read. I know she's spent years hiding inside of herself, but she doesn't need to do that anymore. Not with me.

I shouldn't be leaving, but I have unfinished business to take care of in Los Angeles. That business being Chelsea. She's been sending me non-stop text messages since I got back in Beaumont, and even though I've ignored her, I can't continue to do so. She's a loose cannon at times and the last thing I need is for Jenna to see her texts. I don't even know why I feel the need to tell Chelsea. I shouldn't, but I also shouldn't have slept with her the last time I was home. That was my mistake and I know that she's going to want more now. I'd been able to avoid her for three years, but all it took was one lonely night, a weak will, and a text from her and I was back in her bed, full of regret.

I pull my hand luggage behind me, and the closer I get to my apartment block, the more anxious I become. I don't want to be here. I want to be back with Jenna, making her flat ours. I need to feel her around me, have her in my arms where I feel content and she's safe. This trip has to be short, in and out, just enough time to tell Chelsea that I can't see her anymore and to pack all of my crap. I never thought I'd move to Beaumont, but with my wife there, carrying our baby, it's where I need to be. It's where I want to be. I also need to call my mum and dad and tell them everything, especially my mum. I want her to meet Jenna, and maybe stay in town for a while and be there when the baby is born. I don't want her to miss out on anything because of where I live.

Music wafts through the hall. 4225 West is being played, and while my neighbours know who I am, I can't say many of them are fans. By the time I'm two doors down from my own, I know the music is coming from inside. I try to think back to before I left ... Did I set a timer on my stereo? No, I didn't. I stop in front of my door and don't even bother to fish out my key. I know she's in there; I can smell her perfume out here. Turning the knob hesitantly, I open the door.

I don't know what I expected to find, but it isn't this. Chelsea is dancing around my lounge. There are boxes piled along the wall and her ugly artwork is hanging behind my sofa.

"What the fuck is going on?" I say loudly over the music. She stops and turns. Her hands immediately go to her hair, making sure it's presentable. God forbid a single hair is out of place when someone is staring at her. Jenna was make-up free for two weeks except when we went out to dinner and there are not enough words in my vocabulary to describe how gorgeous she looked. But the one standing before me in barely-there shorts with bleach blonde hair and a fake tan really doesn't do it for me anymore.

"You're home."

"Yeah, that usually happens every few weeks. What are you doing here?" I ask, as I close the door behind me.

Chelsea looks around the room nervously. Did she really think I wouldn't notice all her crap in my flat? "I sort of moved in."

"So I see. Why the fucking hell would you do that?"

"Jimmy— "

"Don't 'Jimmy' me. We aren't together, Chelsea, and I have no intention of getting back together with you." Putting my hand in my pocket, I feel around for my ring. I hate the fact that I took it off, but the last thing I want is for the paps to see it and start digging around, looking for Jenna. She needs to be stress free ... well, as much as she can be when she's married to me.

"Well I thought you'd change your mind after I shared some news with you."

"I doubt it," I say, moving away from the door. I lean against the wall which separates the kitchen from the rest of my living space. My fingers play with my wedding band, wishing she'd leave so I could put it on and call my wife.

"I'm pregnant, Jimmy, and it's yours."

You know that moment when your heart and stomach fall to the floor and you feel all empty inside? Yeah, I'm having that moment.

18

JENNA

Only after I drop my mom off at Liam's do I let a few tears fall down my face. I didn't think I'd care that Jimmy went back to L.A. without me, but I do. The nagging voice in the back of my head won't stop yelling at me that something's wrong. Why didn't he take me with him and why didn't I insist on going?

Because I'm not sure this marriage will work, that's why. Tabloid images of him with various women are at the forefront of my mind. We don't know each other and yet here we are, married and having a baby. There are so many reasons why I don't want his identity to be known and this is one of them. He's famous, I'm not. No one will ever take my child seriously and he or she will always be considered a product of a one-night stand. I never thought drastic measures would have to be taken, such as marriage, but they have and he knows I'm powerless to say no to him. Just like that night. I wanted him, and for the first time in years I was ready and willing to give myself to another man. I knew he wouldn't hurt me, not the way Damien had. I wanted the pleasure I knew he could bring and he fulfilled my fantasy. He did so willingly without even knowing he existed in my thoughts. That's how we should've left it.

Things should not be this way. I should not be driving back to my apartment wondering what my husband is doing. Wondering whether or not he's going to call me when his plane lands or when he's about to go to sleep. I shouldn't care if he's thinking about me because honestly, he's only married to me because of the baby. He doesn't love me and I don't want to love him.

At least that's what I'm telling myself, but those feelings don't hold true. The way he makes love to me and touches me, the way he holds me in his arms—like he's afraid I'm going to disappear—I've never had that before. With Damien, everything was automatic. We met, dated, fell in love. Marriage was the next step in the equation. At night, we went to our sides of the bed, crawled in together and made love because that was what we were programmed to do. Damien only held me after he hit me, never after sex or before and definitely not while he was sleeping.

But with Jimmy, everything is different.

Each caress is done with feeling. Each kiss is done with the intent to show me that he's real, that we're real. These feelings building up inside of me are about to explode and I think he knows that. I think he's waiting. I can't give him what he wants though. I can't go through the hurt or the pain. I've been there and I have a feeling he has, too, because a few times he's acted like our bubble is going to burst at any moment and everything will come crashing down around us. He's holding on for dear life, and as much as I want to hold on with him, I'm afraid.

I'm afraid of what Los Angeles holds for him and I shouldn't be. I need to stand tall and not worry about what he's doing there because I know in my heart he's doing what I think he is. If I don't admit it, if I don't see it, it doesn't happen and we can pretend that this happy union is perfect and nothing can tear us apart. I need to be the trusting wife because he hasn't given me any reason not to trust him. Yet.

I pull into my designated parking spot and realize that I shouldn't be here. I'm supposed to stay at Liam's, but I need some time to myself. Ironic, since I just returned from a long vacation. I sit and stare out the window of my car. When we went to Liam's today, I handed Jimmy my keys out of habit even though we've never had that routine. With Damien, he controlled everything. No, I shouldn't say that. In the beginning, things were very equal. It was only after we were married that my life suddenly changed.

I know I only have minutes before Liam comes barreling into this parking lot to save the damsel in distress. I'm not his damsel to save, though, and the one who should be saving me when I need it is hundreds of miles away without a care in the world. I look down at my phone knowing he hasn't texted, but secretly hoping that I just missed it. My head moves forward on its own volition, resting against the steering wheel. I need to stop getting worked up over something I can't control. I knew about Jimmy's reputation when I said I'd marry him, so if anything, it's my own fault.

Sighing, I get out of the car and walk somewhat quickly to the entrance of my apartment. Even though Paul said Damien isn't around anymore, I can sense him close by. He may not be standing behind me, but he's watching, reminding me what he's capable of. When I open the door to my apartment building the first thing I notice is that the hall light is out. No biggie, except there's someone sitting on the steps. This is where my fight or flight instinct should kick in, but it doesn't. I stop and stare at the figure on the steps, letting my fears come to life. I can't look behind me because there's no one there. My nightmare is staring right back at me. Even with the tiniest of light coming through the entrance window I can make out his features.

"Where ya been, Jenna?"

The way he says my name used to make me soft inside. I used to want to hear his voice whether on the other end of the telephone or when he'd wake me softly in the mornings. I close my eyes and count to ten. What are my options? I have none because I was too stubborn and stupid and now here I am face-to-face with my ex.

"I asked you a question." He doesn't yell or even raise his voice. He sounds broken. His voice wavers and I hate that my heart responds to him. It beats just a bit faster wanting to soothe his pain. How can it not remember the pain he caused me? How can it not remember that it now belongs to another man?

I adjust my hand discreetly so he doesn't see my rings. I don't want to set him off even though I know it's inevitable. There's a viciousness roiling under his skin and my neck prickles in response. It pains me that I can't touch my belly and reassure my growing baby that I'll be okay because I won't be. I'm going to die on this floor, in this dark hallway, and no one will know who did it because according to Paul Baker, Damien Mahoney is nowhere near Beaumont.

Damien stands, walking down the three steps that separate us. I take a step back, adding more space between us.

"You're trembling, sweetheart." He reaches out, his fingers touching my arm lightly and leaving icy trails on my flesh. "Don't be afraid of me, Jenna.

"I've missed you." I nod, playing his game. "I just want to talk, okay? We can even sit on these steps and talk out in the open."

Out in the open? Has he looked around? This isn't open. This is isolated and dark. My chances that Mr. K, my landlord, even knows we're standing out here are slim to none. I could yell, but his hearing aids are probably sitting on his dresser. He'll never hear me.

But I concede and nod, allowing him to pull me to the steps. I try to walk tightly against the wall, but he's not having that. He wants me next to him, our bodies touching.

"Remember when we met?"

Even though I want to resist smiling, I can't.

"Jenna, do you see those guys over there?" I look, coyly, not wanting to draw attention to my gawking, but yes I see them. Anna giggles and I can't help but smile when the one with brown hair waves.

"Oh my god, Anna, he waved." I cover my mouth and squeal as quietly as I can.

"Oh, crap bags, they're coming over. Which one do you want?"

"The brunette," I reply. "Definitely the brunette. Wait, do guys have brunette hair?"

"Yeah, he's hot," Anna says, adding a bit of Southern twang. The guys swim over to our dock. When they climb up the ladder it's like watching one of those stupid gum

commercials in slow motion. Only this time it's the girls staring at the guys, not the other way around.

"Mind if we join you?" the dark-haired one asks. I glance at Anna who is staring. I pinch her leg to get her attention. She nods slowly, her mouth hanging open.

The boy I have eyes for squats in front of me. I can see the ripples in his abdomen. Abs. He has abs. He must be over twenty already. My parents will freak if they find out.

"My name's Damien Mahoney."

"Jenna Hardy," I say automatically.

"Care if I sit?"

I eagerly nod, earning one of the biggest smiles I've ever seen.

"Do you ladies come here often?"

"Every summer since I was five." Closing my eyes, I berate myself for being so stupid.

"How old are you?" he asks.

I look over at Anna. She and her newfound guy are lying on their sides talking to each other. I wish I had the courage she has when it came to guys, but they make me so nervous.

"Sixteen," I say, quietly. "You?"

"Eighteen. We just graduated from high school and are spending our summer here."

Damien touches me; my skin sets alight with a sensation I've never felt before. We sit and talk, occasionally diving into the lake to cool off. He holds me in the water, my legs wrap around his hips. Everything feels natural.

When the sun goes down he kisses me lightly on the lips and I'm in love.

I can't fight the smile and he knows it. His shoulder bumps into mine, breaking my reverie.

"Anna is pregnant. She misses you."

I don't say anything. It's best to not acknowledge those from my past, especially the ones who knew about the abuse but did nothing to stop it. Her husband, Brad, Damien's best friend, turned a blind eye.

"You need to come home, Jenna. You've been gone far too long and I miss you."

"We're divorced," I mutter, my voice breaking.

Sighing, he shakes his head. "We can fix that. You know you love me and you know that I love you. If you come home, I promise I'll never hurt you again."

I scoff. "You hurt me the other night at the coffee shop."

"I was nervous."

I nod. There's always an excuse.

"But I'm not nervous anymore. It's simple really. I want my wife back and I'll do anything to get her back. Her life is mine and her place is beside me." He leans over and kisses my cheek. I'm rigid, the fear setting in. "Ah, I see I have some work to do, so be it then. I'll be back to win your heart. In the meantime, remember that I own you."

Before I can respond he's up and out the door. My breathing becomes ragged. My heart races and I know I need to move, but my legs are cemented to the steps. My ringing phone echoes through the hall, making me jump.

"Hello?" I say after fishing it out of my bag.

"Sweet lips?" His voice is quiet, like he's hiding. I close my eyes and chide myself for thinking the worst already.

"Hi," I say, attempting to clear my throat.

"What are you doing?"

"Nothing." I swallow and take a deep breath. "Just stopping by the apartment to get some stuff before going back to Liam's for the night."

"Are you missing me?"

I roll my eyes and realize that I do miss him, that I need him to hold me right now because I'm shaking so bad I can't move.

"Of course."

"Liar," he says. "I just wanted to call and say goodnight. I'll call you tomorrow."

"All right."

"I lo— tell my baby that I love her."

"What if it's a boy?" I ask.

"It's not, just tell her okay?"

My heart stops for a moment. I can't comment on what he just said because he hangs up. I refuse to think he was going to tell me he loves me. He doesn't and likely never will. So why does he have to say something like that over the phone and not me or the baby when we're together? When he says stuff like that I want to believe his intentions are real. I'm happy that he loves the baby, but sad that he'll never love me. I know one thing's for sure: I need to keep myself from falling in love with Jimmy Davis because he's nothing but pure heartbreak waiting to happen.

19

JIMMY

I bang my phone against my head. I don't know what possessed me to say that to Jenna. I can't tell her that I love her. I don't even know if I do. I do know that I wish she was here, but I'm equally thankful that she's not. I don't how she would've handled Chelsea. Christ, I don't even know how I'm going to handle Chelsea. I look out of the window over the night sky of Los Angeles, the bright lights and sound of traffic bounce between the buildings. After being in Beaumont and spending time in Bora Bora, this concrete jungle is less than appealing. Now I know why Harrison lives on the beach.

I bend over the railing, watching the cars below when the sliding glass door opens. I'm really trying not to think about Chelsea, but she's like a fucking flashing warning light in my face that won't turn off. I'm so fucked. Chelsea will expect ... no, she'll demand that we get married and that isn't going to happen. I'm happy being married to Jenna, even if it has been for just two weeks.

"Who were you talking to?" Her sickly sweet voice makes my skin crawl.

"None of your business," I reply, but that doesn't stop her. Her hand finds my shoulder as she moves closer to me. *If I don't touch her back, it's not cheating.* That's what I tell myself. Closing my eyes, I say the words that need to keep me level headed, *I won't cheat on Jenna,* over and over again.

"It's late, Jimmy. I don't want to fight, but you need to tell whoever it was that you were talking to that you're taken."

I move away from her touch. "I'm not yours to have, Chelsea."

"We're having a baby. I think that entitles me to some respect."

Shoving my hands into my hair, I pull at it and scream loudly. Why the fucking hell is this happening to me? I did the right fucking thing when I found out about Jenna, so why the hell am I being punished?

"How'd you get into my flat?"

She turns away from me and looks out over the city. "Do you want a boy or girl?"

"Hi, Mum." I'm excited to call my mum and tell her all about Jenna. I know she probably won't understand given what she thinks about marriage, but I'm hoping that she'll support my decision.

"Jimmy, to what do I owe the pleasure of hearing my only son's voice?"

"Ah, easy on the dramatics. I call you all the time."

"I know, I just miss you. How are you?"

"Perfect," I say.

"Perfect? How come?"

"I got married."

The long pause at the other end of the line is more than I bargained for.

"Jimmy, please tell me you didn't go to some Vegas drive-thru?"

"No, Mum, we got married on the beach in Bora Bora, but that's not all."

The line goes quiet again, so I continue, "We're going to have a baby."

"Oh, Jimmy," she says, her voice breaking.

"Mum, don't worry, it's a good thing."

"Listen, you don't need to marry her because of the baby, you can work something out, maybe even live together and raise the baby."

"Mum, Jenna is the one woman that I can see myself falling in love with. I didn't marry her because she's having my bub, I married her because she makes me feel whole."

"Are you sure about this?"

"I've never been surer about anything. I can't wait for you to meet my wife."

"Me neither, Jimmy. Be a good husband and father. That's all I ask."

"I don't want anything with you. Why can't you get that through your head?" I want to add that I'm married and having a baby with a woman who has more class in her little finger than Chelsea has, but I can't. I wouldn't put it past Chelsea to go to Beaumont and find Jenna and Jenna definitely doesn't need the likes of Chelsea hanging around.

She turns, her eyes sharp and deadly. "Just weeks ago we were back together."

"We shagged, there's a difference, love. No different from me shagging the bird down the street. I was stupid but I wore a johnny so maybe you should consider the fact that it's not mine."

"You don't believe that," she says, reaching for my hand. I recoil and move farther away from her.

"How'd you get in here?" I repeat

She shrugs. "My uncle."

"Fucking marvellous, breaking in when I'm not around. I'm outta here," I say, walking back into my now despised home. It pisses me off because I wanted to bring Jenna here and fuck her on every single surface. She'd be the first and last, but that can't happen now. Jenna can never come to Los Angeles.

"Where are you going?" I know she's standing there with her hands on her hips. I know her that well.

"Again, it's none of your business." I say, slamming the door behind me. I head toward the stairs, not wanting to wait for the lift and give her a chance to follow me. I'm so fucked. That's going to be my new mantra. Maybe if I keep saying it I'll wake up from this bloody nightmare and be in Jenna's arms. That's what I should do; get the next flight back to Beaumont. Say fuck it and leave it to my dad to sort out this mess. God only knows I've cleaned up enough of his fuckery, it's about time he's cleaned up mine.

As soon as I'm in the garage, I'm sprinting to my Wrangler. I've only driven it a few times since I bought it and I've missed it. Jenna needs a new car. The banged up motor she drives now won't suffice, especially when the baby comes along. I don't know how she'll feel about me buying her a car; she'll probably freak out. Just like she'll do tomorrow when I call and tell her that I've added her to my bank account. I was serious when I told her father that I'm not going anywhere, even if Chelsea is now being a thorn in my side and standing in my way.

I don't know where I'm going when I drive out of the garage. I shouldn't have to run away from my home, but it's easier than having to deal with her. When we were together nothing was easy. We fought constantly about her parents and how they felt about me and it annoyed the crap out of me that she never took my side. I don't even want to imagine what's going to come out of her dad's mouth when she tells him that she's pregnant and that I'm the father.

Am I?

I pull over and bang my head against the steering wheel. Am I even the dad? With Jenna there's no doubt in my mind. She was trying to keep the identity a secret, but I knew instantly. I could feel it in my bones that she was carrying my baby, so why don't I feel like that with Chelsea? Nothing makes sense. We slept together once, weeks ago, and to be honest I don't remember coming because I was thinking about Jenna the entire time and how I wanted to get back to Beaumont to see her. I have to tell Chelsea that I'm married, that I'm taken and happily so, but I'm scared shitless about what she'll do now. If she really is pregnant and I'm the father, her claws will come out and that's not something I really want to subject Jenna to.

I'm so fucked even the sound of Chelsea's annoying laugh is constantly invading my thoughts. I look up to see who the fuck else laughs like that only to find it is her ... and my dad.

My dad?

Chelsea and my father stand on the pavement embracing like lovers. His hand cups her arse as he pulls her closer to him. Her arms cling tightly around his neck. When he pulls away, he puts his hand on her stomach before grabbing her hand and walking into the coffee shop.

I think I just vomited in my mouth.

I'm not the father of her fucking child, my dad is. I don't know what's worse right now.

Pressing down on the accelerator, I maneuver back into the traffic. I need to get the fuck out of here. I need to get my arse back to Beaumont where my wife is waiting for me.

Before I know it I'm in front of Harrison's complex. I drove for over an hour and I don't even remember how I got here. I get out, hoping that at least Yvie's at home and I can use the toilet and raid her fridge. I knock tentatively and wait. It'll be just my luck that no one's here and I'm going to have to take a leak in the bushes.

The door swings open and I'm face-to-face with one of the best women I know—Mrs. James, as in Harrison's mum. I look at her and shrug pitifully and she knows instantly that something's wrong. She puts her arms around me and she pulls me inside. She rubs my back and whispers that everything will be fine. I want to laugh and tell her there's isn't a hope in hell that anything is going to be fine, but instead I keep my mouth shut and let myself be comforted by the woman who has been there for me since I joined the band.

"Where's your wife? Harrison told me you got married."

"She's in Beaumont. I came back to take care of some stuff before I head back to her."

"And I hear she's having a baby."

"Yes, she is, and she's so amazingly beautiful."

Mrs. James kisses me on cheek and holds my face in her hands as her eyes roam, studying me. "In time you'll tell me what's bothering you. Until then, Harrison, Katelyn, and all my grandbabies are out back."

"He's here?"

"Yes, spring break or something for the kids. Go on, they're about to eat."

She doesn't have to tell me twice. I kiss her on the cheek and give her a tight hug. I know that I can tell her about Chelsea and she won't judge me, but there's no way I can say those words aloud without wanting to choke myself. I still don't know what the fuck to believe. I can't, for the life of me, imagine my dad betraying me like that. Chelsea, yes, but not my dad.

As I look around Harrison's, I wonder if Jenna would like to live in a place like this; being able to walk out to the beach whenever you want. It'd be just like our honeymoon, only permanent, and we'd be here, away from the cold weather.

I walk out onto the decking and what I see sends a dagger right through my cold heart. Harrison is so in love with Katelyn it makes me wonder if I can have that. I was in love with Chelsea at one time in my life, but she ruined that and continues to do so. I sought solace in women and lots of them, until now. I have to change, stop being a womaniser, and as much as I want to drink away my sorrows and bed the first bit of totty I see, I can't. I won't.

Watching Harrison and Katelyn gives me some kind of hope. He's holding her, his arms are wrapped loosely around her shoulders. She leans against him, her hands hanging on to his arms. Her smile is so huge and her focus split between him and the kids playing in the surf. He kisses her repeatedly, and it shows me a side of Harrison I've never seen before.

"Ahem," I clear my throat to get their attention. Harrison turns, inadvertently turning Katelyn with him. "Fancy seeing you here," I say, waving.

"Hey, man, grab a beer and join us. Quinn is teaching the twins to body surf."

I open the fridge in Harrison's state-of-the-art kitchen and grab a beer. I really don't want to intrude on their family time and should probably leave after this.

"How's Jenna?" Katelyn asks.

"She's good, although I'm thinking I probably should've brought her with me." It's a lie though. I'm glad I didn't bring her because I know for a fact that her reaction to Chelsea would be to file for a divorce.

Katelyn kisses Harrison and starts to walk away. He holds on to her until they can't reach each other anymore. His eyes never leave her as he watches her walk over to the kids. When she's out of earshot, I blurt out, "I'm in a shit-load of fucking trouble. Or at least I think I am."

He shakes his head and goes over to grab a beer. As he sits next to me, he takes a long swig. His eyes are still trained on his family.

"Why'd you get married, JD?"

"The baby's mine."

"No reason to get married. Are you regretting it?"

"No, I like Jenna and want the baby to have a family."

Finishing his beer, Harrison gets up to get another. He brings one back for me and this time sits opposite me. "What's going on?"

I shrug. "Like I said, I'm fucked."

"How so?"

Leaning back, I rub my hands over my face. "Chelsea's pregnant and she's going to pin it on me. Everyone's going to believe her because we have a history."

Harrison looks back at his family. He waves and smiles. He has what I'm trying to give Jenna but I'm already failing miserably.

"Let's go for a walk."

After taking off my shoes and socks, I follow Harrison out onto the sand. It only takes a few moments for the kids to come running up to me. They're wet and sandy, but I don't care. The short time I spent with the twins was enough to earn me the title of uncle even if I was using them to pick up the birds by the pool. After saying hello, they run back to Katelyn, their laughter echoing along the beach. Anyone who walks past will know that this is a happy house, a house full of love. That's what I want to give Jenna, I know I'm not going to even get close to what Harrison has because he and I aren't cut from anywhere near the same cloth.

Harrison and I walk down the beach. The last time I was here we went surfing, but that's the last thing I want to do today. Today I'm hoping he actually takes me out into the waves and drowns my pathetic self for fucking up the lives of everyone around me.

"So you're married to a woman you hardly know who is pregnant, and your ex-fiancée is also pregnant."

"I know Jenna very well," I rebut.

"Oh yeah, what's her favorite song?"

I roll my eyes and kick the sand in front of me.

"Did you tell Chelsea that you were getting married?"

"No. I didn't know I was until I found out Jenna was pregnant and how many months she was. I whisked her to Bora Bora, proposed, got married, and we had a honeymoon. It was great, perfect actually. Until I went back to being a complete numpty and came back. Now all I can think about is how happy I am that I didn't bring her with me to LA."

"When did you and Chelsea get back together?"

I shake my head. "We haven't. We shagged before I went back to Beaumont, but since I had that night with Jenna at Liam's wedding, I've been thinking about Jenna non-stop. When I was with Chelsea everything seemed fake and forced. I wasn't into it. I pushed her off me."

"Damn, man, that's harsh." Harrison laughs.

I shove him, but realise that he's right, what I did was harsh. Apparently that hasn't put her off, though, as she's in my flat, making herself at home.

"I think the baby might be my dad's."

Harrison chokes on his beer. "Say what?"

"I saw them kissing and shit. I don't know, mate. Would my dad do something like that?"

Harrison shakes his head. "I want to say no, but Chelsea might. I don't know, man, the whole thing seems fucked up."

"What am I going to do?"

We stop walking and stare out into the sea. "The way I see it, you can tell Jenna about Chelsea. She'll understand. She's a good person, and if I know her, she'll tell you to go and be with Chelsea."

"I don't want to be with Chelsea."

"What do you want, JD?"

"My wife."

"Then why the fuck are you standing on my beach? Go back to Beaumont and get her. We have a month before we leave on tour. Go spend time with her, cherish her. Fuck like rabbits if you have to, but just go to her."

"When did you turn into a smart arse?"

Harrison laughs. "When I started plugging into Katelyn."

20

JENNA

I told him what today is, what it meant to me. I thought, as my husband and the father of my child, he'd be here, but he's not. Sitting by myself in a doctor's office full of expectant women would be much easier if I was alone and single. I am, alone that is, in every sense of the word, except they all look at me briefly before turning away. It's the pity party that I've wanted to avoid. They look at the ring on my finger then to the empty chairs on either side of me and shake their heads. Their husbands sit there without a care in the world, reading the most recent edition of *Sports Illustrated*. Their job is done. They fertilized the egg and make their mandatory monthly appearance just to keep their wives happy.

I want my husband to do the same thing. Or at least tell me he's not going to be one of those dads that takes time out of their day to attend doctor's appointments and that I shouldn't have any wild expectations about what our marriage really is.

A sham.

A cover.

A publicity stunt.

I'm sure he is trying to avoid having his name spread all over the tabloids saying that he knocked up some random chick and didn't do the right thing. It's probably bad for his image and will mean the hook-ups will be non-existent for him now. I know I was random, but he married me. He made me feel special, wanted. He told me he wanted this baby and was in this for all the right reasons.

Then he left.

I don't know what I expected, but it's definitely not this: three days maybe, a week at the most, but two weeks? Two weeks to get your affairs in order? When I left Damien, it was quick. I didn't haggle over my bills or anything like that. I didn't even change my address, but Jimmy, I don't even know what he's doing. How long does it take to get one's affairs in order?

Affairs. That's the word that lingers in the back of my mind. Is that what he's doing? Sowing his wild oats in L.A. because I'm not there? I try to clear my head of those thoughts, reminding myself that as much as he said we'd have a conventional marriage, it's not happening. You don't leave your newlywed wife at home while you gallivant back to your home state where the contents of your little black book reside.

The office door opens and for one brief second I allow my heart to beat a little faster thinking it's Jimmy; that he's here and isn't going to miss this appointment. What I don't account for is the instant let down when yet another pregnant woman and her husband walk in, hand in hand. I hate admitting it, but that's what I want. It's what I need and desire deep in my heart. I'll never tell him, though. I'll never tell anyone my true feelings because those are left bottled up and buried deep in the sand. I can't pressure him to be something he's not. I knew this and yet I fooled myself enough to believe his words.

"Jenna Davis?"

I look up at the nurse standing in the doorway holding my file. She smiles, waiting for Jenna Davis to stand and make her presence known. I want to rewind the last twenty minutes of this day and not tell the receptionist that my name has changed. Davis. My child will be born with that last name. And while that pleased me weeks ago, now I'm not so sure. I rise slowly and am met with looks from the other women. They judge me openly. We all do it whether we intend to or not. I'm the poor wife whose husband can't be bothered—that's what they're thinking. They aren't thinking that my husband is a doctor or even his true profession, a musician, and he can't get away from work. No, they're thinking I'm single and doing this on my own. They want to commend me but they don't because that means they understand even though their husbands are sitting next to them. Some were probably willing, but I have no doubt there are a few here that were forced to take time off from their days to be at their wife's side, as they should be.

I glance at the office door one more time before making my way to the nurse. She smiles again when I pass her, the door shutting loudly behind us.

"This way," she says in her 'I'm so happy to be doing my job' voice. We step into a room and she shuts the door behind me. This is routine. I take a seat in the chair until

I'm told to change into the thin piece of fabric that doctors call a gown.

"I see you recently married. Congratulations." The corners of my mouth turn up in the fakest smile I've ever had to plaster on my face. She reaches for my arm, slipping the blue blood pressure cuff up my forearm. "How are you feeling?"

"I'm fine. I haven't had morning sickness in a while."

"And you're sleeping okay?" she asks without eye contact. I know she's in a hurry, she has a waiting room full of patients, but a little acknowledgement would be nice.

"I don't have any problems sleeping." It's a bold-faced lie. Ever since Jimmy left and my run in with Damien I haven't slept at all. Every sound, every little creak in the steps and my body tenses. I lie awake at night with my phone in my hand waiting for the front door to open and for Damien to appear. I leave all my lights on so that shadows don't scare me. I could go back to Liam's, but that's admitting I'm scared or telling him that Damien was around and I'm not sure I'm willing to do that.

"Your husband won't be joining you today?"

I shake my head and look up at the fluorescent lights, giving me an excuse to have watery eyes. I won't cry, not in front of her and not over my missing husband. "He's working," I say as nonchalantly as possible.

"Stand on the scale please."

Slipping off my shoes, I step on the scale. I watch, in horror and delight, as the number increases. Gaining weight is a necessary evil. The higher number should make me feel happy, but it doesn't because at the forefront of my mind are toothpick skinny women draping themselves all over my very willing husband.

"Did you drink your water?"

"Yes."

"Okay, go ahead and lie back on the table, Jenna. The technician will be in first to do your ultrasound and then the doctor will be in. Be sure to tell the tech if you want to know the sex or not."

The nurse is gone before I can say anything. I lie back on the white paper and let my legs dangle over the end. I jump when the door opens, followed by a young male technician. He smiles brightly when he sees me. I try not to stare, but I can't help it. He's tall, at least I think he is, with a gorgeous smile and a head full of curls; the kind that make you want to reach out and run your fingers through them. His eyes are bright blue, like something you'd only see in the daylight and if the sun was shining just right.

"I hear we're looking at your baby today."

I nod, my voice nowhere to be found. He pulls out the rest of the table, allowing my legs to lie flat. He sits in his stool and rolls over to me, pulling the ultrasound machine behind him. I glance at his nametag and shake my head slowly. His name is James, and while that isn't Jimmy's name, it's close enough.

"I'm going to lift your shirt and put on this gross and very cold goop on your skin."

I shiver, not when he touches me, but when the blue blob hits my skin. I shiver when Jimmy touches me.

The technician puts the wand on my stomach and hits a few buttons. The room comes alive with the sound of the baby's heartbeat. It sounds like there are a hundred horses galloping all around me.

"Now that we've heard the heartbeat, let's see your baby."

Before I know what's happening, the ultrasound machine is pushed into the technician and the wand is hanging from my leg.

"Whoa there, buddy," James says. I look over my shoulder to find Jimmy staring at me. The grin on his face tells me that he's happy to be here, to see me, but it quickly morphs into something else. Concern? He steps over to me and kisses me full on the lips.

"Sorry about that, mate. I'm Jimmy Davis."

I look over at James. He's staring at Jimmy with his mouth open. "I know who you are. It's a pleasure to meet you. I'm a huge fan." They shake hands, completely ignoring me.

"Hi, sweet lips," he says, kissing me again.

"Hi."

Jimmy moves so he's on the other side of me and picks up my hand. He kisses my rings before locking his fingers with mine. If we were any place else I'd punch him in his junk, but I can't really do that right now since I'm stuck and I want to know if my baby has ten fingers and toes.

"Have you seen our bub, yet?"

"No, Mr. Davis, we were just about to look."

I want to throw up at how sweet James is being to Jimmy. I mean, really? I'm the pregnant one. Shouldn't he be sugary sweet to me?

"Call me JD."

I roll my eyes and face the screen. "Can we see the baby now, please?"

James pulls his eyes away from Jimmy's and looks for the wand. He fumbles with it a few times before setting it back on my stomach. The baby's heartbeat fills the room again, relaxing me.

"What's that noise?"

I look over at my husband and see his eyes wandering. This is why I wanted him here, not only to be by my side, but to experience this together.

"That's our baby," I say, quietly, my voice breaking. Jimmy's face breaks out into the most mesmerizing grin I've ever seen. More than when I said yes to his marriage proposal. He kisses me hard, holding my face to his.

"I need to record this sound," he says, pulling away. He lets go of my hand, takes out his phone, and holds it in the air. I want to laugh out loud at how silly he's being, but know this is something I'll listen to over and over again.

"There you go. I think I've got it."

"I hope so," I say, knowing I'll need to hear the heartbeat again once I get home.

"Do you want to know what you're having?"

Jimmy and I stare at each other, both our faces morphing into smiles. As much as I want to be mad at him right now, and believe me I plan to let him have it after we're done, now that he's here, I want to know as long as he's sitting by my side.

We both look at James and nod.

21

JIMMY

I'm pushing it, I know I am. I can't help it. No, that's not right. I can help it, but I don't know how. I feel like my head is going to explode and it doesn't matter what I do, or what I say, it's going to be the wrong thing.

Chelsea's pregnant. She reminds me of this fact on a daily basis, throwing it in my face like I'm supposed to care. She tells me that she loves me and is ready to get married. The smart thing for me to say is 'I'm already married', but I don't. I don't say anything. I act like a fucking mute when she's around. I hate it. I hate that when I'm in L.A. I can't leave my flat without her following me. At what point do women wake up and smell the coffee? When do they realise that they're being ignored on purpose and that it doesn't matter how much whining and crying they do, if a bloke isn't into them, he's not going to change his mind suddenly?

She asked me to go to her doctor's appointment. I declined politely by saying I didn't want to go. She burst into tears. I fucking hate it when women cry so I gave in and said I'd go with her. I don't even know why I went. I know this baby isn't mine, yet I sat there in the waiting room, reading a magazine and shying away from her every time she tried to hold my hand. The only problem with that is I never asked when it was and, sod's law, I was delayed in getting back to my Jenna.

Yeah, *my* Jenna. I miss her. I miss holding her hand and kissing her luscious lips. I miss rubbing my hand along her stomach, knowing our baby is in there thriving off her. I know she knows something is wrong. Our phone conversations were short and I had to speak so quietly that she had to ask me to repeat myself. I couldn't risk Chelsea hearing me, and since I'm a total idiot, I couldn't ask Chelsea to leave.

But I'm here now and I'm holding my wife's hand as we walk to her car. I open the door for her, but she doesn't get in. She stands against the side of the car and crosses her arms under her glorious boobs. I reach out to rub her arm, but she shies away from me.

Fuck me.

I run my hand through my hair. It's in dire need of being cut, but I wanted to ask Jenna her opinion. I want to get a Mohawk, but I want her to like it.

"Jenna—"

"Don't. You don't get to Jenna me. You left me, Jimmy. You said you'd be right back. To me that's ... I don't even know, but not two weeks and not with those sorry ass excuses for phone calls."

Jenna bites lower lip and I want to pull it from her offending teeth and kiss the crap out of it, but having her move away from me again isn't something I want to experience.

"I'm sorry. I know it's a shit excuse, but I am. I didn't

mean to be away for this long. I tried ... look it doesn't matter. I'm back and am not going anywhere."

"You're right, it doesn't matter." Standing up straight, Jenna unfolds her arms and looks up at the sky briefly before leveling her gaze back on me. "I want a divorce," she says in a whisper.

"Where have you been, James?"

My mum thinks I'm sleeping, but I've missed my dad and he's home now. I creep down the hall to their bedroom and peek in. My mum is sitting at her table, the one that has all the make-up on it, that she tells my nana that she needs so that my dad will look at her. I think my mum is beautiful just the way she is.

"James, I asked you a question."

"I heard you."

I can't see my dad, but I hear him. He sounds like he's so far away.

"Are you going to answer me?"

"You don't need to worry about where I was, Brigette. I was at work. That's what I do. I leave at night and go to work so you can live like a queen and so Jimmy can go to the finest boys' school. Stop with the questions."

My mum turns around in her chair and puts her hands in her lap. She looks like she's been crying. "I'm tired."

"Come to bed, love."

"No, James. I'm tired of the cheating. I'm tired of whoever it is hanging up on me every time I answer the phone only for it to start ringing again for you to answer. I'm tired of you coming home and smelling like you bathed in the perfume counter at Harrod's. I'm tired of being an after-

thought in your life. I want a divorce. I want you to move out, tonight."

I jump when something slams against the wall. My mum stands. "What are you doing, James? Jimmy's sleeping."

"Do you think I care? My wife is telling me that she wants a divorce and is kicking me out of my house and you want me to be quiet? Are you mad? I give you the life you ask for. I provide the finest jewels and furs that you drape yourself in at every social event. So fucking what if I get some on the side."

"Get out," my mum shouts.

I jump back away from the door, afraid that she'll see me.

"You're mad, woman. We've been married for fifteen years. I gave you a child. I provide you with a home. You don't want me to leave."

"I've called a lawyer, James. You need to leave, tonight. I want you gone."

"You want me gone?"

Their room goes silent for a moment.

"Fine, Brigette. I'm going, but don't you dare call me and beg me to come back. You want me gone, so be it."

I don't want him to go. He's my dad. He needs to stay. He promised he'd take me to football practice tomorrow. Who's going to take me now?

The door swings open and my dad steps into the hall. I look up at him and he shakes his head. He turns and looks at my mum. "I hope you're happy, Brigette."

"Don't leave me, Dad," I say, grabbing his hand.

He pulls it away and rests it on my shoulder. "Listen

closely, Jimmy. Never get married. Women are only good for one thing."

"James!" my mum screeches.

"What, love? Isn't that why you're kicking me out?"

"Jimmy, go to bed, please."

"No, Mum. I'm going with Dad. I'll pack my suitcase."

I run down the hall, ignoring my dad calling my name. I don't want to live with my mum if she doesn't like my dad.

"Jimmy," my dad shouts. I turn to find him shaking his head. "You can't come."

"Why not? You told me you'd take me to football tomorrow. I want to come with you."

"I don't want you to come with me."

I freeze in my doorway. My mum covers her mouth as her eyes go wide and fill with tears. My dad shakes his head. He turns and walks away. We both jump when the door slams shut. My mum rushes to me, drops to her knees, and pulls me into her arms.

"Don't listen to him, Jimmy. He's been drinking and doesn't know what he's saying. He'll always want you. You're his son."

Only he doesn't want me.

"Why?" I ask, stepping closer. I feel the need to pin her against the car so she can't escape. She can't leave me. I know I'm a loser who doesn't deserve her, but I need her. I want her in my life. I want to raise our baby together and be a family. I won't let her get away. I refuse to just walk away from her like my dad walked away from my mum. He didn't stay to fight, but I will. I am. She's not leaving me because I'm a fucking idiot.

"Because you don't want to be married, Jimmy. I don't want you to stay out of obligation and I don't …"

"Don't what, sweet lips?" I move closer. I know I'm being devious and underhanded, but I need to feel her against me. I'm going to find every way to show her that I'm hers. I know there's stuff I need to take care of and I will. I won't let anything come between us.

She shakes her head, covering her face. I pull her hands away and put them around my waist. "I'm sorry, Jenna. I'm so fucking sorry. There was so much crap I had to take care of and I'm no good at this relationship thing but I'm going to work at it so that I am. I'm going work at it and make sure you can count on me and trust me. I promise you that I was faithful because I know that's what you're thinking. You're my wife and I'm taking my vows very seriously."

"I don't know, Jimmy." But she does know. Her hands are clutching the back of my shirt. Her nails are digging into my skin. She knows that she wants me just as much as I want her.

"I know, and I'll fix it," I say as my lips touch hers. She's rigid, fighting me. "I'm not perfect, but I'm trying to be better for you," I add, moving my lips against hers. "I want to be the best husband and father to our baby." She finally opens up and accepts me, meeting me halfway. I feel alive when her tongue touches mine. Her body doesn't want a divorce, I'm sure about that. I'm going to have to step up my game and make sure she knows that she's my one and only. I was stupid to stay in California for so long. I let myself get sucked into Chelsea's drama and I need to learn to say no.

"What brings you by?"

Looking at my father makes me cringe, but I'm here,

being the man my mum brought me up to be. Maybe what I saw was two people comforting each other because I was being an arsehole. Or maybe I saw exactly what I think I saw, which was my dad snogging the face off my ex-girlfriend who has just happened to tell me that she's pregnant.

I walk in and sit down on his leather sofa only to stand up again. Images of him and Chelsea invade my subconscious and it's not a pretty sight. I walk over to the window and look out over Los Angeles. My dad's place is pretty much like Liam's was—floor to ceiling windows—but no one can see in. It's the best of both worlds in my opinion; at least it used to be. Now I see a two-storey house with a fenced-off garden in my future.

"I'm having a baby," I blurt out.

"I heard. Congratulations." He's moving around behind me, no doubt pouring himself three fingers of Scotch.

"Who told you? I doubt my mum called you."

"Chelsea told me. I see her every now again." I nod and want to add, Of course you do.

"I'm not talking about Chelsea. I'm with someone in Beaumont and we're having a baby together."

He pats me on the back, causing me to jump. "That's my boy, one here and one on the side. Nothing wrong with that at all, son."

Except there's everything wrong with it. Doesn't he know that he's wrong? Doesn't he know that when you find the one, everything in life falls into place? The morning after I woke up with Jenna in my arms, I smiled. And it wasn't some stupid cheesy smile. It was a real, genuine one. She makes me smile.

"Dad, I don't have anyone on the side. I'm married, off the market."

"Now why would you go and do something stupid like that? Get an annulment. I have a good lawyer who can help you."

"Because I want to be with her and I want to raise my child with her. I don't want my kid going through the same crap I went through. My child will grow up knowing me."

"And what about Chelsea, doesn't she deserve the same from you?"

I shake my head. "Chelsea's not having my baby. I went with her to the doctor's, I saw the chart. I may be a bloke, but I can add numbers up. Chelsea was pregnant before her and I slept together."

Jenna pulls away too soon for my liking. "I want you to change your number."

"Okay, let's go do it right now," I say without hesitation. If changing my number will make her feel better, I'll do it. At this point I'll stand on top of a building and tell the world that I'm happily married and about to have a baby. I'll do anything she asks except leave. I'll never leave my child. She's going to have to leave me if she wants out.

"Can I ask you something, wifey?"

She rolls her eyes playfully as she moves her hands so that they rest on my shoulders. "What?"

"Would you like to meet my mum? She really wants to meet you and wants to come and visit."

"Yeah I'd like that. What about your dad?"

"Nah, sweet lips, you don't want to meet him. My mum, though, she's fantastic. You'll love her and she already loves you because you're making her a grandma."

"Jimmy?"

"Yes, Mrs. Davis?" God, I really love the fact that my surname is now hers.

"Why did it take you two weeks?"

I could give her some stupid bullshit excuse, but I won't. I'm never going to lie to this woman. Withhold some facts, yes, but it's for her protection.

"There was a shit storm in L.A. I had to meet with some people, see my dad, empty my flat, and make some financial arrangements to protect you. It took longer than I thought and I'm sorry."

All I get from her in reply is a nod. I don't know whether she believes me or not, but I'm never leaving her side again for as long as I live, and one of these days I'm going to have to tell Jenna about my shitty father. Yes, I came to live with him when I turned eighteen, but that was because my mum made me. If she hadn't, I'd still be a busker in Covent Garden or something. Mum made sure my dad and I established some kind of relationship, but that doesn't mean I want him anywhere near my wife and baby.

"You know, wifey, we need to decide if we're going to tell people what we're having." I help her into the car and shut the door. When I get in, her hand automatically finds mine, making me wonder just how serious she was about asking for a divorce. The only thing I know is that I never want to hear those words come out of her mouth again.

"Let's keep it a secret."

I bang my head against the headrest and look at her. She's glowing, her hand rubbing her stomach. I lean over and kiss her before starting the car.

"Your wish is my command, sweet lips."

I lean my head back on the headrest and turn my face toward the window. The afternoon sun shines through the window, warming my face. My hand rests in Jimmy's lap, our fingers locked together. His finger taps in beat with the song on the radio against the top of my hand. If this were weeks ago, I'd be looking at him and imagining what our child will look like; but it's not, and as much as I want to trust what he says, I can't get over the suspicion that something is off.

I know I'm a fool for getting into the car with him. I caved when he turned on his British charm and wooed me into believing that everything is okay. He didn't say I was overreacting though or that my hormones are getting me riled up and that concerns me. I've never been the jealous type. With Damien, my friends never let on that they were attracted to him or desired him in any way, but Jimmy? With him I know. I see the way other women look at him. The way they throw themselves at him expecting, and at some point receiving attention in return. Is he going to be like that when he goes on stage the next time? Will he touch their faces, caressing them like he does me?

It can't be easy changing who you are in the blink of an eye and that is what he did or should've done. I wasn't kidding when I took my vows and I hope to God he wasn't either. We may not be in love, but I want us to at least be faithful.

My lips curve into a smile when I feel his hand caress my stomach. My shirt lifts and his lips are there. Jimmy places kisses along my growing belly from one side to the other, whispering words only the baby can hear. My fingers thread though his hair, my nails scraping softly along his scalp. In our short time together, I've learned that he loves this and that it turns him on.

My eyes remain shut. I feel like I'm dreaming and that when I wake up everything will be ugly again. Damien will be standing outside my window with the murderous look on his face, and next to Jimmy will be hordes of women claiming to be his mistresses. Keeping my eyes shut and my face toward the window is the best option for me right now. I want to relish in the attention he's giving me before it goes away. Before my bubble is burst and some skinny girl shows up in Beaumont telling me that she's been sleeping with my husband.

When his lips find mine, I close my eyes tighter and submit to him. He controls me, drives me to the brink with just the simplest of kisses. I wish my body would fight him, ward him off, but it craves him. My body desires his touch and it has since we first met a year ago when he came to

Beaumont. How I ever made it without coming onto him before the wedding is beside me. Having him in my arms that one night was the result of years of therapy teaching me to love myself again. Helping me discover that Damien and his fist could no longer hurt me, control me. When Jimmy came to me that night, I knew what I was doing. I wanted a piece of him like every other woman his path had crossed. I was no different in that way. I took him and everything he was willing to give me in an empty room on a pool table. Our story is definitely one for the grandkids.

I cup his head, holding him to my lips. I want him to crawl on top of me and take me in the car. I've missed him and my need for him grows more urgent with each flick of his tongue against mine.

"Jimmy," I say against his lips. My hand travels down his neck, over his chest, and to his belt buckle. I tug, pulling it out of the loop on his jeans. I palm his hard-on, squeezing gently, and I'm rewarded with him biting down on my lip. He stills my hand and I squeeze again, letting my thumb brush up and down against his bulge.

"Wifey, you're killing me. I've missed you so much, but right now we have somewhere to be."

"Why'd you stop the car then?" I ask, opening my eyes for the first time and looking around. Is it too much to ask for a little backseat action? I know I'm pregnant, but I'm not above breaking the law if it means I can get freaky with my hot ass husband.

"Because we have plans and we're here." Jimmy looks out the window. I follow his gaze and realize we're in a parking lot. I was so lost in my daydream that I wasn't paying attention. Refusing to pay attention is more like it, but still the same nonetheless.

"What are we doing at the Beaumont Country Club?"

Jimmy shrugs. "Liam told me that we should meet him here."

"Do you play golf?" What a stupid question for a wife to ask her husband, but it shows that we don't know each other very well. "I really don't want to sit in there while you play golf with Liam."

"Sweet lips, I doubt Liam plays golf or is even allowed on the course with his tattoos. Can you imagine someone telling him to cover them up?"

"No, not really. So why are we here?"

"I haven't got the foggiest, let's go find out."

Or not, I want to say, but he's out of the car before I have a chance to open my mouth. I drop the visor and look in the mirror at my make-up. My lips are red and plump from his razor burn and my eyes look like I just woke up. Clearly people will know we've been fooling around in the car and I'd rather not leave that impression, despite my desire to screw his brains out in the backseat. I pull out my lip-gloss and apply a fresh coat, and run my fingers under my eyes to get rid of the excess make-up particles.

Jimmy opens the door and holds out his hand for me. I will give him credit; he's a gentleman in the truest sense of the word. His mother raised him proper and I can't wait to thank her for that. We walk hand in hand into the club. Josie's brought me here for lunch before, but we haven't been here much since Liam has come home. Something about his parents being members and it's too awkward for him.

Jimmy gives our names to the hostess who tells us to follow her. We are heading to a part of the club that is away from the restaurant. She points to a door and walks away, leaving us standing in the hallway by ourselves.

"What's going on?" I ask. Jimmy shakes his head but opens the door anyway. We step into a dark room. I clutch at his hand, hanging on for life. This is a set-up. Liam didn't plan this, Damien did. He's here in this room. I can feel it. Something moves behind me and I have to bite my lip from screaming out.

We've just walked into our death. My other arms grips his forearm, my nails digging into his skin. If I could crawl into his body I would. I move as close as possible, hoping that this will be quick and painless.

When the lights flick on I let out a blood-curdling scream at the hordes of people yelling at me, "Surprise!"

My heart pounds a thousand beats per second as I try to catch my breath. There are tears rushing down my face as my chest heaves.

"Jenna, what's wrong?" Josie asks as I cover my mouth to try and contain a sob.

"I thou-thought you were going to kill us."

Josie deadpans. "Oh shit, I'm so sorry. I didn't think of that. We just wanted to give you guys a reception since you eloped and didn't give us a chance to have a party."

"Okay." I'm a blubbering fool being held up by her husband. Jimmy rubs my back as he tries to act calm, but I feel him shaking. He thought we were set-up, too, and it's nice to know that I'm not the only one walking around paranoid.

"Come on, darling, let's go get you cleaned up. You have a party to attend." I nod and reluctantly let go of Jimmy's hand as Josie and Katelyn lead me out of the room. They lead me down the hall and behind a closed door. Once it's shut I let out a sob that makes my whole body shake. I'm directed to sit on the couch with both girls rubbing my back.

"What's going on? Because I'm getting the feeling you're bottling up some pretty deep emotions to be crying like this."

"Nothing," I say, wiping my tears. "Just my hormones."

"Bullshit," Josie and Katelyn say in unison.

"You can talk to us, you know. Just because you married into the band doesn't mean we're not friends," Katelyn says, stroking my hair. Josie nods.

I take a deep breath and blurt out, "I don't want to believe Jimmy is having an affair and I know he doesn't love me, but we took these vows and he was gone for two weeks and I'm really freaking out inside because my mind is telling me to run and file for divorce but my body is telling me to go screw his brains out in the backseat of the car." I cover my mouth in horror and look at my two friends. "Oh god, I'm so sorry. Ever since my second trimester it seems I have no filter."

Katelyn and Josie start laughing, which honestly doesn't make me feel any better. "Jenna," Katelyn starts, "I don't think Jimmy would cheat on you. At least I would hope that he's smarter than that."

"But he is Jimmy," Josie adds, which makes everything Katelyn just said go out the door.

"Oh great," I say, throwing my hands up in the air.

"No, listen. At one point we've all thought it. I would lie awake in bed at night and imagine Liam with other women. I had visuals from the many magazines and even Sam's face would pop-up. But he asked me to trust him and I did. Does it mean that I didn't think about it? No, it doesn't. Each time he went back to L.A., I was a wreck because I thought 'what if he's so lonely that he needs that painkiller?' Those women don't care if he's with someone, they all want a piece of someone else's pie."

"I felt the same about Harrison even though I knew he hadn't dated much and even stopped dating when he moved to Beaumont. The thoughts were there, but I know Harrison would never do something like that, nor would he allow Jimmy to do it on his watch. Trust that the guys will keep him on the right path as long as Jimmy wants to be there."

I try to smile at Josie and Katelyn and, while their words offer some reassurance, the thoughts still linger. The door opens with a small knock. We look up to find Jimmy peeking his head in.

"Hello, my lovelies, I'd like to have my wife back if that's okay with you?"

"Yeah, we're going to get her all pretty and then she'll be out," Josie says, standing. I smile softly at Jimmy before he finally closes the door.

"He's not cheating," Josie says.

"How do you know?"

She looks at me, her Cheshire Cat grin getting larger. "That boy is in love with you. I've never seen him look at another woman like that before."

My heart soars with her words. She would know, she's

spent the most time with him. Maybe I need to let go and just go with the flow and take each day as it comes. If I live in fear that he's cheating, I'll probably drive him into another woman's arms and I wouldn't be able to live if I did something like that.

23

JIMMY

My wife is crying and it's all my fault and my two best friends are shooting daggers at me as I walk down the corridor toward the bar. It's not going to matter what I say to her or to them. I've fucked up and there's no changing it. I'm as stupid as my mum was when she took my dad back. I don't know how I'm going to fix this. If I knew I would not be in this situation in the first place.

I approach the bar with some trepidation. They have questions and will expect answers. If this was any other woman they probably wouldn't care as much, but it's Jenna. I crossed the line during the night of the wedding and if the condom had done what it was supposed to do and not split, then no one would even know.

Except one time wasn't enough for me, and while being a dad wasn't something I was looking to be, I'm happy that she's my wife.

I take the beer that Liam is offering me. He and Harrison are leaning against the bar and watching the crowd. It makes a change that we are the spectators watching the crowd instead of it being the other way around.

"You scared the shit out of Jenna," I say, before taking a long swig of the beer. The cold amber liquid feels good as it slips down my throat and I quickly finish it. I can't get drunk, not tonight, but I can hide the fucking bullshit loitering at the back of my mind. Harrison knows my secret, but I trust him not to say anything to Liam. If I'm being honest, I'm hoping that he's forgotten and hasn't told Katelyn either. I don't want the little tidbit about Chelsea being pregnant to get back to Jenna before I have had a chance to say something to her first.

That's if I have the balls to even sum up the courage to say anything to her. Right now, I don't. I'd rather have my nuts twisted into a vice grip than explain about Chelsea being up the duff.

"I don't know much about women, but I do know those tears were a culmination of a few things."

"What does that mean, Liam?" I ask, taking another beer from the barman.

He puts his beer down and looks at me. "What the hell could take two weeks that you couldn't do from here? You left her the second you came back from your honeymoon. Why didn't you just take her with you?"

"It's not as easy as that, and you know it."

Liam knows it's not simple. There's a reason why he never took Josie home to L.A. Sam. Chelsea is my own personal Sam. If I took Jenna to Los Angeles I wouldn't be standing here today. Jenna would've left me. She would've walked out of my life and never looked back and I can't risk that happening.

"You can't be messing around on her. She's pregnant and not feeling sexy."

I look at my friend and shake my head. "How do you know this crap?"

Harrison laughs, lifting his beer bottle to his mouth. "This is why Katelyn and I aren't having any more kids. I can't deal with the emo shit that comes with it."

"She told Josie she's fat."

"She's pregnant," I say a little more loudly then I intend to. A few people I don't know, who I'm assuming are friends with Liam, turn and look at me. I tip my bottle at them and smile before looking back at him. "You're turning into someone who's pussy-whipped, Liam."

Harrison sprays beer out of his mouth and starts coughing. Liam looks like I've kicked his dog.

I shrug. "All I'm saying is that you've been getting in touch with your feminine side lately and it's starting to show."

"That's what happens when you're in love."

I see my bride scanning the room, and hope that she's looking for me. When our eyes meet, her face lights up. I take a sip of my beer and put it down. "Yeah, I know what you mean," I say before walking away from both of them.

Her smile becomes bigger, her eyes brighter, the closer I get. I know I fucked up, but I'm going to do whatever it takes to make sure she knows that she's my number one priority. I can't continue to mess up because I know if I do, she'll leave. She's already threatened divorce and I've hopefully talked her out of it, but if she says that word again I don't know what I'll do except to get down on my hands and knees and beg her not to leave me. I'll do more than my father did, that's for sure.

My dad has been gone for a month. My mum cries every night, but I don't understand why. She kicked him out so why is she crying? I only talk to her when she asks me questions. I'm mad at her for telling my dad to go away. I've tried calling him, but he never answers. I don't know when I'll get to see him again, but I'm saving all my money so I can go and live with him. Maybe he'll take me to America to live with my grandpa. He's always saying that everything is better over there and that he only lives in England because of my mum. But we don't need her anymore so my dad and me can just leave.

I climb the steps to my mum's flat. I don't call it home anymore, not since my dad left. I open the door and walk straight up the stairs that lead to my bedroom. I'll hide there until dinner. I don't want to watch the television with my mum.

"Jimmy."

I freeze when I hear my dad's voice. I turn and see him kneeling down with his arms open and waiting for me. Dropping my backpack, I run into his arms. I knew he'd come back for me. He loves me and promised he'd take me to football practice.

"I'm really happy you're here."

"Me too, Jimmy. I wanted to see you before I left."

I step back. "What do you mean?"

"I'm going to the States for a while, but I'll be back."

"I'm coming with you," I blurt out as I run toward the stairs.

"Jimmy?"

"Be right back, Dad, I just have to get my case; it's already packed." I run up the stairs and push the door open. I run to my bed, fall to my knees, and pull out my suitcase. I won't miss anything in my room. My dad can buy me new things when we get to Grandpa's.

When I go back downstairs there's a girl sitting on my dad's lap. She wasn't there earlier, but I already know I don't like her. She's kissing his neck like I've seen Rebecca do to Peter's older brother. Peter said his brother likes it and that it means the girl is ready to get busy. But I don't know why she's kissing my dad. Only my mum should be doing that. I don't like this girl at all.

"I'm ready," I say loudly.

The girl turns and looks at me, but she doesn't smile. She rolls her eyes and gets off my dad's lap. If you ask me, she's a little too big to be sitting there anyway. Even I don't do that anymore.

"You said it would just be us," the girl says. My dad moves her to one side and I see him touch her bum. I look at my dad with confusion. He closes his eyes, and when he looks at me, he beckons me toward him.

"Jimmy, you can't come with me."

"Why not?" I won't cry because I'm a tough boy.

"Because I need to get my place set up and get back into the studio. I can't do that with you hanging around. I keep late nights and that's not a good lifestyle for a little boy."

"I'm not little."

"Jimmy, come on, bud. You need to stay with your mom and help her out."

"No! She's making you leave. I'm coming with you."

My dad stands and puts his hand on my shoulder. The girl comes up behind my dad and grabs his hand.

"Don't touch my dad," I say, pushing her hand away. I push her until she's no longer standing next to us. "Tell her to go away."

"I can't."

"Why not? You love Mum, not her."

"Jimmy, listen. I love your mom, but I love Tiffany, too. I'm going to marry Tiffany as soon as the divorce is final."

"You can't, Dad. You love Mum."

"James, we're going to miss the flight."

My dad nods, as he listens to her. I hate her. My dad ruffles my hair. "See ya around. Be good to your mom."

As soon as the door shuts I start banging on it, shouting for my dad. "Come back," I say over and over again. I'm trying not to cry, but I can't help it. I want my dad.

My mum pulls me into her arms. She holds me while I cry against the door. She doesn't say anything. She doesn't have to.

I pull my wife into my arms and look in to her eyes. From this moment onwards I'm going to be better. I never want to hear the word divorce come out of her mouth again. Linking my hand with hers, I pull her to the middle of the dance floor. I don't know what song is playing, but from here on it will be ours. My arm moves around her waist and I pull her closer to me, holding our linked hands to our chests. We sway back and forth, dancing in front of our friends and family as husband and wife.

"I know I made you cry."

Jenna shakes her head.

"I did, I know I did. I'm stupid. I'm a stupid guy who

has made a life changing decision and I plan to follow through with everything I said on our wedding day. I promised you then and I promise you now, I'll cherish you, I'll protect you, and I'll be only yours. The only thing that can separate us is death, and we're going to live until we're old and grey and our great-great grandchildren have to come and visit us in a nursing home."

Jenna nods as I wipe away a tear. "You say the sweetest things."

"You bring out the best in me, sweet lips. I just need you to be patient with me. I'm going to fuck up, but you have my permission to kick my arse when I do."

"Okay."

"Yeah, okay," I say, kissing her. "Come on, I want to take you home and ravage your body. I've missed you."

"I'm fat."

I stop us from dancing and put my hands on her cheeks, forcing her to look at me. "You're beautiful and sexy. So fucking sexy that I've got a hard-on just thinking about you. I've wanted you for so long before the wedding and when I finally had you, I needed more. I'd be here even if you weren't pregnant. I don't want to hear that you're fat or not beautiful because you put all these other women to shame."

Taking her hand, I lead her out of the room. I know this party is for us, but I've just got back and I need to be alone with my wife.

24

JENNA

I roll over and look at my sleeping husband. He kept me up late last night saying good-bye and memorizing every inch of my body, and as much as I'd like to be sleeping right alongside him, the baby is running a marathon inside of me right now. I could wake him and ask him to sing to our child, but I like watching him sleep. It's a glorious sight with the sheet barely covering him, and I like being able to stare at his body freely. If I wanted I could trace the lines of his abs perfectly with my fingers and watch him wake from my touch.

I hate admitting it, but he's been the model husband since he came back from Los Angeles and I love having him here. He's been attentive, caring, and doesn't leave my side unless it's for band practice. He's leaving today, after being home for a month. Not back to L.A. but to go on tour. When he told me, I freaked. My body shook. I cried and shut myself in our room for hours until he couldn't take it anymore. It's the stupid pregnancy hormones, I know it is. I let my mind get the best of me and believe that he's going to return to the old Jimmy and that this past month was nothing but a show. I know my mind is being irrational. He's not going to leave me for a groupie, but it's hard. I want to live in a bubble and pretend the outside world doesn't exist. The irrational side of me needs to shut the hell up and enjoy the man next to me. He says he's not cheating and I need to trust that, trust him.

This tour will be different and the first one where the wives aren't going. The thought never crossed my mind about going with them, but Josie and Katelyn usually travel with the band. They're staying back for my benefit. I told them I'd be fine, but they wouldn't listen. With my parents gone and my third trimester looming, they felt it better that they stay with me. I'll be moving into Josie's house today until the guys get back. Not something I wanted to do, but my husband asked and even batted his damn eyelashes at me. Who am I to refuse?

My fingers have a mind of their own and follow the image engraved in my mind as they trace the ridges on his stomach. He stirs and mumbles something, but I don't stop. I try not to laugh, biting my bottom lip to keep from giggling. Side to side my finger moves, lightly touching his skin. His skin pebbles from my touch, encouraging me to keep at it.

His hand stills mine. I look at his face for any sign of displeasure but see none. He slides my hand under the sheet and onto his hard-on. He moves my hand up and down a few times before letting go. I watch as the sheet moves from the motion. I push it aside so I can take in the glory that is my husband. I glance at him; his eyes are shut and his arms are resting behind his head. I know he's awake by the sexy smirk spreading across his face.

Leaning down, I lick the valley between his abs. My tongue traces through the light path of hair leading to where I want to be. My lips replace my tongue. His fingers thread through my hair. If I look up, I'll be done for. His eyes do me in each and every time. I know what he wants and have no problems giving it to him.

"Come here and kiss me, wifey."

I chuckle, but don't move toward him. I straddle him as I kiss the top of his cock and replace my hand with my tongue. Jimmy hisses as his hips move forward. I chance a look and see his head thrown back. Seeing him like this spurs me to do this for him. If I can make him feel good, maybe he won't leave me in the end. I take him fully in my mouth, my hands spread out over his abdomen, my nails scratching lightly as they move.

His hand cups my arm pulling me away. "I need a kiss," he says as he brings me to his lips. In one swift move he impales me and sets a quick and fast rhythm. I scream out in pleasure as he rocks into me. "Christ, sweet lips, I fucking love your pussy."

A moan escapes, causing him to laugh.

"You like it when I talk dirty, don't you?"

"Yes," I reply, breathlessly.

He rolls us over and sits back on his haunches. His thumb presses against my clit. My eyes roll back as he continues to work my body into a frenzy. I've never felt like this. I've never felt like I'm standing on the edge and the only relief I'll get is if I fall over the side. He does this to me. He brings this out of me. Jimmy's masterful in the art of sex and I'm his student. He's teaching me to listen to my body, to feel what pleasure he's giving me. This is a class I want to flunk, repeatedly, so he has to start all over again.

I scream out as my orgasm rolls over me. Jimmy moves faster, more urgent. The pulsing is almost much too much to bear and I dig into his skin, looking for relief. He falls on top of me, panting.

"What am I to you?" he asks.

"My husband."

"Damn straight. Now kiss me."

"DO YOU THINK YOU HAVE EVERYTHING?" I ask, folding another shirt before putting it in his suitcase. We've stalled long enough, avoiding the inevitable. He's leaving for months and the timing couldn't be worse. They'll be gone most of the summer, arriving home a few weeks before my due date. I won't lie, I'm nervous the baby will come early and he won't be here.

I want him to stay, but I don't tell him this. I can't. Touring is part of his job and as much as I'm going to hate it, he has to go. I know I won't be alone, but I've grown rather fond of having Jimmy in my life every day. Waking up, walking to work, and crawling into bed has become a treat for me.

"I've never taken this many things before. You're spoiling me." Jimmy kisses me on my cheek and slaps my ass. He's sweet on one side, dirty on the other. Honestly, I wouldn't change him.

"I want to make sure you have enough clothes."

"You know we always use the facilities at the hotels we stay in and our manager will make sure our clothes get washed, right?" he playfully asks over his shoulder as he walks into the bathroom.

"What's his name again?" I know Josie and Katelyn were beyond happy that another "Sam" wasn't hired. I hid my elation that the new manager is a man. The last thing I want is some other woman doing Jimmy's laundry. I've become quite fond of the boxers he wears.

Jimmy comes out of the bathroom shirtless. My folding falters as I watch him move around the room. "He's called Gary. He's from New York, so not involved with the L.A. scene which is what Liam and Harrison wanted. He's also married and has kids so he gets it."

"Yeah, that's good," I say, my voice breaking. Jimmy comes up behind me, rests his chin on my shoulder, and places his hands on my belly. His thumbs move up and down over my shirt.

"For the first time since I joined the band I don't want to go," he whispers against my neck.

I nod, agreeing with him because I don't want him to go either. Or I wish I was going with him, but it's just not possible. "Would you be mad if I said I wanted you to stay?"

"No, I want to know that you want me here and that you need me here."

"I do, so much." I turn and wrap my arms around him. I won't cry, not in front of him. It's not fair to him if I do. He knows what this is doing to me. I don't need to pour salt in the open wound. "I think our—"

"Are you ready to tell everyone?"

I can't help but smile. We've been keeping the sex of the baby a secret and refusing to acknowledge it for fear we might slip in front of our friends.

"I think so. Josie and Katelyn want to know so they can plan a baby shower and I'm sure our moms want to know what we're having."

"My mum can't wait to meet you. She'll be arriving as soon as the tour ends and will stay to help out if you need her."

My mom has offered the same thing, but we can't have both of them here. "I think I'll take your mom up on the offer and tell mine she can come after."

"Whatever you want, wifey."

"I think we should tell people."

Jimmy's smile is infectious. I bury my head in his shoulder and hold onto him. In a few minutes we have to drive over to Liam's and say good-bye. We'll be living a life of webcams, texting, and phones. I've also been told to stay away from gossip sites and that if I'm starting to have a freak out, I'm to call him immediately.

He pulls away all too soon for my liking and bends down. His hands hold my stomach while he peppers me with kisses.

Jimmy looks up and winks, causing me to laugh. "I've recorded the song I've been singing so you have to play it every morning. I read online that you can put headphones on your stomach. I want to make sure my baby girl hears her daddy's voice every day."

A single tear falls from my eye onto the top of his hand. He stands, placing both hands on my cheeks. "I love you, sweet lips. I'll be home soon."

My breathing stops momentarily. "What did you say?"

"You heard me, Jenna. I love you. I love our daughter and I love our life together."

25

JIMMY

4225 West is back on tour! #Liam #Harrison #JD
Gonna rock with 4225 West tonight!
OMG!! Did you see Jimmy wink at me last night?? ☺ #4225West
I LOVE Jimmy Davis. He's delish
I so played out my fantasy last night at the after party #JimmyDavis #Love #bestnightever

I throw my phone down next to me. I really hate Twitter. I miss life in Beaumont. It's like Twitter and Beaumont go hand in hand for me. If I'm there, my Twitter feed and mentions are quiet. When I'm on the road, it's a 'trending topic' mess.

I want quiet.

No, what I want is my wife, in our bed, snuggled up in my arms. She's what I need. I miss touching her tummy and singing to our daughter, and even though I'm trying not to think about it too much, I do. The days are long and the nights are even longer. Before Jenna, I lived for my nights, but now I can't wait to get off stage so I can call her or see her beautiful face on Skype. I know she's staying up odd hours so we can talk and I appreciate it, but I hate seeing her so tired when she comes online.

Who knew I'd change this much in such a short amount of time? Not me. I knew marrying Jenna was a risk, but it was one I was willing to jump into feet first. I love her and not because we're having a baby, but because she's every-thing that I'm not. She completes me as a person and treats me as her equal.

I know she worries about me being unfaithful, but I saw what cheating did to my mum and I'd never do that to anyone. Chelsea did it to me and that alone pushed me to the lowest point in my life. I refuse to even look at another woman, so those tweets are all fucking bullshit. It's just nothing but a bunch of women trying their hand at a bit of shit-stirring.

Our tour bus pulls up and stops along the street in New York City. We are spending an extra day here to watch Yvie James perform. She's been here for a while working on Broadway, and now that her big brother is in town, we're going to watch her show. Yvie is like a sister to me—spunky, loud and annoying—but I wouldn't swap her for anything. She's my age and we've been through a lot together. Yvie knew Chelsea wasn't right for me before I could break free.

The bus door opens and we file out. I'm thankful that our arrival has been kept on the down low. It's not that I don't like the fans, it just that sometimes it's nice not to be noticed. Stretching, I take in the early morning sun. It's going to be a scorcher today, but all I'm doing is shopping. I'm forcing the guys to go with me to the toy stores and we'll be stocking up. Jenna's going to kill me because our place doesn't have a lot of space, but my little one needs toys and when her daddy gets home, he'll be moving her mum to a new house.

I've been searching for a house online. I'd like one like Harrison and Katelyn's. It's big enough for us to expand as a family and has a decent-sized garden. Liam and Josie's garden is too big for me. I look around at the buildings that surround me and think about how I wanted to live in the City. Not so much just me, but also Chelsea. When I bought the bungalow just a few blocks away from Sunset, I thought we'd be happy there. I was wrong, and standing here today I can say thank God Chelsea did what she did and I caught her because I wouldn't swap Jenna for anything.

The high-pitched squealing catches my attention. Before I know it, brown hair is flying by me at mock high speed and launching herself into Harrison's arms. He catches her without missing a beat and spins her around. Her legs wrap around his waist and to Liam and me this is normal and we expect it. But to the guy standing off to the side with the telltale sign of being utterly pissed off, he was definitely not expecting this on his leisurely stroll down a New York City side street.

This guy ... he's interesting. I watch him because he makes it easy to do so. He's glaring at Harrison as he stands against the building with his foot pressed up against the façade. The only thing missing is a cigarette hanging from his mouth and this bloke would be a James Dean wannabe. Sadly for him, he's not. He's middle-aged, with this week's style mop top and dressed like a twenty-something model out of GQ.

Harrison puts Yvie down, but doesn't let go of her. I

turn back and watch her friend with his eyes full of anger. He thinks he owns her. Funny. Last time I checked no one owned Yvie James, except maybe Quinn.

Yvie makes her rounds, Liam next then me. I pick her up and give 'Mr. Angry' the eye as I give her a long, hard kiss on her cheek. He doesn't know who he's messing around with, but let me tell you something; she's mine ... ours, and we protect what's ours.

"I'm so happy you guys are here. I've missed you," Yvie says as she falls back into Harrison's arms. He has his baby sister engulfed in his arms. Their bond is undeniable. "Come meet Oliver. He's my producer."

"And shagging partner," I mutter loud enough so Liam can hear me. He raises an eyebrow when Yvie glares at me. I shrug. I'm not sorry. The dude is a bloody dickhead and needs an attitude adjustment.

"Oliver, these are my brothers. That's Jimmy, Liam, and Harrison." She points at each one of us, and while all three of us stand there, each with a different expression, I can tell Ollie here isn't a fan.

"Nice to meet you, mate. I'd like to say that Yvie has told us lots about you but she hasn't." Oliver doesn't want to shake hands so I don't offer mine. I can see through his veneer; he's a twat and is probably shagging Yvie to get ahead in the industry. Maybe he'll piss off Harrison and we can have a fight later. It's been a long time since I've enjoyed myself in a bar fight.

"I'm sorry, what did you say your name was?" Harrison's words have a bit of bite to them and I know he saw the way this fuck was looking at us with Yvie. I'm trying not to laugh, but seeing him in overprotective mode is hilarious.

That's one thing about Harrison James: you don't mess with his family or he makes you pay. And if he's making you pay, you can be damn sure that I'll be right behind him, and so will Liam.

"I'm sorry, who are you?"

Taking a step back, I shake my head. This man is about to get his arse beaten. Harrison looks up sharply. This won't end well.

"Who are you?"

"As if it's any of your business. I'm Yvie's boyfriend and producer." Yeah, things are going downhill fast.

Harrison rubs his chin and Liam rolls his shoulders.

"Hold up, guys," Yvie says with her hands on her hips. "Oliver, don't be an ass to my brother. And, Harrison, stop acting tough. He's not like you guys."

"Every man should have respect for his girl's family," Liam says. I agree; it's the most important value to have.

I think 4225 West should do a celebrity wrestling match or something like that. I'll volunteer for the greater cause of humanity. Anything that allows me to release this pent-up aggression building inside of me. I know where it's coming from ... Chelsea. I was so grateful when Jenna asked me to change my number. I didn't hesitate. I did it because my wife asked me to and she's the most important person to me. What I didn't count on was Chelsea bombarding my email with pleas. I can clearly picture her in my mind. The tears running down her face, begging me to call her. The thing is, I don't want to. I know that makes me the biggest shit in the world, but I'm not convinced the baby she's having is mine.

I asked her for a paternity test, at Harrison's insistence.

He said he had one done with Quinn because he had to know. I have to know. I can't go to Jenna with this news, without knowing for sure. She'll leave me and I won't be able to handle that. When I told her that I loved her, I meant it without a doubt. I'll do whatever I can to make sure she knows that, but Chelsea is in the way and threatening my happiness and I can't have that.

Yvie promises she'll meet us at the side door of the venue before the show so we can let her in. I hope she leaves the douche behind. I don't want her night with us ruined by this arsehole.

I LOVE BEING ON STAGE. For me it's like an orgasm building and waiting to be released. When the lights go off and the first note is hit, the sensation takes over my body. Tonight is no different. I'm bouncing on the balls of my feet, anticipation crackling in the atmosphere. The chants are loud, they want Liam and that has never bothered me. They can have him in all his glory and he'll happily give it to them as long as he's on stage. I look at the three of us standing side by side, and think about how we've changed in the past two years. All of us are parents, even if my little one isn't here yet. I love her and can't wait to hold her in my arms. Harrison's a family man, doing the baseball and cheerleading camps and soccer practices in his mum mobile, and Liam ... our founder, he's setting the bar so high that I'm afraid I'll never achieve what he has, but I want it. He's the example of what dreams are made of, how you can change your path, but still end up where you started.

We go out on stage—Harrison to his drums, Liam to the microphone with his guitar hanging on his hip, and me to the keyboard. I take out my harmonica from my pocket and get it ready. Tonight, we're starting with "Tobacco Sunset," the song I wrote. Lyrics, for me, are a struggle. It can take me months to write a song, but lately, I've been writing them once a week. But this one is special. I sing it to my little one every day and I sang it to Jenna before I knew she was pregnant. Or maybe I did know. Maybe that's why I couldn't get her out of my head, or my system. Something was pulling me to her and whatever it was, whether our daughter or just life, I'm fucking grateful.

Liam steps up to the mic and the crowd roars. I smile, loving the vibrations they're sending our way. I play a few keys on the keyboard to get them going and make them cheer louder.

"New York, how you doin'?"

Liam's play on words are his version of Joey from *Friends*. Jenna and I have been watching the repeats lately. She says we're Monica and Chandler, but I tell her there's no way I'm going to be known as Bing. I called her my lobster. My sweet-lipped lobster who's made just for me.

"4225 West is happy to be here tonight. And right now we're going to start you off with a little something from JD. He's been a busy man lately." I look at the back of Liam and wonder what the fuck he's talking about. When Harrison hits his drums, ba-dum-tsh, I know something's up.

"Our little JD went and got himself all married and they're having a baby and this song we're about to play was written for his wife!" Liam yells into the microphone. The crowd erupts as anger and dread wash over me. It's not that

I didn't want people to know, but I didn't want Chelsea to know. I'm thousands of miles away, and will be for months, and there's no fucking way I can stop her from finding out. Even though I have doubts that her child is mine, she'll still go off the deep end if she's convinced herself that her baby is mine.

26

JENNA

I press play and let the soft melody lull me to sleep. If it works for the baby, why can't it work for me? A harmonica plays. He's gone all out on this recording.

"Hello, little one," he says. I can't help but smile at his words. He's not taking any chances and is making sure the baby knows he's talking to her. "I had to go away for a little while, but wanted you to have your song. Well, actually it's your mum's song, I just haven't been able to tell her about it yet. I wrote this song right after your mum and I made you. It was such a perfect night and I knew right at that moment that your mum had stolen my heart. You are just the added bonus."

Happy tears stream down my face. I reach for my phone, only to remember that he's on stage and will be calling me in a couple hours. I can wait until then. It'll be painful, but worth it. What I have to say to him needs to be done face-to-face—it can't be left on voicemail.

"Little one, I love your mum and want you to be very nice to her while I'm away. When I get home, it will almost be time for you to make your entrance and we can't wait to meet you."

Jimmy starts singing. It's the song he sang when I was sick. He said, and I remember this clearly, that his mom used to sing it to him when he was sick. He lied, but I'll forgive him, this one time.

After we set sail, there's gonna be storms
Just don't lose faith in me cause I'll keep us on course
Remember this day, it's written in the stars
We're on our way to forever, girl, it's not that far
I've never felt like this before
I see our ship comin' from the shore
And that horizon in your eyes
Is like tobacco sunburst
Is this gonna last, I wanna know
I gave you the key to my heart and it was hard to let it go

I'm stingy. I can admit that. While I should have the headphones on my stomach so she can hear her daddy sing to her, I'm listening to them instead. I've had the song on repeat for the last few hours. When he left, he told me he loved me. I didn't say it back. Not because I don't love him, I do, but I thought it was a knee-jerk reaction to the emotional moment we were having. This song tells me otherwise.

For a while I've questioned why I married Jimmy. It wasn't impulsive even though it seemed like it at the time. It definitely wasn't his charm, that's what got us into this situation to begin with. I married Jimmy because I wanted to. I wanted a new chapter in my life. One that isn't filled with fear and constantly looking over my shoulder. I never thought I'd find someone to fill that void in my life, but I have. I know getting married because you're pregnant isn't the smartest thing to do and we may not last, but for now I'm going to love him as long as he'll allow me to.

My phone rings from its resting spot, on top of my ever-growing stomach. I hit answer and sigh.

"Hello," I say, dreamily.

"Hey, sweet lips, how are my girls?" He's turned on the charm and he's not even here. Damn that man.

"We're good. Just waiting for you to call. How was the show?"

"It was great. We had a good crowd. They were really getting into it. I need to tell you something, though."

I can't imagine what he's about to say. Did he go crazy and jump off the stage only to fall onto the floor because his fans didn't catch him?

"What?" I choke out.

Jimmy sighs. I imagine him running his hand over his perfect face. His fingers rubbing his soulful brown eyes. "Liam ... I'm sorry, Jenna ... Liam told everyone that I'm married and having a baby."

"What?" I cry out in relief. My heart pounds and I swear if I open my mouth wide enough I'll be able to expel it onto the floor. "That's what you have to tell me?"

"Yeah. Why, what did you think I was going to say?"

"Not that," I say almost too excitedly.

"Oh shit, Jenna, you thought I was going to tell you I fucked up, right? Seriously? After the vows we said to each other?"

"Jimmy," I try to interrupt.

"We took those vows and I meant every fucking word of them."

"Jimmy?"

"What?"

"I'm sorry," I say, laughing. "Jimmy, I'm sorry. I love you and I just thought you were going to tell me that you crowd surfed, but only that the crowd didn't catch you."

"You love me?" His voice is tender, questioning.

I smile and nod, not realizing he can't see me. "I should've told you before you left. I'm an idiot."

"Well I won't argue with you, but you're my idiot and you're fucking sexy and beautiful and I miss the crap out of you already."

I start to laugh. My husband, the poet. "You have a way with words, Jimmy. Speaking of ... I listened to the song."

"Hey! That's for the little one. If you wanted a song you should've asked for one. Don't deprive my child of me while I'm gone you evil wench." Jimmy's laughing so hard he snorts, causing me to snort as well. We make a great pair.

"Little one?"

"Yeah," he says softly. "You're my sweet lips and that's my little one. I can't wait to meet our daughter, Jenna. I can't wait to hold your hand and help bring her into the world."

"Me too. I love her nickname."

"Good, because I'm going to use it a lot." I love that the names he's given us are unique and not common. I can see him saying 'little one' at the park and our little girl come running because she'll know it's her daddy calling her.

"Thank you," I say when he's calmed down. "Thank you for loving me and our baby."

"You make me feel whole, Jenna. I love you."

"I love you, too."

We talk until I'm yawning. He sings me to sleep, making me wish we had these moments inside of the apartment and not on the phone. Jimmy being gone right now is the most unbearable thing I've had to deal with in a long time.

SATURDAYS ARE busy at the shop. Josie has tried to make me take a leave of absence, but I told her she'd need to fire me if she didn't want me around anymore. When I said that, she got tears in her eyes and shook her head. I've been with her for a long time now, I can't imagine not working with her. I like to think of myself as one of the catalysts that got her and Liam back together. If I hadn't shown her the flyer and encouraged her to go to Los Angeles, who knows what would've happened?

I can tell you this: there wouldn't be a Harrison and Katelyn, no Jenna and Jimmy, and that is far too depressing to think about.

I'm a cliché, I've realized. I married into a rock band. First Josie, then Katelyn—even though they're not married, she's his wife—and now me. The writing was on the wall if you think about it. It was only a matter of time.

Katelyn and Aubrey are working today as well. Josie mans the flower shop while Katelyn is in the coffee shop. Aubrey and I move back and forth between the two, depending on which side is busier. The older patrons, the returning customers, have learned that they can get lunch and order their flowers all in one sitting. It's an oddity, really, but it works.

In the corner, we have a young kid playing his guitar. Liam booked gigs before he left. He didn't want Josie to have to worry about it and didn't want the newly established music scene to think she wasn't catering to everyone. This one is good, a little sweet on the eyes. He'll go far I'm sure.

I walk to my next table with my order pad ready. "Hello, what can I get for you?"

The customer is hidden behind a newspaper, covering his or her features. I can't really lean up on my tiptoes because that would be considered rude so I wait.

The newspaper ruffles and the customer—a man—speaks in a low, hoarse voice. "Coffee, black."

Typical businessman. "Can I get you anything else?"

"No," he replies, barely looking over his paper. His hat is covering most of features so I can't see what he looks like. "Fucking fat," he mutters.

I bite the inside of my cheek to keep the slurs from escaping. *Sexiest pig.*

"Jenna?" I look over at Katelyn. "Jimmy's on the phone. Says it's urgent."

I roll my eyes. He knows I'm working. I can't imagine what would be so urgent. "I'm sorry, I'll be right back after I find out what my husband wants," I say in a snotty tone. *That's right, asshole, I'm married.*

I pick up the phone and say hello.

He laughs. "Hi, sweet lips. I missed your voice so I wanted to say hi."

"I'm working, Jimmy. I just left a customer at the table, although he called me fat."

"Fuck that, you're fucking sexy and I miss you."

"I miss you, too. Skype tonight?"

"I don't know, wifey, will you take off your shirt for me so I can see your tits?"

"Incorrigible," I say, knowing I'll do whatever he asks of me.

"You love me?"

"You know I do and so does your little one."

"I miss you. I'll call you later." He hangs up before I can say good-bye. I don't know what that call was about, but it's enough to put a smile on my face. I walk back to my table with the asshole's coffee, hoping he's ready to order. Today might be the day that I actually spit in someone's food.

"Sorry about that."

"I'm sure you are."

I roll my eyes and set down his coffee. I'm not going to take his shit. I don't have to. If he's not careful, I'll have one of the kids come wait on him just so I can see them piss him off.

"If you need anything, let me know."

"Excuse me, miss."

I'm not two steps away before he calls me back. I turn and freeze. The paper is down and this man is not just any customer, but Damien.

I look around to see if anyone is watching. Of course, no one is in sight. My pulse races with fear. He knows I'm pregnant. This is something he's wanted.

"You're fat, Jenna. You know that's unacceptable."

"You need to leave, Damien. There's a warrant for your arrest. If anyone see's you, they'll call the cops," I lie, easily.

He scoffs. "I'm not afraid of your Podunk friend." He points to my belly. "When did you turn into a whore?"

"I'm married—" I stop talking. I don't need to tell him anything.

"I'm coming for you, don't forget." Before I can say anything he's up and out the door. His paper left behind. I step forward and look. It's a picture of Jimmy and I that was taken on the street before we got married. There are slash marks and the word dead is written all over it.

I reach to pick it up, but it's taken from my hand quickly. "Sorry, I forgot my paper," Damien says as he walks out the door again.

27

JIMMY

I've come home a day early to surprise Chelsea. It's our three-year anniversary. She thinks I'm going to be on tour until the end of the week, but that was a little white lie I told her. It's all part of my master plan. We're leaving tonight for a holiday in Jamaica. I've been planning this for months now. I want our anniversary to be special.

Liam drops me off outside our house. I get out and stare at the brick building. I love this place. The lights are on so I know that she's still awake. When I spoke to her earlier today, she said she was staying home because the thought of going out without me was pure agony. She likes to exaggerate every now and again. She's never had a problem going out on her own before, but I get it, especially today. We want to be together.

I unlock the door and put my bags down in the hall. The house is quiet. I'm hoping she's not asleep, although if she is, I can't understand why she's left the lights on.

As I walk down the hall, the sound of skin slapping and moaning seeps from our bedroom. I rub my hands together.

My bird is watching porn and is probably getting really turned on by it. She's missed me. I love this side of her. She likes to get kinky and I'm a very obliging partner. My early arrival is bound to break the record for best 'surprise, I'm back, did you miss me?' ever.

I turn the handle and open the door a little. The sounds seem very lifelike and a lot louder. She has the TV switched on with the volume turned up on full-blast, but I can still hear her moans. I know the sounds she makes and can tell she's nearly coming. I bend over and unlace my boots, slipping them off my feet. My belt buckle is undone. The buttons pulled away from my jeans. My hand rubs my cock, it's hardening the closer I get.

Everything moves in slow motion as I walk around the corner. My fiancée is on her knees being fucked from behind. My eyes travel from his nakedness over her body to her face. I can't see her though because the face that I love so much is buried in another bastard's crotch.

"What the fucking hell?" I shout loudly. The three of them stop suddenly and look at me. Chelsea's eyes widen in horror as she realises she's been caught with her pants down. Literally. I do up my jeans and stare at the three of them. My eyes begin to fully assess the scene, taking it in bit by bit. She's fucking cheating on me. And in my fucking house, no less.

"Jimmy," she says and her voice is laced with both exhaustion and nerves.

"Don't say a fucking word. You don't need to explain." I turn and walk out, picking up my boots as I go. I don't stop to put them on before grabbing my suitcase and leaving. Fishing my keys out of my bag, I head to my car.

"Jimmy," she screams. I look up to find her outside in a T-shirt, one that is barely covering her backside. Her two friends follow out behind her and leave without saying anything.

I open the door and throw my bag in. I don't know where I'll go, probably to my dad's or even a hotel. I can't go to Liam's place and Harrison lives too far away.

"Jimmy, wait!" I don't acknowledge her and she doesn't take that as a sign. She runs over to me and grabs my arm. I shake her off. "I can explain."

I close my eyes. Those are the words I don't want to hear. "Really? You can explain why I just walked into my house and found my fiancée being fucked by not one, but two men? What happened, Chelsea, did they just happen to fall into your mouth and cunt?"

"Jimmy," she whines.

When I look at her again, she's not Chelsea. Her blonde hair has been changed to red. Her brown eyes are now green. Blood drips down her face like tears. She opens her mouth to speak, but nothing comes out. I look at this strange woman and my worst fears come to life.

I awake suddenly. My shirt is soaked with sweat. I look around, taking in my surroundings. The walls feel like they're closing in. I reach for Jenna, feeling for her body so I can hold her, and realise that I'm on the bus and I'm still on tour. I sit up and swing my legs over the side, hoping to regulate my breathing.

It was a nightmare. Why I was dreaming about Chelsea, I don't know, but seeing Jenna at the end ... that fucking scared the shit out of me. I know she'd never cheat on me, but this dream means something. I look at the clock and calculate the time difference. It's three a.m. in Beaumont, but I don't care. I need to hear her voice. I need to know that her and little one are okay.

I dial her number and wait. It rings five, six, and seven times before she finally picks up. "Hello," she says, groggily. I know I've woken her, but I need this for my sanity.

"Hi, wifey." I close my eyes and wait.

"What's wrong, Jimmy?"

"Nothing, I had ... had a dream and I needed to hear your voice and make sure that you and the bub are okay."

"We're fine, but now you have me worried. Are you okay?"

I lie back in bed and cover my eyes with my arm. "I am now that I've heard your voice. I miss you, Jenna. I didn't think this tour would be so hard, but it is. I don't know how Liam and Harrison are handling it, but I'm falling apart."

"Do you want me to come see you?"

The thought of having Jenna here with me, even if it's for a weekend, is enticing. She didn't come on tour with us last summer and part of me is grateful about that. I wouldn't have been able to control myself around her, but I also wouldn't want to embarrass her in front of Josie.

"I'd love that. I want you here, even if it's for a few days."

"Okay, Jimmy."

I tell her where we are going to be and help her book her ticket online. This time tomorrow she'll be in my arms and won't have to leave unless I'm on stage. When we hang up, I dial the number of the other woman who has been on my mind.

"Morning, Mum."

"Jimmy? How lovely to hear your voice. How are you?"

Hearing the excitement in my mum's voice makes me happy. Since I was eight and realised how poorly my dad treated her, how uninterested he was in having a family, she's not only been my mum, but my best friend.

"I'm okay."

"Are you sure? You don't sound okay, what's wrong?" This is exactly why I called her. She knows when something is bothering me. Blame it on motherly instinct or just being an amazing person. Either way, my mum can fix anything.

"I miss Jenna and I miss touching her belly every day."

"It's amazing, isn't it?"

"What is?"

"Watching your wife grow and look after your child inside of her."

I look at the photo of Jenna that I have stuck to the wall. This room is so small and I've had to forfeit the bedside table to display photos on. This picture was taken of us on the beach in Bora Bora. My hand rests on her belly. Her hand is cupping my cheek. We didn't pose for this. A passerby caught us in a moment with their camera and asked if they could send us the image. I'm grateful that they did because it's a reminder of why I'm turning my life around.

"It's not just that, Mum. I sing to little one and she calms down. She kicks Jenna terribly in the morning and my singing was helping that. I feel like I'm failing them both by not being there."

"Little one?"

I can't help but smile. I've always used nicknames, but

they're never normally special or meaningful. Not until I met Jenna, that is. She brings out the best in me.

"That's what I call her ... the baby. I think she likes it."

"I'm sure she does, you're her daddy." My mum sighs. "I can't believe you're going to be a father, Jimmy."

"I know, Mum, but this is a good thing. I love Jenna. She's makes me a better person and I really can't see myself without her, even if we weren't having a baby. I was always trying to find ways to talk to her and be around her."

"And what about how you felt about Chelsea?"

I close my eyes and my nightmare flashes before me. It's not so much that I'm reliving that day, but more the ending, seeing Jenna with blood on her face that freaks me out. I know her ex is out there, lurking. I can feel it, but I'm afraid to say anything to her. I don't want to put the fear of God in her if he's not around. But my instincts are telling me he's not done yet. He'll be back.

"Chelsea was a distraction. I never saw myself having kids, more like living this rock star lifestyle. I saw her more like a trophy wife. I knew that she'd be the wife that spends all day at the spa getting pampered and making sure she looked perfect."

"Are you saying Jenna's not like that?"

I rub my hand over my face and through my hair. It's due for a cut so I can make my Mohawk stand up again or maybe I'll surprise her and get it done before I see her. Maybe I can talk Jenna into cutting my hair when she's here. I knew my comments about Chelsea would be taken out of context, but I also know my mum won't repeat what I've told her.

"It's not like that mum. When I look at Jenna, I see a

future with her. I see home and warmth. Jenna's nothing like Chelsea. She doesn't care about the fame and fortune. She just wants to be loved and I want to love her until she tells me that I'm not worthy of her."

"Oh, Jimmy, I don't think she'll do that."

I hope not, I want to say.

"I really miss her. I rang her before I rang you and woke her up. I need to see her so she's going to fly out and come and see me tomorrow. I'm not going to be able to last three more months without being with her and holding her. God, Mum, I need to touch her tummy and talk to little one so she knows I haven't abandoned her." My voice breaks. I bite my lip to keep my emotions in check.

"Jimmy, you're not your father. I brought you up to be better than him."

"I know."

"Just love her and I'm sure she'll love you back. I know that I can't wait to meet her and hold my granddaughter."

"Little one is going to be beautiful. I'm hoping she has red hair like Jenna."

"She'll be beautiful. You're going to have a beautiful family and you should be proud of that."

"I am."

As soon as I hang up, I start counting the minutes until Jenna's here. I don't know if it's safe for pregnant women to fly, but I think she'd tell me if it wasn't. If she can't come here, I'll just fly to her. Not seeing her isn't going to work for me.

28

JENNA

I feel like I'm being watched ... or followed, which is the stupidest thing ever, since I'm walking in a crowded airport with hundreds, maybe even thousands of people. But I can't help but feel eyes boring into the back of my head. If I stop and look around, eyes follow me, no doubt wondering what would possess the pregnant woman to suddenly stop in the middle of the walkway and look behind her repeatedly.

Everyone rushes by, shoulders bumping into mine as they pass. A few people grunt and even give me a dirty look, but I know someone is there ... here, watching me. My body can feel eyes roaming all over it and it makes the hair on the back of my neck stand on end. I turn back and walk toward the exit. Jimmy will be waiting. I just need to get there. My pace quickens, short of a full-on jog. Anxiety increases, my skin ... it itches as if a spider is crawling on it. As soon as I see the doors, I'm running. I look back in time to see someone—a man—turn quickly. He's wearing a dark hat that covers his face and a nondescript trench coat.

I turn back to the door and step out. Freedom. Peace. Jimmy is standing against a black car with dark tinted windows, much like you see on television. I'm freaking Cinderella right now and my prince is staring at me. Gawking, really. His legs are crossed at his ankles. His left hand in his pocket. In his right, he holds a sign—*Sweet Lips* is written in big red letters. Standing back, I take in everything about him. I appraise him. Memorize him. My teeth find my lower lip as he shakes his head and smiles. He knows I'm checking him out. His hair stands on his head, the sides shaved. His Mohawk is back, thank god. He laughs and looks down at the ground before looking back at me with those eyes ... the eyes that say you know you want me, and he's right I do. Being pregnant has its perks sexually. I want it, him, all the time. He's making me insatiable. He's teaching me to enjoy what he can do to my body.

My mind tells my body to move forward, even though my eyes want me to stand here and watch him. His hand comes out of his pocket and he dangles a necklace from his fingers. It sways back and forth until I hold out my hand to stop it. A diamond locket rests in my hand. He slides it away from me, only to reach around my neck and clasp it. His hands linger at the back of my neck, his fingers pushing into my hair. I knew I loved this man, but this ... this hammers it home.

"I've missed you, wifey," he says as his lips graze mine. It's not enough, but we're in public and he has an image to keep up.

"I've missed you, too."

Jimmy places his lips to mine, but pulls away too quickly. "Hey."

He chuckles, placing his hand on our daughter. "Let's go." He pulls my hand into his and opens the car door, allowing me to slide in before him. Once he's in and the car is in traffic, his hands are all over me.

"I fucking need you," he says as his teeth nip into my skin. I never thought about how much alone time we'd get while I'm here. The guys travel by bus and since none of the families are with them they haven't been staying in hotels this time around.

Jimmy rests his head on my shoulder. I snuggle into him, afraid to let go. Closing my eyes, I lean into him. He can make all my demons go away. I haven't seen or heard from Damien since that day in Whimsicality. Is it too much to hope that something has happened to him and I'll never see him again?

"When did you cut your hair?"

"Yesterday, after I finished talking to you and then my mum. I remembered that you mentioned it in Bora Bora and I thought, what can I do to drive my missus crazy? I'm hoping this is it."

"I love it and I love you, Jimmy."

"I love you, Jenna, and I love our daughter. I want to give you the world. I know we got married quickly, but I feel like I've known you my entire life. And the way you were so obviously checking me out back there ... I can't wait to get you onto the bus and have my wicked way with you."

I roll my eyes, shaking my head at him. "You're so rotten."

"But you love me."

That I do.

"STAND RIGHT HERE. You'll be able to see Harrison and Liam, but I'm on the other side so you'll only be able to stare at my arse."

"Jimmy," I say, hitting his shoulder.

"What?" He leans in. "Do you remember digging your nails into it earlier today telling me to take you harder and faster?"

No, I don't need that reminder. The reenactment is playing like a dirty porn clip over and over again. Reuniting with him was everything I wanted it to be and more.

"Yes I remember."

"We remember, too, Romeo," Liam says as he passes by. I stifle a laugh, as Jimmy turns red. I never thought I'd see the day where Jimmy Davis blushes from embarrassment, but now I have. My worst fear came true when we got to the bus. Harrison, Liam, and Tyler were all there. They all snickered when Jimmy pulled me down the aisle and into his room. When we came out, Liam mimicked Jimmy, complete with a British accent.

"Fuck off, mate," Jimmy says as he pulls me closer.

"Time to go on," Harrison says, stopping next to me. Leaning down, he kisses me on the cheek. "It's really too bad you couldn't bring Katelyn. Maybe you ladies need to alternate weeks so we can get some service up in this piece."

"I'll tell her when I get back." Harrison winks and walks away. I lean into Jimmy and kiss him.

"Good luck and have fun."

"I will now that I know you're waiting for me." He kisses me before taking the stage. Jimmy stands next to his keyboard. On one side is his guitar. He hasn't said much about his father, but I know who he is. Everyone does. I'm assuming he's learned to play these instruments from his dad, although I can't be sure. Some people are musically inclined. They're gifted.

The music starts and the crowd erupts. You'd think they've all just woken from a winter's slumber with how quiet they were, but now the noise level is deafening.

I look over at the guys and take in their presence. This is my first time seeing them on stage like this. It's magical. No wonder we've all fallen for rock stars. They command the stage, even Jimmy, who is simply playing the piano. He owns it. It's part of him. My eyes wander to Harrison. I've listened to Katelyn describe what it's like to watch Harrison, but to actually see it, to feel the drumbeat rise from the floor and wash over your body is indescribable.

Liam walks over to me and plays his guitar for me. The crowd, somehow, becomes louder. He winks and walks back to the microphone to sing. I start to sway, moving to the music while watching Jimmy. He switches from the piano to the guitar to the harmonica.

When the familiar sounds of little one's song starts, my hand immediately goes to her. She pushes against me. I push back, letting her know that yes, it's her daddy, and he's about to play it for her.

Hearing Liam sing the song that Jimmy sings for our daughter is different, but I like it. His voice is perfect and it's clear why he's the singer. I still prefer Jimmy's voice, but hearing Liam takes it to a whole new level.

I look out into the crowd. There are mostly women and a few men, no doubt brought by their significant others.

That seems a bit awkward, these women yelling everything they can think to get the guys' attention and their men just standing by aimlessly. Unless of course they like 4225 West then it's not strange at all.

As I scan the first few rows, smiling as I do, my gaze lands on him, the man from the airport. He hasn't bothered to change. He's still wearing the same hat and trench coat. I close my eyes and shake out the cobwebs. I'm just tired. I'm seeing things. But when I open them, he's still there, staring at the stage. I try to follow his line of vision, but can't. He's either focused on Liam or Jimmy.

It's Jimmy who he's staring at. Why? Why was this man following me in the airport and now boring down on my husband?

Damien!

I try to inch closer, but the bodyguard stops me. I'm not to come out on stage. I'm to stay behind the curtain for my own safety. But I need to see. I need to know. Is Damien here? How did he find me in the airport and how the hell did he make it to the front of the stage without being noticed?

The anxiety I had earlier is now back in droves. My palms itch and my skin feels like there's a thousand needles trying to get in or out, it doesn't matter. It's driving me nuts.

"Are you okay, Mrs. Davis?" the bodyguard asks. I look down and see my nails digging into my arms. Damien's here. He's wearing a trench coat to a rock concert. Who does that?

He does because he's here to cause harm. Instantly, the image of the defaced newspaper article that I saw him with that time in Whimsicality comes back to me. I look around, frantically. I step toward the stage, only to be stopped by a large arm.

"Mrs. Davis, what's wrong?"

I point to Damien who is now closer to the stage. The bodyguard shakes his head, he doesn't understand.

"He's my ex," I say, barely audible. He leans down so I repeat myself. He turns and looks to where I'm pointing. His body goes rigid. He moves in front, trying to shield me, but I move. I need to see. The bodyguard says something into his hand. Men move toward Damien.

"Gun," I say, as I tug on his shirt. "Gun," I yell louder.

Damien raises the gun and points it at Jimmy who doesn't have a clue what's going on. Neither do Liam and Harrison. They're playing, as they should be.

I get past the bodyguard and run onto stage. The crowd yells louder. Liam stops me, placing his arm around me. I beat on his arm. I kick and scream in his ear. "Gun, Liam!" He looks at me with utter confusion.

Jimmy drops to the ground. My ears feel like they've been filled with cotton and there's a panicked scream bursting out of my chest. My feet are heavy, but I need to run to him. I need to be there with him. With my husband.

Liam turns in slow motion, dropping his guitar to his side, the dissonance ringing out over the sound system. Strong arms pick me up from behind and carry me away from my husband. The roar of the crowd is deafening, but the only sound I can focus on is the rush of blood through veins in my temples. I scream out for Jimmy as Liam and Harrison rush to his side.

Lights come on and people start screaming. The crowd's so loud no one can hear me. "Put me down," I yell, kicking whoever is carrying me. I'm set on my feet and the moment I'm touching the ground, I'm running back to Jimmy, my heart pounding against my ribcage.

"Jimmy!" I scream, but Harrison is there to stop me.

"Let me go, Harrison!"

He wraps his arms around me, holding me tight to his chest. He leans down. "Calm down, sweetheart, think about the baby. Let the paramedics work on JD."

"He's been shot." I don't remember crying, but there are hot streaks running down my cheeks and pooling into his T-shirt.

"I know. I know," he says, running his hand up and down my back. The gesture that's meant to be soothing only serves to agitate me more. He's holding me back.

"He needs me."

"Right now, he needs them more, Jenna." He pulls back and cups my tear-laden face. "He needs them, okay? They need to help him."

Harrison's eyes, the ones that are always calm as still water, are frantic and dark. I press my hand to my chest as something inside of me breaks.

"Is he going to be okay?" I'm unraveling, like twine from a spool, falling away from myself into disjointed pieces, tangled and messy.

Harrison looks over his shoulder and back at me. "I don't know."

I fall into his arms, clutching at his shirt as sob after sob rolls through my body. My ex has done the unthinkable and there isn't anything I can do to help. Harrison pulls me off stage when the paramedics pass by with Jimmy.

29

JIMMY

I love having my missus here. It's like I have a new energy flowing through me. Being on stage has always been a high for me, but now, knowing she's just off the stage watching me perform takes it to a whole new level. The only thing I'd change is our stage set-up. I want to be near her so I can watch her all night and not the crowd. These women out there, the ones who are wearing shirts that are two sizes too small? The ones who used to do it for me and float my boat? They don't even compare to Jenna.

I glance at Jenna as often as I can. Liam is doing a bloody excellent job at keeping her entertained, but if I'm honest, I wish it was me being the front-man today. I need it to be me. Maybe tonight I'll give Jenna her own personal show. I can play her body like a piano and make it sing. That's if I can get her to undress for me again. I got a little carried away when we got back to the tour bus, but I couldn't help myself. My dick has a mind of its own when it comes to her and he wanted to be buried deep inside of her. He didn't care that my band mates were sitting a few feet outside the room. He wanted her, and I'm not one to deny him and his needs.

I'm a no one without Jenna. I should tell her this, but finding the right words to do so is pretty much impossible. Admitting my feelings to her, albeit suddenly, has been such a relief. It's like we've been together for years now and not just months. With her at my side, I know I'm going to be a better person, lover and musician. She makes me feel like I can conquer anything I put my mind to.

Taking out my harmonica, I start the beginning of "Tobacco Sunburst" and take a sneak peek over my shoulder. Jenna's hand is on her tummy, her fingers dancing along. I wink, but know she can't see me. I wasn't planning on telling her that the song I sang to her when she told everyone she wasn't feeling very well was one that she inspired. I should've known she'd listen to it as soon as I went out of town. I've been so quiet when singing to little one because I didn't want her mum to hear. She's sneaky, that one.

Liam belts out the lyrics as Harrison adds the beat. I look out to the crowd quickly before bringing my harmonica back to my mouth. I think the only thing that can make me happier right now is to hold little one in my arms. I'm not going to be afraid to hold her like some men are. I'm excited. I can't wait to have her snuggled into my neck while I rock her to sleep. I'm going to be a hands-on dad, I'll do everything Jenna needs me to do, even the disgusting stuff that involves nappies and shit.

Pain suddenly rips through my chest. Hot, searing, and torturous. I try to move my hand to touch the throbbing, but I can't. It's immobile, dangling uselessly at my side. I look down at my shirt and see a wet red spot forming. I hear screaming behind me. Jenna. It's her voice.

My head rests on the stage. How did I get here?

My eyes look at the man standing in front of me. I know him from somewhere. I try to reach out to him, but he turns, leaving me.

"Holy fuck, JD," Liam says, hovering over me. The stage lights behind him make it look as though he's glowing and there are black spots dancing in front of my eyes. I don't like this new lighting effect.

"Somebody get the motherfucking paramedics here," Harrison yells.

Paramedics? Is Jenna okay? I look for her, my eyes searching the stage, but I can't see her.

"Wh—"

"Hold on, man."

I don't know what the fuck he means. Hold on?

Everything starts turning black. Someone is closing the curtains, but the show's not over. My song ... I didn't finish it.

The screaming dulls into a hushed roar. Thank god because it was fucking hurting my head. I think I need a coffee or something. I'm so tired.

I look at Liam and smile. He's my best friend, my brother.

"Don't you fucking leave me, JD. You fight. You have a wife and daughter on the way. Do you hear me, man? You fucking fight to stay with us."

Where am I going?

30

JENNA

Harrison rushes us from the venue and into the waiting car. I don't know how the driver knows, but he does. Once the door is shut, we're speeding behind the ambulance. The very one that is transporting my husband.

Harrison holds me against him. His leg bounces up and down. The edge of his phone is pressed against his lips. Is he waiting for a call? Call ... I need to call Jimmy's mom, but what do I say? I don't even have her number.

I sit up in a panic. My breathing becomes erratic.

"Whoa, what's wrong? You have to calm down, Jenna."

"His mom ... she's in ..." I shake my head, realizing that I don't know where his mom is. I don't know anything about his family.

"She lives in London. I'll call her for you." And just like that Harrison comes to my rescue. I feel like such a moron for not knowing. As his wife I should know these things. Like his blood type, I don't know that. What if he needs a transfusion?

Before I know it, Harrison is opening the door and tugging at my hand. He pulls me through the glass doors and to the nurses' station.

"Hi, excuse me. The ambulance just brought in my husband."

"Have a seat," the nurse says without looking up. Harrison puts his arm around me and tries to direct me to a chair, but I hold onto the counter.

"Jenna, give them a few minutes. Let's find Liam."

Harrison's demeanor is calm where I'm freaking out on the inside. I'm about to scream and pull at my hair. My ex-husband has shot ... he freaking shot my husband. I don't know where Damien is now, but he's out there and probably waiting to finish the job. If he hasn't already succeeded.

I knew I should've left the minute Damien first showed up at the café. I've put everyone in danger and now Jimmy is somewhere in this hospital. I don't know if he's dead or alive. Why can't the nurse just tell me what they're doing? They must know, right?

We walk down random halls. I see paramedics and wonder if they're the ones that brought in Jimmy. They look at me as I pass, their eyes full of sorrow. I can't imagine what they see on a daily basis.

"Excuse me," I say, stopping Harrison from walking any farther. "Did you bring my husband in?"

"Who's your husband?" the lady asks, looking at her clipboard.

"Jimmy Davis," Harrison answers before I can. "He was shot while on stage tonight. Our friend came with him."

The lady looks over her clipboard and shakes her head. My heart drops a bit further into the pit of my stomach.

"Try down the hall that way." She points ahead of us. "That's the critical wing and if he was shot, he's likely there."

Harrison doesn't wait for more instructions before he's pulling me behind him. We turn the corner and I gasp, my hand flying up to cover my mouth when I see Liam leaning against the wall. He's covered in blood.

Jimmy's blood.

"Liam," Harrison says. He looks up and that patented smile he has for his friends is gone. It's replaced with so much pain, more than when Josie was dismissing him when he first came back to town. Tears rush to my eyes as I take in the sight before me. Liam looks broken.

"Liam?" My voice breaks. He doesn't acknowledge my silent question, but pulls me into a hug. He holds me tight, his tears dampening my neck. I don't want to take his tears as a sign, but I can't help but think my husband is gone.

Pulling away, I cover my eyes, wiping away the tears. "Did he ... is he—" I choke on my words as strong arms keep me from falling to the ground. I can't keep the tears at bay any longer. Jimmy and I were just starting to build a life together and now it's gone.

"He's in surgery, Jenna. I don't know anything else until they come and find us."

I look up quickly. "Surgery? That's good, right?"

Liam shrugs. "I don't know, but he lost a lot of blood and wasn't conscious."

"Oh god," I cry.

"Come on, let's go sit down." Harrison has to drag me away. I don't know if Jimmy is behind that door or if Liam just stopped there, but I don't want to leave. What if

Jimmy needs me? I don't want to be too far away from him.

The guys lead me to a waiting room. It's much smaller and quieter than the one we were directed to when we first came in. I sit down and melt into the couch. Deep down I know it's not comfortable, but I have a feeling my body knows we're going to be here for a long time. I won't leave Jimmy's side.

"I'm going to go make some phone calls," Harrison says, placing a kiss on my forehead. "I'll bring back some coffee." I watch him walk away. He gets about halfway from us and falls against the wall. You can see the sobs take over his body. It slips my mind sometimes that Jimmy has another family away from little one and me.

"I'm sorry, Liam."

He looks up at me, his eyes glazed with tears. "What on earth are you sorry for?"

I take a deep breath. "For bringing Damien into your lives. I should've left when he showed up. I knew he was dangerous and now Jimmy's in surgery and I don't even know if he's going to make it, and it's all because of me." My voice cracks at the end, my body splintering, shattering. I don't know how to keep it all in.

Liam pulls me into his arms, rubbing my shoulder. "People are sick, Jenna. You can't predict what they're going to do. This could've easily been me if Sam was around. I love you like a sister and am so thankful that you pushed Josie back to me, so don't ever be sorry. You didn't ask for this."

Liam turns toward me so he can look at me. "I'm a man blessed with a lot. I have the love of my life, my son, my career and my family ... that includes you, Jimmy, Katelyn, the girls, Quinn, and Harrison. Without these things in my life, I'm nothing. Each one of you gives me something to look forward to. You ... you're the one who not only makes my wife smile, but you gave one of my best friends a new life. Don't be sorry, Jenna, be determined to bring that fucker's ass down for doing this to our family."

I'm speechless. I've never had friends like Josie and Liam before. They're rare gems and when you mix in Katelyn and Harrison, Liam's right. We're a family.

I lean into Liam and close my eyes. His hand returns to my shoulder, holding me there, giving me the comfort that I need. I hope that I can offer him a little bit of support. I know he's hurting, we both are, each in our own way.

"Hello?"

"Sorry to call so early, but the shop is closed today."

I sit up and look at the clock—it's four a.m. "What's wrong, Josie?"

"It's ... oh god, Jenna, Mason ... he was in an accident and he ..."

I swallow hard and hold my breath. I know she's going to deliver the worst news ever. I'm supposed to keep the girls overnight so he can surprise Katelyn with dinner. He said that during football season he loses his romantic side and needs as much help as possible.

"Josie?"

"He's gone, Jenna. Oh god, he's gone." Silent tears fall as *I listen to Josie cry on the phone. I don't know what to do. I've never been faced with death. Josie, Katelyn, and Mason are my only friends.*

"I'm on my way. Where do I go?"

"I don't ... I ca—"

"Where are you?"

"Katelyn's," she says through a shuddering breath.

"I'm on my way." I hang up and immediately cross my arms over my chest and hold myself. He can't be gone. He's the only guy I can trust. He knows everything about me and I didn't even have to tell him. He just knew. He said he'd protect me and now he's gone.

I move around my apartment as if on autopilot. I'm going to put on a brave face for everyone. I'll be their rock, as they have been for me.

I pick up the picture of all of us that we took last year. Noah and the twins were so small. I can't even think about what it'll be like for Katelyn now.

"Here," Harrison says, holding a cup of coffee. I know it's not good for the baby, but I refuse to sleep. I need to know my husband is okay before I close my eyes. Sitting up, I take the paper cup from him. I wipe at my cheek, trying to rub away the make-up running down my face. I look around briefly, and see a few more people in this room waiting. Are they all here for the same reason, or something different? It makes me wonder who is here because of a car accident or another shooting. They happen more in the city than in a place like Beaumont. But I can guarantee you, 4225 West never thought they'd be part of a shooting during one of their shows.

"I called the girls, they're on their way. Mr. Powell is going to stay with the kids. I also asked Gary to get a charter plane so they can get here faster."

Liam nods. I know he wants to hold Josie and I can't imagine what's going through Katelyn's mind. She's been in this position before, and as much as I love her, I want a different outcome. At the end of the day I want to go home with my husband by my side. I want just a little bit of happiness, especially for little one. She needs to know her dad.

I sip my coffee gingerly. It's something to settle my stomach, but I know I'll need food even if I'm not hungry. Crackers, those will have to do—until I know Jimmy's going to be okay. I can't ... I won't leave his side until I know.

We sit in silence. The television is showing the nightly news. Liam curses when the newscaster talks about the shooting at the concert. I'm sure this is a public relations nightmare for Gary. He'll probably tell Jimmy to ditch the extra baggage and take my baby away from me. Jimmy wouldn't do that though, right?

"Mrs. Davis?"

I look up when my name's called. I stand on shaky legs, only to be flanked by Liam and Harrison. "That's me," I say.

"Go ahead and have a seat," the doctor says as he sits down across from us. We sit back down. I can't look at the doctor. Instead,333 I focus on the ring on my finger and the way Jimmy looked when he put it there.

"Your husband is in critical condition. The bullet entered from the right, passed through both lungs and exited on the left. He sustained considerable damage to his lungs. We've operated and right now he's on a respirator. For the next twenty-four hours everything is touch and go. We have to watch for blood clots forming and detaching. He'll have a nurse with him the whole time until the threat is gone.

"I'm very sorry, Mrs. Davis, I wish I could provide better news, but this is all I have."

"When can I see him?"

"He can have one visitor at a time. You can go in when you're ready."

I nod. "Thank you."

He takes his leave. Once he's out of the waiting room, I collapse into Liam's arms and break down. My husband isn't going to make it and there isn't a thing I can do about it. Harrison wraps his arms around me as well. His tears wet my back, while Liam's meet mine. Both these strong men hold me as we cry for the one we love.

31

JIMMY

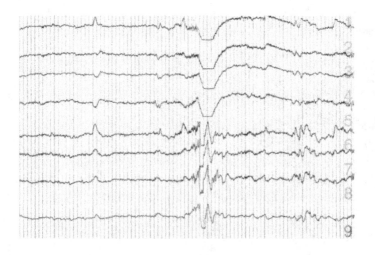

32

JENNA

I stand on shaky legs, with Liam on one side and Harrison on the other. I'm taking liberties and going in first. Maybe I haven't earned it. I haven't known him long enough, but we share something that he can't share with Liam and Harrison.

They walk me toward his room. How they know where it is, I don't know. Did the doctor tell me and I not listen? We bypass the nurses' station. I can't bear to look at them. I don't want to see the pity on their faces. I don't want them to look at me as if I'm about to lose my husband. I don't want to see their eyes wander to my mid-section and have them shake their heads because I'll be a single mom soon.

That's what I wanted, right? To be a single mom? Is this karma coming back to bite me in the ass because I was going to keep this baby a secret from Jimmy? Is he going to pay the price because I'm a selfish bitch and brought all this evil onto him? I should be the one lying in that bed. I should be the one who is in critical condition, fighting for my life. Jimmy doesn't deserve this.

Harrison pushes the door open slowly. My senses become alive as I stare at the floor, my eyes moving slowly until I can see the wall in front of me. The room smells like antiseptic and Lysol. The walls are white. Jimmy hates white. He needs color. He wants vibrant displays of life. I close my eyes when I finally hear the beeping that's telling me his heart is still beating. It means that his blood is still pumping through his body, keeping him alive. But it's the whoosh of the machine helping him breathe that makes my knees buckle. He can't breathe.

"Oh god, he can't breathe." Liam and Harrison grab my arms to steady me. I don't like hospitals and the bad things that go along with them. The whish and hum of machines designed to mimic human functions. The constant beep, beep, beeping of vital signs being measured.

"Come on, Jenna, be strong. Think about the baby. Jimmy needs you to be strong for the baby right now." Liam's voice is too calm. I look at him briefly and know he's holding everything in.

We step farther into the room. I see his nurse first before I see him. I take a step back when I finally lay my eyes on him. His Mohawk is flattened, his eyes closed. There's a tube coming out of his mouth, and wires everywhere. My hand covers my mouth as I cry out, which gets the nurses attention.

She looks up from her computer screen with a scowl on her face. "Only one visitor at a time."

"We know," Liam says. "This is his wife, and as you can see, she's pregnant and unsteady on her feet."

"Shh," she says, pointing to the curtain behind us. "Someone is sleeping in there."

The three of us turn our heads and look. I look at Harrison, who shakes his head, then to Liam who looks pissed off as hell.

"Why isn't he in a private room with security?" Liam asks.

"He's just a patient. I'm going to have to ask you to leave. Only one visitor at a time."

Liam nods and leads me over to Jimmy's bedside. Harrison slides a chair over for me to sit in. You'd think the nurse would do this, but apparently it's not her job.

"We're going to go see about getting JD moved. We'll be right back," Liam whispers in my ear. I don't know what he's going to do, but I have a feeling this nurse isn't going to like it.

I lay my hand on top of Jimmy's and rest my head by his leg. I really want to crawl into bed with him and hold him like he holds me, but I know that isn't possible. Tears fall silently from my eyes as the pain in my chest builds. I want to talk to him, but not with this nurse in here. What I have to say is private, for his ears only. Who knows what this chick will blog about when she gets home at the end of her shift or who she's texting.

"You should talk to him." Her tone is snotty, which pisses me off.

"I want to, but you're here." My words have bite but I don't care. I know he needs to hear my voice, but damn it if I want only him to hear me. Thing is, I wouldn't care if Liam and Harrison were with me.

"Where's his wedding ring?" I ask.

"Behind you. His personal belongings are in that bag."

I get up and go to the bag and dump its contents on the

counter. His ring clanks on the hard wooden top, along with his wallet, chain and watch. I open his wallet to pull out the picture of little one. I think he needs it. He needs to feel close to her.

"He had a picture in his wallet, it's not here."

"I don't know what to tell you."

When I look back, she's smirking. She knows damn well where that picture went.

"It's okay," I say, sliding his wallet into my purse. "I'll just let his doctor know that someone went through his wallet."

She scoffs. "Maybe he took it out."

"Or maybe he didn't because he showed it to me before he went on stage." I stand tall and lean over Jimmy. "My husband carries that photo everywhere he goes, it's his daughter. Funny how he's not able to account for his belongings at the moment, isn't it?"

"Well, I'm sure it'll turn up."

Turn up? What's she going to do, put it back in the bag after I leave the room? Does she actually think I'm going to leave his side?

I sit back down and pick up Jimmy's hand. He's warm and for me that's a good sign. I hold his hand to my face, placing my lips there. I don't know if he can feel my tears, but I hope they aren't annoying him.

I don't know how long I sit there like that, with him. Minutes? Hours? For me time has stopped. The constant whoosh and beep are somewhat soothing, although I'd give anything for him to open his eyes and smile at me.

Every so often the nurse stands, presses some buttons, and sits back down. I want to look at her computer screen and see if she's playing Solitaire or if she's actually working. She's probably checking all her social media sites.

Liam and Harrison walk back into the room followed by a tall man.

"Jenna, this is Dr. Bryant, he's the Hospital Director. We're going to move JD to a private room and he's going to waive the one visitor rule."

I've never been more amazed by Liam than I am now. Standing, I pull him into my arms. He knows that I need him and Harrison right now, just as much as they need to be near Jimmy.

"Mrs. Davis, I'm sorry about your husband."

"Thank you," I choke out as I shake his hand. "I just want him to wake up so I can take him home."

"Yes, of course, we're doing all we can for him."

And just like that the glass wall to Jimmy's room is collapsed. Men and women come in and transfer wires to another machine that they set on top of him. The nurse, who unfortunately has to come with us, pushes her cart out. Jimmy's bed is pulled from the wall and we follow behind. I can't look at anyone while we pass. I don't want to see their faces or know that they recognize who is in that bed.

His new room is much larger with windows that overlook the courtyard. At least now we'll have something to look at.

"Mrs. Davis, I'm assuming you'll be staying here?"

"We all will be, and his mom will be here soon," Harrison answers. "We also have two more coming, our wives, that will need access. I'm not sure if they'll stay, but at least for a few days they'll be here."

"It's against—"

"I told you, we'll pay and we'll make a fucking donation to the hospital if he walks out of here alive," Liam fires back.

"Of course, Mr. Page."

Mr. Page? Looks like Liam used his status to get his way. I know he doesn't like to do that, but I'm thankful he did.

"This nurse," I ask, pointing to her, "does she have to stay or can she set up outside his door?"

"Oh no, she can set up in the hall like the others do."

"Perfect." I arch my eyebrow at her. *Take that you wench.* "Also, my husband had a picture of our daughter's ultrasound in his wallet. He showed it to me before he went on stage and now it's not there. I'm wondering if you can ask the staff that handled his belongings if they've found it."

"The lawsuit, if it's leaked, won't be pretty," Liam adds, making me wish I could think quickly on my feet like him.

Dr. Bryant nods before leaving us to Jimmy. I let Harrison and Liam go to his side while I stand at the foot of the bed. My hand rests on his foot, while the guys pick up each of his hands. Liam's shoulders shake and Harrison is gasping for air. I don't know who to go to first so I stand there and watch as these brothers cry for one of their own. I'll never pretend to understand their bond, not after witnessing this.

33

JIMMY

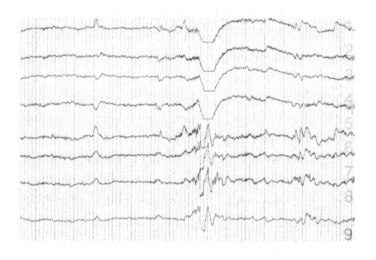

34

JENNA

I lose track of time. I'm stiff, sore, and hungry. My arms ache from the position they've been in. My back burns from the strain, and little one is kicking up something fierce. I didn't bring my headphones because Jimmy would've just sung to her, but he's not singing ... yet.

Hours, that's how long we've been here. The sun is up, or maybe it's setting again and I'm really not with it. Harrison's head rests at the end of Jimmy's bed, while Liam is opposite me. Both of them are asleep, exhaustion finally taking over, but neither of them are willing to leave this room.

I can't blame them. I'm not leaving either. I hate getting up to go to the bathroom as it is. Gary has moved the tour bus to the parking lot. I can see it from the window. People—mostly women—gather around it. I had suggested that Liam and Harrison go and sleep in there, but they just shook their heads. We know the first twenty-four hours are critical; those are the words that we recall, and each time he twitches or the machines beeps a little more rapidly, I panic. And when I panic, they panic. The cycle is endless.

I sit in the windowsill watching the small vigil form by the bus. They must be the fans that saw the shooting happen. It won't be long before the press is outside and the bus is surrounded. Gary said the detective is coming by today; he needs my statement. I have to relive the nightmare. I have to recall every second of what I remember from last night as it unfolded, in slow motion, right before my eyes. The only thing I want to know is, where's Damien?

The door opens slowly and the nurse, a much nicer one, waves me over. I slide off the windowsill carefully and walk to her. She holds the door open for me to follow her out. I look at Jimmy and back at her and she knows. She places her hand on my shoulder and leads me to the window where I can still see him.

Months ago, I wouldn't be standing here. I'd be at home, taking care of the kids if this had happened. But he knew ... he knew that we were having a baby and wasn't going to take no for an answer when he asked me to marry him. The whole time during the ceremony I thought he was doing it so I wouldn't be alone, but that wasn't the case. He did it because he wants us to be a family.

"I'm sorry to bother you, but I wanted to give you this." She hands me little one's ultrasound picture. Tears fill my eyes immediately. The nurse rests her hand on my shoulder, giving me the comfort I need. "I'm sorry you're going through this, but we've taken steps to eliminate the issue from arising again."

"Thank you," I say with a broken voice.

"I think I have something that will make you smile, Mrs.

Davis. There are two women out front who are asking for you."

"Did they say who they are?" My luck is they're crazed fans trying to get in to see Jimmy.

The nurse fishes a piece of paper out of her pocket. "Katelyn Powell and Josie Westbury, is what I have here. They seem very eager to see you." She smiles softly. She knows what those two names mean to me.

I know a smile is breaking out across my face and it's going hand in hand with tears. "Thank you, you can let them in."

She nods and walks away. I look back into the room; Liam and Harrison are still sleeping so I leave them be. I'm going to be selfish and fall into the arms of my best friends before their men come to take them away from me.

Their strides are long and powerful and they race to me once they get around the corner. They drop their bags and pull me into their arms. The definition of a group hug is nothing compared to being held by your two best friends. Words don't need to be said, the emotion is enough. I can feel their shoulders shake, and hear their labored breathing. We are all sharing the pain and anguish of not knowing.

Josie breaks first. She wipes her eyes before picking up her bag. She leaves me with Katelyn. When I look at her, it's not pity I see in her eyes, but knowledge. Katelyn's been here. She knows what I'm going through.

Katelyn takes my hand in hers and holds it to her heart. Not only can I feel her heart beating, but under my palm are her wedding rings. They hang from a necklace the twins bought her for her birthday. She places her hand over mine and closes her eyes.

"I went to see Mason before we got on the plane. Sometimes when I'm there I don't say anything and other times I talk about the girls, Harrison, and Quinn. But this time I told him what you're going through and asked him to help. No one knows this, but I asked him for a sign that being with Harrison was going to be okay and it started snowing. Right there with me lying on the ground a snowflake fell, so I took that and ran with it. As you know, Mason was pretty amazing and he loved you so I know he's watching over Jimmy.

"I'm here for you, Jenna, whatever you need. You were there for me so many times when I was going through everything. I hate seeing ... this type of place with us here."

"You don't need to stay, Katelyn, I know it's hard."

Katelyn shakes her head. She lets her tears fall. "I need to be here. This is where I'm supposed to be."

I know it's hard for her to be here. I know it's going to be difficult for her to walk into Jimmy's room and see him looking similar to the way Mason looked. I won't be upset if she can't handle this. I hope she knows this.

Katelyn and I walk hand in hand back to Jimmy's room. Josie waits for us by the door. I step in first. Liam and Harrison are still out cold. I think it's sweet, to see them like this, but once they know the girls are here things will become emotional again.

Josie wraps her arms around Liam, and Katelyn leans down and kisses Harrison on his cheek. Harrison wakes first and moves out of his chair lightning fast. Katelyn is off the ground before she knows what's hit her. He has his face buried in her neck. Her legs are wrapped around his waist and her hand holds his head to hers. He carries her out of the room. Only when I sit down do I see Liam wake, but he's not moving. He's holding onto Josie's arms while she whispers in his ear.

Liam wasn't here when we went through this with Mason and neither was Harrison, but they both know the magnitude of what this moment means for Josie and Katelyn.

"What are they saying?" Josie asks.

I shake my head. "They monitor everything. Right now they're watching for blood clots. And ... and I don't know. I just want him to wake up so we can go home," I say, trying to keep my voice from breaking. I pick up Jimmy's hand and hold it to my lips.

"The press is outside and there are fans in the parking lot. Gary says there isn't much he can do about it because they're not disrupting anyone and they're staying out of the way. There are a lot of flowers and gifts by the bus. Gary said he'll leave them there until people stop showing up.

"The shooting is all over the news and media channels. A few of the channels are outside. I think they're waiting for you and Harrison to say something."

"They can wait," Liam says sharply.

"Okay, babe. Gary will take care of it." Josie rubs his shoulders, trying to soothe him.

"We brought you some more clothes, Jenna. Katelyn and I will make sure you guys have food and whatever else you need so you only have to leave for a few minutes at a time. What do you need right now?"

"For my husband to wake up."

"She needs food and a shower."

I glare at Liam. "No, I don't. You need to go shower."

"Why are you wearing scrubs?"

Liam looks at Josie over his shoulder before looking back at Jimmy. "I was there. I held him until the paramedics arrived."

"Oh, Liam," Josie cries as she wraps her arms around him. "Come on, let's go and get cleaned up and when we come back, I'll take Jenna to get some food."

I open my mouth to balk, but the look Josie gives me shuts my mouth. I don't want to leave, but the thought of food makes little one kick. I can't neglect her. I need her.

As soon as they're gone I lay my head on Jimmy's leg. I want to be near his heart, but I can't touch his chest. It'll cause him pain and I can't have that. I hold his hand and take a deep breath.

"Jimmy, I need you to fight and come back to us. Little one and I need you. She wants to know her daddy and I know you want to meet her. If you didn't, you wouldn't have taken me to Bora Bora and asked me to marry you. You made me think you were asking because I was having a baby, when you knew the whole time that we were going to have our baby.

"The night of Josie and Liam's wedding, you were my fantasy come true. I had told the girls that you were on my list, but I never imagined days later it would happen. When you came up to me, I didn't have any fear. You were someone I wanted. The only one I wanted since I left my other life. I asked myself many times since that night, why you, and the only answer I can come up with is that my body craved you. When I would look at you, I could see myself with you and as much as that scared me, I wanted it. If anyone were to ask me then why I married you my answer would be because you charmed me. You have this way about you, it's hard to describe.

"That day at the doctor's when you showed up late and I asked for a divorce, you were adamant that we weren't getting one. I wanted to walk away, but you wouldn't let me. I've wanted to ask you about Los Angeles, but I haven't. Half of me doesn't want to know, but the other half does. But right now I just want you to wake-up and sing to me, sing to our baby because she misses you. I miss you."

"You must be my daughter-in-law."

35

JIMMY

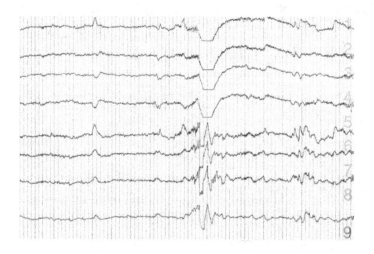

36

JENNA

"Why isn't he awake yet?" I pull at my hair as I pace back and forth. "It's been two weeks. He made it through the twenty-four hour mark. His brain activity is normal, so why isn't he awake?" I ask the doctor who's flashing his pen light in Jimmy's eyes.

"We aren't sure."

"What do you mean, 'you aren't sure'? You're the damn doctor and my husband has been like this for fourteen days."

"I understand, Mrs. Davis," he says as he pockets his pen. If Jimmy was awake I know he'd say something about the pocket protector. Who wears those anymore?

"No, you don't understand." Sighing, I rest my head against the wall. I'm frustrated and scared. I don't understand their nonchalance about all of this. Why isn't he awake?

Brigette comes over and rubs my shoulders. She's been a godsend since she arrived. I know I have Liam and Harrison here with me, and Katelyn and Josie on the weekends, but

Brigette has been a rock for me. When she walked in the door, I didn't know what to expect.

"You must be my daughter-in-law."

I turn and look behind me. A woman stands in the doorway—she's petite, blonde, and very well put together. Her dress fits her body perfectly, stopping just above her knees. She screams money. If I didn't know better, I'd say she's someone who snuck in here to be close to Jimmy. She doesn't look like a mom, but she does look like Jimmy. Or rather he looks like her, except with dark hair.

"Hi," I say, meekly. This is not how I wanted to meet my mother-in-law. She's supposed to be here a week before little one arrives and Jimmy is supposed to introduce us. I wipe my hands on my pants and stand on shaky legs. I walk closer to her, blocking her line of sight to Jimmy. I extend my hand. "I'm Jenna."

She looks at me with an unreadable expression. I feel like a moron standing here like this. She probably hates me. I would, it's my ex that did this to her son. She drops the over-sized bag she is holding and wraps her arms around me, catching me off guard. Her embrace is tight and welcoming. I close my arms around her and hug her back as if we haven't seen each other in years.

"I'm Brigette," she says, pulling away. She sets her hands on my shoulders and appraises me. "Well, Jimmy said you were beautiful, but he obviously forgot to add that you're also stunning."

Blushing, I shake my head.

"I'm gross," I say. "I think he'd say something else if he saw me right now."

She shakes her head. "He'd say, 'Hey, Mum, look at my

wife, isn't she gorgeous?' And you are. You staying by his bed holding his hand and saying those words to him, makes you the most beautiful woman in the world, in my book."

"I'm really happy you're here."

"So am I. I just wish we were meeting each other in happier circumstances like the birth of my first granddaughter. Can I?" She looks down at my stomach and back at me. Just as quickly as I give my okay, her hands are on my stomach.

"Hi there, baby, I'm your grandma." And as if she knows, little one kicks nice and hard. Brigette's mouth drops open in surprise as I choke back a half laugh, half cry. Jimmy's missing this and that breaks my heart.

"You'll have to forgive my daughter-in-law, she's tired and uncomfortable. I know it has nothing to do with that tiny little bed you've given her and the lack of sleep she gets because the night nurse is still checking on my son every few minutes."

I try not to smile, but in this moment I love Brigette. She takes shots at the doctor and night nurse every chance she gets, but she does it with a smile and British words that make them think she's being nice to them.

"We can send in another bed."

"That would be lovely," she says without missing a beat. "Also, send in an obstetrician. I can't see her flying home any time soon to attend an appointment when her husband is like this."

"I'll send in the necessary forms—"

Brigette stops rubbing my shoulders. I turn and watch as she faces off with the doctor. "You should call her doctor in Beaumont to make things easier for her. She's under a lot of stress and is very close to her due date. Please respect the fact that she doesn't want to leave her husband's side and send your colleague down here."

I can see the doctor sigh and try not to laugh. "I'll have someone come down to see Mrs. Davis." The doctor takes his leave, shutting Jimmy's door behind him.

"You're brilliant."

Brigette shrugs, walking over to Jimmy. She threads her fingers through his hair and smiles. "I was going to be a solicitor when I met Jimmy's dad. I was young and stupid and thought I could tame him, and maybe I did at first, but it didn't last very long."

"Jimmy doesn't talk about his dad."

She shakes her head. "No, I don't imagine he does. James treats Jimmy as a friend or drinking partner, but never as a son. I sent Jimmy to live with his father because he wanted to be a musician. I had hoped Jimmy would grow out of it, but he didn't. Not that I don't appreciate what he does, but this is how I saw him, with a wife and a baby on the way. I didn't want him to end up like his father, but the music is in his veins.

"When Jimmy rang me and told me he was married, I prayed it wasn't some drunken Vegas wedding conducted by one of those Elvis impersonators. The minute he started telling me about you, I knew he had found someone to love him the way he deserves to be loved."

"We're the cliché one-night stand who ends up pregnant."

Brigette smiles. "And that night changed his life. I can remember all the phones calls after that. I didn't know what happened, but I knew something had changed. He started talking about hanging around in Beaumont more and for the life of me I had no idea why until he told me about you. One-night stand or not, you changed his life."

"WHAT THE BLOODY hell are you doing here?" I jump at the sound of Brigette's voice and her book slamming. I look groggily around the room before another body comes into focus. Standing in the doorway is Jimmy's dad. Even though I've never met him, I know who he is, everyone does and there's no mistaking him now.

"It's good to see you, too, Brigette. I see my money is treating you well." Brigette stands, setting her afghan and book in her chair.

"James, what are you doing here?"

"Is that not my son lying there?"

Brigette looks at me to Jimmy and back to me. Her eyes tell me everything; she's sorry. "You don't get to pick and choose when you're going to be a father, James."

James stares her down as he walks by her, taking the empty seat next to Jimmy's bed. "Who are you? You let some groupie in here, Brigette? That's unlike you."

"I'm his wife," I say, proudly.

He scoffs. "I thought I told him to leave you curbside."

"Excuse me?"

He cocks an eyebrow. "Same trick his mother used to trap me. I told my boy he shouldn't be falling for this shit."

"For the love of god, James, you don't even know the full story. There is no way Jimmy would confide in you. Don't listen to him, Jenna, he's full of crap."

"My son thinks with his dick. I know him better than you think."

This can't be happening. It can't be. What kind of heartless person is this man?

"That's enough, James." Liam comes into view and I swear he puffs out his chest. "If you think for a minute that you're welcome here, you're sadly mistaken. And if you think you're going to disrespect Jenna and Brigette, I won't need security to escort you, I'll do it myself."

"How in God's name did you even get in here?" Brigette asks.

James smiles and I know how without him even saying the words.

"Unbelievable," she mutters.

"I think you owe Jimmy's wife an apology," Liam says as he sits down on my bed-turned-couch during the day.

"No, it's fine. I don't want him to pretty up his ugly-assed words with a half-assed apology."

Liam and Brigette laugh, which causes James to shake his head. It's clear now why Jimmy never talked about his dad. I wouldn't talk about him either. Jimmy is nothing like him; at least he's not now. I can't imagine Jimmy ever being this way though. I know he was a man-whore, but the way James is, it's too chauvinistic and patronizing.

"I'll let you stay—"

"You'll let me stay?"

I stand, not that I can do anything to this man, but he needs to know I'm serious. "Yes, I'll let you stay. This is my husband, you have no say here. If you're in here, it's because I say so. Tough shit if you don't like it, I don't care. My husband is in a damn coma and I won't have you in here thinking your shit doesn't stink, Mr. Davis."

I sit back down and bite the inside of my cheek when Liam starts clapping. "No wonder Jimmy loves you," he says. I try not to smile, but I can't help it. I bury my face into Jimmy's side, not wanting to look at anyone.

"James, were you coming to get me or what?"

I roll my eyes and look over my shoulder. This face I know. I've seen her before. Liam stands and so does Brigette. My eyes travel down to her mid-section and see it protruding, just not as big as mine.

"What the fuck are you doing here?" Liam blurts out.

"You're pregnant?" Brigette asks. She looks at James, who shrugs.

"Who are you?" I ask, breaking up the back and forth.

"I'm Chelsea—"

"She's Jimmy's ex and a vapid little whore."

Chelsea rolls her eyes. "You never change, Liam."

"I see that you don't either. Let me guess, you're here to pin that on Jimmy?" Liam points to her belly. My stomach turns, my mouth drops open. This can't be happening.

"It's not Jimmy's." Harrison walks into the room with our lunch. He sets it down on the table and proceeds to kiss Brigette on the cheek. "Don't worry about her. He loves you," he whispers in my ear, before kissing me on the cheek.

Harrison surveys the room. "Before you even open your mouth, Chelsea, to blame Jimmy for your pregnancy, I know the truth."

"Truth?" I ask.

"His father knocked up his ex."

"Oh good Lord, you're going to burn in hell, James."

37

JIMMY

Beep ... beep ... beep

Beep ... beep ... beep

Beep ... beep ... beep

Beep ... beep ... beep

Beep ... beep ... beep

The voices I hear sound familiar, but I can't see their faces.

A hand touches mine, keeping me warm. This touch is familiar and comfortable, but I want to know who it is.

Fingers run through my hair. I want to move my head into that warm hand. I try, but to no avail.

My throat hurts. I've swallowed something big and it's stuck. How am I breathing?

Beep ... beep ... beep

Beep ... beep ... beep

Beep ... beep ... beep

Beep ... beep ... beep

What is that noise?

I need to see it.

I need to make it stop. It's hurting my head.

My chest hurts. It's a dull pain, but nonetheless it hurts and I have no idea why.

Why am I hurting?

Where the hell am I?

Why are the curtains … The curtains aren't closed.

Pain rips through my side, cutting off my air. I can't breathe.

My eyes flash open.

I gag on the foreign object that's down my throat.

"Calm down, Jimmy, let me help you."

I look into a pair of brown eyes that I don't recognise. Her hair is grey and pulled back away from her face.

"I know you're scared, but I need you to listen to me. This is a tube to help you breathe. You've sustained some damage to your lungs and before we remove the tube we'll need an x-ray. Now there's a room full of people waiting to see you so I'm going to sit you up, but no talking. If you feel the need to cough, please do. I'll be back in a few minutes."

The moment she moves out of my line of vision, I'm searching for the green eyes that light up my world. My bed rises and I blink rapidly to clear my eyes. She'll be here, right?

Her smile, that's what I see first. I try to smile back, but this fucking tube is in my way. Her beautiful eyes are watery and red-rimmed. She's been crying and I haven't been around to comfort her. I raise my arms, well as far as my left one will go. I look down briefly, and see multiple tubes coming out of it. I'm a fucking wreck.

Jenna moves closer. Her fingers touch my cheek and move down to my chin. I lean into her touch, needing to feel her on my skin. She rests her forehead against mine. I feel her body shake. My right arm moves slowly. Once I'm touching her, I'm not going to stop. I hold her head to mine and try to get her to kiss me. I may not be able to move my lips much, but I know she can and right now I need them to touch me.

She knows what I want because she wants it, too. When her lips touch my cheek, it's like an explosion. Fireworks go off in my chest. My skin tingles. I don't know if I'll ever survive without her. I guess I'll never tempt fate to find out.

"I'm so sorry, Jimmy. I love you so much." She pulls away far too soon for me. I know there are other people in the room, but right now I don't give a shit. I only want her. I have no idea why she's apologising and I don't care. I don't want her to leave me.

I move my hand down to her stomach and push against little one. My heart races when she pushes back. She knows her daddy's touch. Jenna holds my hand there for a moment before backing away.

My mum comes into view and she looks more beautiful than the last time I saw her. "Oh, Jimmy," she says as she kisses my cheek. She's crying, too, and I'm starting to realise that I might not be okay.

I grunt, getting Jenna's attention. I pull at the tube in my mouth, but she knocks my hand away. I fight around her hand, trying to pull it out. I need to ask what happened. I don't remember how I got here.

"Jimmy, stop," she says, holding my hand down. I know I'm stronger than her, but right now I can't get out of her grip. "I know you're upset, but it's okay. We aren't going anywhere."

I shake my head. That's not what I'm upset about. I need to know what the fuck happened to me. I relax so she will let go of my hand and when she does, I make the phone sign, holding my fingers up to my ear. She knows exactly what I need and starts searching through her bag for her phone. She hands it to me and I type my question.

What happened to me?

She pulls away the phone and reads my message. Her eyes find mine and I can see the pain and hurt in them. She looks so sad. I hate thinking that I'm the reason she looks like that. She picks up my hand and holds it, locking our fingers together.

"You were shot," she says, taking a deep breath. "Damien was there. I saw him and he had a gun. He shot you and escaped. The bullet went through both your lungs and exited. You've been in here a month."

I listen to what she says, grabbing for her phone again.

Where is he?

She shakes her head. "They haven't found him yet, but the detectives have been very good and stop by every day to see how you're doing. We've all given statements. They're looking for him.

A month?

She nods. "Yeah, and I haven't left yet. The guys are here, too. And Katelyn and Josie come on the weekends. Gary's outside with the bus and you have fans waiting for you to wake up. Liam and Harrison have even done an acoustic set for them. The press was here for a while, but they left after a week, but I'm sure they'll be back. Your dad and his girlfriend are here."

My eyes widen. I don't want Jenna to be anywhere in the vicinity of my dad.

"Don't worry, I know, but you can tell me your side when you're better. We're good, Jimmy."

I love you, I type to her.

She smiles. "I love you, too."

Little one?

"She's good. Josie brought my headphones so she could listen to you. It's almost time though, Jimmy."

You're bigger.

Jenna laughs and even though I can't remember not hearing her for a month, I've missed her laugh. "Yeah, I'm as big as a whale."

I shake my head and type: **You're fucking gorgeous, sweet lips.**

"I've missed that."

I'll never stop.

Before I can find a way to get her into my bed so I can show her how much I love her, the doctor walks in. I hate that Jenna has to move aside, but all the machines are right there and that's where he needs to be.

"How are you feeling, Jimmy?"

Does he expect me to grunt my answer? Does he want me to act like a bloody zombie? Because I can. That's what I feel like—like I've been run over repeatedly.

"We're going to take you down for an X-ray now. We usually do them here, but getting your wife to leave the room is a bit of a hassle."

I try to shrug, but fail miserably. I'm not gonna lie,

knowing she was here the whole time makes me love her even more.

"Here," Jenna says, placing a piece of paper in my hand. I bring it up to my eyes and warmth surges through me. It's my little one and I don't give a shit that in that picture, she looks like an alien life form. I know she's growing inside of Jenna and ready to make her debut. I place the picture on my chest and squeeze Jenna's hand as the nurse starts moving my bed.

I attempt my half-arsed smile at her. She loves me. I wink, which makes her giggle. Yeah I need to get the fuck out of this bed, and fast.

38

JENNA

Jimmy's been having his X-ray for over two hours. I was told they'd be right back and to stay here, but he's been gone too long. Between my hair pulling, lip chewing, and constantly looking at my watch, I'm going crazy. Everyone else is as cool as a cucumber. I'm the only one freaking out. He just woke up and now he's gone.

Someone from the hospital is a snitch. The press is gathering outside and none of us have contacted them. I watch as they assemble in the space that was designated for them after Jimmy was shot. More fans are starting to show up, too. They linger by the bus, waiting for one of the guys to come out and talk to them.

Liam and Harrison have been so accommodating to them. I told Jimmy about the acoustic show, but it's been more than that. The guys have had catered meals sent out to them and even held a three-hour meet and greet. When I asked them why, they said if they were going to sit outside and wait for word on Jimmy, this was the least they could do. I agreed, but opted to stay inside next to my husband instead of thanking them myself. Maybe when we leave, Jimmy and I can thank them together.

"You should sit down, honey. He'll be back soon."

"How do you know?" I ask Brigette. When Jimmy's dad and his ex-girlfriend showed up pregnant, I thought she was going to come unglued. But she's held strong and kept her head held high. Whatever James did to her, it doesn't show.

"James, what did you do?"

"I don't know what you're talking about, Brigette." I watch them, back and forth. James is smug and uncaring. I can tell by his tone. I look at the woman in the doorway. Her face flashes before my eyes. I've seen her so many times in the articles about the band. I was a fan of 4225 West long before I knew that Liam was Noah's dad. I'd buy every magazine just to read the newest gossip and she'd been in there. They were engaged. I knew that.

I look back at my sleeping husband and pray that he wakes up soon. I'm not mad that she's here, but curious. And what does James have to do with her?

Brigette doesn't seem to want to answer James and he's not offering up any information. I'm so confused and tired. I just want everyone to leave.

"What are you doing here?" I ask her. I wish I could remember her name, but for the life of me I can't. Jimmy never talks about her and I don't ask. We have exes for a reason.

"I'm here because of Jimmy."

"He doesn't want you here," I put forth.

She scoffs and throws her hair over her shoulder. "Yes he does."

I shake my head. "He doesn't."

"She's right, Chelsea," Harrison adds.

Chelsea, that's right—either he or Liam said it before when she showed up. Chelsea. The rag mags never did say why they broke up, not that it matters anymore.

"You're pregnant?" she asks. I want to say no shit, but I nod. It's clear that I am. "Who's the father?"

"Oh, for crying out loud, Chelsea. Jimmy is the father, you silly girl." Brigette throws her hands up in the air. "Why did you bring her here, James?"

"What makes you think she came with me? Jimmy's the one who knocked her up."

My mouth drops. Liam stands and Harrison yells out, "Bullshit."

"Excuse me?" James says.

This is a back and forth tennis match, all taking place while my husband's in a coma. It's a stupid soap opera.

"Jenna, look at me."

I do as Harrison commands.

"JD did not knock her up. She's trying to pin it on Jimmy, but he thinks his dad is the father of her baby."

"How does he know?" I ask, quietly lacking the confidence that I need to assert myself here.

"Because when he was home, she moved into JD's apartment, but he told her that he didn't want her and that he didn't think the baby was his. He saw Chelsea and his father at a café have a tête-à-tête right before he left." Harrison looks at James. "He saw his father kiss his ex-fiancée and place his hands on her stomach."

"How do you know about this, Harrison?" Brigette asks.

"He came and told me. He was freaking out a bit because

he had left Jenna alone and was in L.A. dealing with Chelsea when he should've been in Beaumont."

"I damn well knew it, James. My god, what kind of lowlife man are you to sleep with your son's ex? I mean, seriously. And you, you're a disgusting piece of work. After everything you did to Jimmy. No wonder he calls you a leech."

"Wow," I say.

"This is why JD didn't want you to know his dad," Liam adds.

"Hey, now—"

"No, James, you don't get to make excuses for your behaviour. I wish I could say I regret sending him to you, but he met the boys and his wife so it must've been for the best."

"I'm happy you're here, Brigette."

"Me too. I just wish we didn't meet like this. I'm worried I'm going to outlast my welcome and you won't want me around when the baby is born."

"Nonsense," I say, pulling her into my arms. She's been a comfort to have here. My mom wanted to come, but I told her it was okay to stay home. I kept her updated daily and told her if I needed her, I'd call, but with Liam, Harrison, and Brigette here twenty-four seven the room is crowded. "Jimmy will be happy that you're here."

Brigette moves my hair off my shoulder. "Don't give him a hard time about Chelsea when he fully wakes. He was in love with her once, a long time ago. He thought she was the one for him, but she put him through hell and back. First with her family and then she cheated on him. I'd never seen him so broken."

"Is that why he started sowing his wild oats?"

She laughs, but I really don't want to call my husband a man-whore even though that is what he was.

"I guess you could say that. He very much did play the field, until he met you. I knew the day that you two ... well, you know, because when he rang me, he was different. He was happy and talking about moving to Beaumont to be closer to Liam and Harrison. Before, he was adamant that he would stay in L.A. because he needed to be a free spirit."

"I'm usually not that type of girl."

"I know you're not."

"What type of girl?" We both turn to Jimmy coming back into the room. His breathing tube has been removed and he's smiling. Once his bed is in place, I rush over and place my lips on his. He pulls away too quickly for my liking.

"What's wrong?" I ask.

"I haven't brushed my teeth in a month, sweet lips. I would really like to before you start kissing me again."

"We can have a nurse come in and give you a sponge bath, Mr. Davis."

I see red when the doctor suggests that. His mom and I have been the ones bathing him while he was in the coma. I'll be dead before some nurse comes in to wash him now that he's awake.

"I'll do it."

Jimmy smiles although it doesn't reach his eyes. He's tired. I can see it in his face. He's trying to stay awake to please us. I brush his hair away from his face. He leans into my hand. I hope that I'm bringing him a bit of comfort.

"I'll repeat what I told you after I read your X-ray. You'll need to wear the oxygen mask until your levels rise, but can take it off to answer questions. You're going to feel tired for a while, and even though it seems like you've been asleep, your body doesn't realize that. So be patient with your recovery."

"Thank you," he says. His voice is hoarse and scratchy. It sounds like he's been yelling for days on end.

"I'll leave you to take your bath," Brigette says, winking at Jimmy as she leaves behind the doctor. I close all the blinds and fill the bucket with warm water.

"You have a couple of scars," I say, when I come back. I roll down his blankets. Untying the top of his hospital issued nightgown, I let it fall open. "They can do plastic surgery if you want them removed, but they're healing nice."

Jimmy looks down at his chest and stifles a cry. I gingerly kiss his chest, away from his sutures.

"I look like Frankenstein."

"You look like my husband." I set the warm sponge onto his skin. He shivers, and as much as I'd love to say it's because I'm touching him, I know it's from the cold air. "They had to go in and stop the bleeding. If they hadn't, we would've lost you." I clean around the cut they made and make my way to the first bullet hole. "He shot you here, Jimmy, while I was watching you perform, while Liam was singing little one's song. I saw him in the crowd, but the security guard couldn't understand what I was saying until he saw the gun. I tried to get to you, but Liam stopped me. He saw you fall to the ground. Harrison carried me away from you.

"The bullet exited here," I say, as I move to the other side. "Liam held you until the medics arrived. He put his knee on one side and his hand here to stop the bleeding. Days later the medics stopped by and told him if he hadn't done that they would've lost you on the way here. He saved my family."

I make my way down his body. He looks at me when I drip water over his semi-erect penis.

"I shouldn't be turned on, but I am."

Laughing, I shake my head.

"The doctor said we can't have sex for a while."

"You asked?"

"Yeah, I haven't been able to please my wifey for a month. I have a lot of catching up to do."

"I'm not going anywhere, Jimmy."

"Can I tell you about Chelsea?"

"You don't have to, Harrison filled me in."

"I want to."

"Okay," I say, sitting down in the hard plastic chair next to his bed. I pick his hand up, careful of the IV, and place it to my lips. This is going to be hard for him and the last thing I want is for him to think I'm angry. I'm not. I almost lost my husband. It's going to take a lot to piss me off these days.

"When I went back to L.A., I found out that she had moved into my flat and was spouting all this crap about being pregnant. We had slept together a few days before you and I got married so I thought for one fucked up moment that I had ruined everything with you.

"I was so stupid, Jenna. I had a bad feeling about it straight away, but didn't leave. I saw Chelsea and my dad together, but couldn't for the life of me understand why my dad would do that to me. I went and saw him and thought that after I told him about you and little one, he'd own up but he didn't.

"I wanted to tell you, but I didn't want you to think that I cheated on you because I didn't. From the moment I asked you to marry me, I've been yours."

Tears drip down my face as he tries to pull me closer. I don't let on that he's not at full strength yet and move to where he needs me. "I just want to hold you, Jenna."

He doesn't know what those words mean to me. It's not that he wants to hold me, but opening up about his dad and ex means the world to me.

I adjust so I can lie with him easily. I've been doing this for a month. I'm a pro now. I rest my head in the crook of his neck and play with the stubble on his chin. It doesn't escape me that this is what I've been waiting for. I've needed this moment since the night of the concert and he knows it.

39

JIMMY

I'm experiencing one of the most erotic moments in my life and there isn't jack shit I can do about it. I'm too weak physically, and because of that I can't even begin to please my wife. I can only remember what she feels like wrapped around my dick and how she sounds when she's moaning my name. Fuck, right now I can't even breathe without the aid of some godforsaken machine. I want to get out of this bed, but I can't. I can't even have a piss by myself. I have to take a leak into a bucket. Thank fuck the plastic tube sticking out of my dick has gone. I hate thinking about everything my wife has seen this past month. I hate that she's seeing the absolute worst from me.

For better or for worse, in sickness and health—those are the vows we said to each other, and look at me taking advantage of those words to the max. I'm going to throw myself my own fucking pity party and ask her to buy me a bloody cake so I can celebrate. Her fucking nutter of an ex shot me like the bastard coward he is. He can't fight like a man. No, he hits women, and when that doesn't do it for him, he shoots people.

If I ever …

I close my eyes as the sponge moves over my body. Her touch is gentle and soothing. I can tell without even asking her, that she's been doing this the entire time I've been here. I'm glad it's her. Not that I want her to stare at my fucked up body, but she has the most reason to take care of me. With my luck I would probably have got my own personal Sam and she'd cut my crown jewels off or something equally as messed up.

I have my wife—one that loves me, no matter what, and if this doesn't prove that we're going to make it through anything, I don't know what will.

I listen intently as she recounts what happened. Her voice … it does something to me, even though it shouldn't. I shouldn't be turned on right now, but I am. My arm, the one without all the wires, tries to move, but it's slow and unsteady. It's unbelievable how one month of no movement renders it useless. My fingers finally get close enough to touch her hair when she smiles at me. She leans forward and rests her head in the crook of my neck. My limp arm falls on her. Romantic, right?

"I just want to hold you, Jenna." I can't even begin to think how she's felt this past month. If I do, I'll go crazy. If she was in this bed and our roles were reversed, I don't know what I would've done.

Having her lie beside me isn't enough, but I know that's all I'm going to get at the moment. She's not going to let me get away with anything.

"You should put your oxygen mask on."

I scoff and roll my eyes. "I'm trying to love you right now." I'm almost out of breath and can't even think about how different my life is going to be now. "I need to hold you."

"I told you, I'm not going anywhere."

She sits up, already breaking her promise.

"You just left me."

Shaking her head, she giggles. "I'm covering you up. You don't want to catch a cold and you don't want your mom to see you like this."

"I think my mum knows we have sex, sweet lips," I say, pointing to her belly.

"Incorrigible, that's what you are. We can't have sex, Jimmy. You need to heal."

"But, my sexy wifey, you can straddle me and hang onto the rails. I'll do all the work, I promise."

She's not buying it, clearly. She re-ties my ridiculous excuse for a hospital gown and covers me back up. Tucking me in like I'm a baby. I like being pampered, but this is going to get old fast.

"Jenna?"

"Yeah, Jimmy?"

"I love you."

I'm rewarded with a smile that puts all the others to shame. "I love you, too."

I smile weakly. "I'm tired."

"I know you are. You should rest. I won't go anywhere." I don't know where the fatigue came from, but suddenly I'm exhausted. Jenna slips my oxygen mask over my nose and mouth and I instantly hate it. I can't kiss her now. It's a sad realisation that I can't do any of the things I want to do with my wife right now, except look at her.

She sits down next to me and holds my hand. Is this what she did while I was in a coma? Part of me wishes I knew, but the other part doesn't want to know. I don't want to know if she cried, although I know she did. I don't want to know that she didn't take care of herself. I can see it in her eyes. She's tired. She should've been taking care of herself and little one, not sitting by my side day in, day out.

But I'm happy that she did. It warms me to know that she never left my side, that when things got rough she anchored down and held us afloat.

She's the last thing I see when I close my eyes. Her head rests on my bed next to me. I want to pull her into bed with me and hold her while I sleep, but I know it's not possible. I heard everything the doctor said, I just don't want to believe it. No sex now, and it'll be questionable later. And because of the damage to my lungs, I'm not breathing at *full capacity* whatever the fuck that means. I'll need physical therapy to help me rebuild my stamina. But the worst thing? I'll be carrying around an oxygen tank with me for a while until I can breathe on my own at ninety percent. Fucking *great*.

When I wake up my blinds are closed and it's dark. There's a small light coming from the corner, but that's the only light I can see. I reach for Jenna, but find her spot is empty. She's not here. She said she'd never leave me. My heart rate increases, causing the machine to start beeping like wildfire.

"Hey, what's the matter?"

My mum comes into view. Her fingers work their way

through my hair. She did this when I was little to soothe me. Closing my eyes, I let her work her magic as I try and calm down. I'm afraid to remove my mask. I can feel my lungs struggling to get air. Tears sting my eyes. I refuse to let the water drip down my face. I will not cry, not now. Who knew bullet holes would cause so much damage?

"Are you okay?"

I nod, even though I'm not. I want my wife to be sitting next to me so I know she's okay. "Jenna," I mumble into my mask. My mum smiles and I don't know if she's doing so because I'm awake or if she actually understood what I said.

"Your wife is lovely, Jimmy. I've watched her take care of you for a month. She loves you so much and is very happy that you're having a baby together. I never thought, after Chelsea, that you'd fall in love again. I had hoped, but also realised that you were young, hurt, and going to do whatever you needed to mend your heart.

"The day you called and told me that you got married, my first thought was that you were doing something stupid and reckless like I read about in the papers. When you said that she was pregnant and you were the father, my words were 'You don't need to marry her because of the baby, you can work something out, maybe live together and raise the baby', and do you remember what you said to me?"

I shake my head.

"You said, 'Mum, Jenna is the one woman that I can see myself falling in love with. I didn't marry her because she's having my bub, I married her because she makes me feel whole.' I've watched her, Jimmy. I've watched her to see how she was around you and do you know what I saw?"

I shake my head again.

"I saw a woman who loves her husband with every bone in her body. You both make me believe that it doesn't matter how you got together, but what you do once you have each other is what counts. Maybe that's the secret. Maybe everyone should marry someone they don't know well and let life lead them wherever it takes them. Whatever journey you, Jenna and little one are on, it's the right one. I can see nothing but happiness for you.

"I do wish I had met her under different circumstances, but I give my daughter-in-law all the credit in the world. You were her priority and she made sure you had the best care possible. But I do think bath time was her favourite."

I smile and move my mask up. "Mine too."

We are leaving Chicago today after being here for six-weeks. Jimmy can't walk without assistance yet and it's driving him batty. Physically, he can walk, but his oxygen levels are still too low to maintain his normal habits. This also means no performing until he's given the okay by his doctor.

I'm not even going to sugarcoat it—I'm ready to go back to Beaumont. I'm tired of hospital life. I'd like to say I'll never be back, but little one's due date is fast approaching. I'm just thankful that Jimmy will be there to help bring her into the world, because if he missed this, I don't think he'd forgive himself.

Jimmy's most recent set of X-rays show his lungs have healed, but there's scar tissue that could be bothersome later in life. He has to work with a physical therapist three days a week until he's cleared. Liam thought it was a good idea for the band to get into shape, so he hired a guy named Alexander Knight to see to the band's needs. He'll be doing Jimmy's training as well. Liam wants to keep it all in the family. If I didn't know better, I'd think that Liam is developing a mob mentality. Not that you're going to hear me complain.

Katelyn and Josie have already dished on his deets. He's single, goes by the nickname Xander, and has the most delectable muscles. This is from Josie. It's a good thing Liam has her wrapped around his finger because Xander might be his competition. Katelyn says his eyes are caramel colored and she might have a hard time focusing when he's showing her how to tone her arms.

Damien is still on the loose. From what we've been told, his parents were under surveillance for a while and were even brought in for questioning. They admitted to knowing about the abuse, saying that he confided in them that he needed help, but they didn't want to meddle. I don't know if I should thank them for not meddling or bash their heads together for keeping their mouths shut.

I'm happy with my husband who is sleeping for the last time in his hospital bed. Tonight, he'll be in the comforts of our new home, courtesy of Josie and Katelyn. Here's what I learned. My husband is a sneaky little shit. While he was on tour, instead of resting or preparing for that night's show he, along with my two best friends, were plotting behind my back to buy us a house. When we return to Beaumont I'll be a suburban housewife complete with a porch swing and white picket fence. As much as I want to yell at him, I can't. He did this for me and little one and I'm grateful.

I've spent many hours watching Jimmy sleep. It's funny, I never thought it would be an activity that I'm fond of, but I am. I think it's the only time his mind shuts down and allows his body to rest because when he's awake, he wants ... no, he *needs* to be a part of everything going on.

His dad will be here soon. I'm dreading this and so is Brigette. James had the audacity to ask for a "private" visit, which I vehemently denied. I don't trust him and I definitely don't want Chelsea in here alone with him. Jimmy is getting stronger by the day, but he's not in a position to fend off unwanted attacks by a psycho ex-girlfriend or the verbal barrage his father plans to let loose.

Maybe Chelsea isn't psycho and that's an unfair assessment. From what I've learned they had a pretty solid relationship, until she screwed up. Maybe I should thank her because had she not, I wouldn't be standing here today. And Jimmy wouldn't be lying in a hospital bed with a machine hooked up to him making sure he's getting enough oxygen. So I'm the bad seed. I brought this onto him. I put him there. Damn him and his intuitive mind knowing that the baby was his.

"What are you thinking about?" His voice is raspy, sexy. I want to hear him talk to me like this all day, but he can't. Right now the most he can go is twenty minutes before the mask has to go on, and sooner if we've been making out like horny teenagers.

I shake my head and walk over to him. I don't want him to know I'm second guessing us meeting. He doesn't need to worry about the guilt that I'm carrying around with me. He's in this bed because of me. His lungs are damaged because I didn't leave when I wanted to. I let people convince me to stay when I knew how dangerous Damien was, albeit I never thought he'd try to kill someone.

My someone.

Leaning down, I kiss him.

"My lips are dry," he says as I pull away.

I nod and reach into the bag of essentials I've placed next to his bed. There's everything here that he needs. Lip balm, handiwipes, lotion, and candy to suck on. I pull out the lip balm and hand it to him. I'm supposed to stop enabling him and let him do things for himself. What the doctor doesn't understand is that I like doing these things for him. It's intimate for us and we need that right now.

"You don't want to do it for me?" he asks, taking the tube from my hand.

"I do, but you're supposed to do it yourself."

"Come here," he demands. I lean forward so that I'm inches away from him. He smiles as he uncaps the lip balm. Placing it on my lips, he rubs it back and forth on my bottom and top lip. He leans forward and kisses me hard. "There, now I'm all set."

"Yes, you are."

"Knock, knock."

"You have company," I say quietly enough for him to hear me. He closes his eyes and nods.

"I love you."

I lean forward and kiss him again before turning and pasting on a welcoming face. I hear Jimmy adjust his bed so he's sitting up a bit more.

"Come on in." I sit down next to Jimmy. Mean, I know, but I don't want James and Chelsea to take up both sides of him.

"You're staying?" James asks in a snide tone.

"She's my wife. You better start accepting it."

"No need to get angry, son. I was just asking a question. Chelsea and I thought we could spend some time with you."

"Well, you can do it with Jenna here. Anything that you need to say can be said in front of her. I'm not exactly in a position to be able to repeat myself."

"Fair enough," James says as he sits down, leaving Chelsea to stand or sit away from Jimmy, which is my preference. "How are you feeling?"

Jimmy shrugs and reaches for his water. I let him do it on his own. The last thing I want is hear his father's sneering comments about me enabling him.

"I'm fine. I'm glad I'm going home today."

"You're going home? No one told me." James looks at me, raising his eyebrow.

"Jenna doesn't owe you anything, Dad, and neither do I. I'm not even sure why you're here."

James leans closer, resting his head in his hands, and takes a deep breath. I have to give him credit he's putting on a great performance for Jimmy's sake. By his expression, he's not buying it. Chelsea huffs from her corner. I can't help but laugh. She lost Jimmy and ended up with his father. It's gross to even think about. What would possess someone to stoop so low?

"I care about you Jimmy. When I saw the report—"

"I saw it first," Chelsea blurts out.

Well, good for her.

James rolls his eyes. "When Chelsea called and told me, we had to come."

Jimmy picks at his blanket. I can tell he's not amused. His heart rate is starting to pick up, too. I watch the monitor for signs of distress. I'll kick his dad out if I have to.

"You should've stayed at home."

"Jimmy—"

"No, you listen to me," he says. I put my hand on him to try and keep him calm. "I went back to L.A. to tie up some loose ends and to tell you that I was married. To share with you that I'm happy and that my wife and I are having a baby. And what do you do? You tell me to get an annulment and ignore her. As if that wasn't bad enough, you," he points to Chelsea, "move into my flat and try to pin your pregnancy on me. Yeah, I was fucking stupid to even consider taking you back before I knew about Jenna, but I couldn't get her out of my head, so I did the right thing and left. But no, you had to go and pull this ridiculous stunt thinking I wouldn't find out, but I did. I'm not your baby's father. And you ..." he says, looking back at his dad. "What the fuck is wrong with you? Chelsea and I were together for three years and you think in your fucked up little mind that it's okay to sleep with her?

"You know I had forgiven you for leaving when I was little, but this ... I've made changes in my life and I think you need to be one of them. What you've done is so low I don't think I can forgive you. I can't look at the both of you across a family dinner and think that this situation is okay, and I'm definitely not letting my daughter be a part of it."

"You have some pretty powerful words there, son."

"Yeah well, you've done some pretty shitty things to me in my life."

"You dumped Chelsea, do you need a reminder?"

Jimmy purses his lips, shaking his head. "No, the vision of her getting shagged from behind with a dick in her mouth is still pretty damn clear."

I gasp and look at Chelsea who isn't making eye contact with anyone. I knew she cheated, but had no idea it was that bad. Jimmy clutches my hand. "I'm sorry," I say to him.

"Why? I'm sure as hell not. If I hadn't caught her I probably wouldn't be married to you right now and this is definitely where I want to be."

My eyes start to water with his confession. I'm sure he's rethinking some of this. Without me he wouldn't be in this bed, unable to breathe fully on his own.

Jimmy turns and looks at Chelsea. "I just want to know why? What would possess you to sleep with my dad and then try and pin his baby on me?"

"I love him," she replies weakly.

He shakes his head and looks like he's in need of his mask.

"Jimmy," I say quietly.

"I'm okay." He takes a deep breath and I'm there, ready to put his mask on if need be, but he doesn't give me the opportunity. "I loved you, Chelsea, until you threw it all away. We had a good life and I treated you like a fucking princess. I put up with the bullshit from your—" Jimmy stops speaking. He tries to laugh, which only causes a coughing fit. I'm about to put an end to this meeting when he smiles at me. I shake my head, but he starts talking again. "I get it now. Your parents don't know you've been shagging my old man, do they?"

Chelsea shakes her head. This is like a never-ending ping pong match with the back and forth.

"I see how it is. I'm the lesser of two evils where the Davis men are concerned, so you thought you'd come back to me and that I'd forgive you, and oops Chelsea's pregnant and Jimmy's doing the right thing. What you didn't count on was me pushing you away or me seeing you have a full-on snogging session with my dad at a coffee shop."

Both Chelsea and James' mouths drop open.

"Yeah, I saw you so that's how I knew. It's why I never called. It's why, when my wife asked me to change my number, I did immediately without hesitation. I bloody knew you were lying. I knew it. The sad part is that I let this bullshit almost ruin my chance with Jenna. Thank God she loves me because if I didn't have her right now because of you two ... I don't know what I'd do. As far as I'm concerned the pair of you are dead to me. You're nobodies. You don't exist in my life anymore."

"Son, you can't say that."

"I can. You slept with my ex, that's low enough as it is, but then you had to take it one step further and encourage her to pin the pregnancy on me when you knew I was married. You knew I was having a baby and that didn't stop you."

I put my hand on his shoulder to calm him down. I knew this was a mistake, but he insisted. Jimmy closes his eyes, as his chest moves rapidly. I pull his mask over his head whether he wants it there or not. These people aren't worth my husband being unable to breathe.

"Just until you're able to catch your breath," I whisper in his ear. He nods, keeping his eyes closed. I have to say, I'm sure the pictures his mind can conjure up right now have to be better than staring at his father and ex-girlfriend.

"I love you," I say, reassuring him that I'm here and not going anywhere. It doesn't matter how screwed up this situation is. I have my own skeletons that he's overlooking. I'm in this for life.

Jimmy pulls his mask down and looks in the direction of James. "I'm disgusted that I have the same name as you." Jimmy covers his face with his hands as I lean on his shoulder. I can't even imagine what he's going through right now.

Jimmy looks at his dad. "You need to leave now. I'm going home today, with my wife and my friends."

"Your home is in Los Angeles. You know you won't be able to stay away."

"That's where you're wrong, Dad. You don't have anything I need or want. Jenna has it all. *She's* my home."

"**O**kay, Jimmy, just one minute left." Xander is standing behind me, ready to catch me if I trip or lose my footing. I've never been a fan of running, and running on this bloody treadmill makes me hate it even more, but it's working, this physical therapy bollocks, so I'm trying my hardest not to complain.

We—I say we because Jenna hasn't left my side—have been home for a month. Jenna's in her last few weeks of pregnancy and I'm determined I'm going to be in the delivery room with her and without my need for oxygen. For the majority of the time, I can walk around the house without any complications. At night, I'm hooked up to a machine and I fucking despise it. Right now, I can't be the husband that I want or need to be and it makes me feel like I'm less than adequate.

Looking at the display on the treadmill, I watch the seconds tick down. My lungs are burning, but thankfully I'm not gasping for air like I was when I first started this regimen. When I started, I didn't last thirty seconds without

Xander having to hold me up so he could slip my oxygen mask over my face. If I ever felt emasculated, it was in that moment. I'm just thankful that no one saw me but him. He works with complete professionalism and he didn't molly-coddle me. He put me straight back on the treadmill and told me to start again. Because of Xander, I'll be stronger and healthier when little one arrives.

The red lights flash, indicating that my training is done. I go from a steady jog to a brisk walk to cool down and decrease my heart rate. My hands find the railings as my lungs start to protest at the amount of work they're doing. I can see Xander as he moves behind me, waiting. The mirror that I'm staring at tells me everything I need to know: he's waiting for me to collapse, but I'm not going to do it, not this time.

"How are you feeling?"

"On top of the world," I lie. I'm okay, but not great and haven't been since the shooting. "I'm getting better." Not a lie, but not exactly the truth either. Yes, I feel better, but this is a painstakingly slow process. I want results instantly, like that miracle diet that you hear about on the radio. Instant results. If you starve yourself to death, that is.

I'm running myself to death, and as much as I'd like to give up and wallow in a self-imposed pity party, I won't. It's not fair on Jenna to have half a husband just because her ex went psycho and tried to kill me. She was already dealt a shitty hand with him. I refuse to let it happen again with me. I'll be whole again before little one arrives if it kills me. And I will make my wife feel good again.

"You're doing well, Jimmy."

"Thanks," I say as I step off the treadmill. My legs don't

protest as much as they did when I started and that's a good thing. My lungs do enough complaining for the rest of my body. They scream for air, and instead of giving in, I go through the breathing exercises that I learned with Jenna at her Lamaze classes.

"Do you have your breathing under control?" Xander asks.

I nod and inhale my next breath before exhaling and relaxing. Who knew her antenatal classes would help me like this? I never would have believed it and I've definitely kept that information to myself. There's no way I'd share my knowledge with Liam or Harrison. Xander knows, though, and I can trust him not to say anything to them.

Xander has quickly become part of the band and integrated well. We've taken to him, too. At first I didn't want to trust him, but he's given me no reason not to. He's honest and very upfront about his life. He recently graduated from university and took the first job he was offered which happened to be in Beaumont. Sadly for the rehab facility, Liam came along and hired him full-time to keep us all in shape. It might not be Xander's dream job, but he's being paid well and he gets to travel.

"What time's your appointment?" he asks as he checks my pulse.

"In an hour," I answer. I'm surprised my voice isn't raspy from the extensive breathing. Jenna's commented many times about my raspy voice, but other than whispering dirty words into her ear, I haven't been able to take advantage of it to its full extent. Another kill-joy if you ask me.

"I think the outcome will be positive. I'll send my report

over after you leave so your doctor can see your latest results."

"Thank you."

"What are you hoping to achieve with this visit?"

"Sex," I blurt out.

Xander's mouth drops open as he tries to compose himself and not to have a reaction at my verbal diarrhea. I realise my mistake by the sheer look of horror spreading across his face.

"I mean with Jenna. I haven't been able to have sex with her for months and the ache is killing me."

"You had me there for a minute."

"Liam would kill me ... if I cheated on Jenna."

Xander nods. "He's protective."

"Fiercely, but I admire him for it. I know if I step out of line, he'll be there to give me an arse kicking."

"Somehow I don't think you'd do that to Jenna."

He's right, I wouldn't. She deserves to be the happiest woman in the world and hell would freeze over before I disappoint her.

"No, I wouldn't. Any woman who's been through what she has deserves to be doted on. I need to be whole again so I can be that man for her. I miss being with her."

"I miss you, too."

Turning around, I see my wife standing at the door. Her hand, the one that has my ring on it, rests on her belly. Little one has run out of space and needs to get here already. Not only am I anxious to meet her, but Jenna is, too. I feel like she's been pregnant forever and I know she feels the same. She's beautiful though. Everything about her shines like a diamond, and when she smiles, it makes me go weak in the knees. I hope that feeling never goes away.

"Am I interrupting?"

My teeth bite my lower lip as she walks closer. Jesus, this doctor needs to tell me it's okay to have sex with her. I need to feel her and be close to her. Holding her at night does not sate my desire. Her arm slides around my waist and I instantly bury my face in her hair. I kiss her neck lightly, enough so she knows I've been thinking about her, but not too much to embarrass her in front of Xander.

"We're just about finished," Xander says. He walks to his desk, thankfully leaving me with Jenna.

"I'm feeling optimistic."

"Jimmy, it's okay if we can't. You know that."

I shake my head. "No, it's not. It's been a month and I'm much better. Even Xander says so. He better have a damn good reason why I can't have sex with my wife or I'm going to freak the fuck out on him."

"Don't be so dramatic."

"I'm horny."

"You're insatiable. You know, I've bragged to Josie and Katelyn about that before."

I cringe. Us guys don't do the kiss 'n' tell thing. I don't want to know about what they do with their women. "You talk about me to Josie and Katelyn?"

She nods as her hand grabs my waist. "I tell them everything ... like that little trick you do with your tongue. Or how you like to—"

I put my hand over her mouth to shut her up. I can't listen to this, not right now. I step forward and grind into her. "If the doctor says yes, I'm shagging you in the car. No foreplay, no dipping my fingers for a taste of your sweet pussy. I'm going to drive us to a deserted road and fuck you senseless," I whisper in her ear.

"Jimmy." Her voice is quiet, wanting. I don't care what she says. She wants it. She wants me buried deep inside of her to ease the ache. That's one very important factor in our relationship. We turn each other on and are both willing to give in to each other, and I plan to take full advantage.

"HI JIMMY, HOW ARE YOU FEELING?" the doctor walks in and speaks without looking at me. His face is glued to his tablet. I know this office is using tablets for their charts, but for the love of God, make eye contact with me so you can see how well I'm doing.

"I'm good."

He sits down and types. Jenna sits in the corner, reading a magazine. I find myself wishing it was Playboy or something to get her in the mood. I wasn't kidding when I told her my plans. Today, foreplay is overrated. I have time to make up for it. Besides, the moment I touch her, I'm going to blow my load.

"Mr. Knight says everything's looking good. Your oxygen level is about ninety percent. I still want to see it higher, but as long as you don't over exert yourself I don't see a need to carry the tank around anymore. I still want you to sleep with it, though, until your level increases."

"Can I have sex?"

"Jimmy!" Jenna screeches.

The doctor starts laughing. "Yes, Jimmy, you're clear to

have sex as long as your tank is near in the event you start to hyperventilate, which I think might happen."

"No kidding," I say. "Are we done here?"

"Yes, Jimmy. We'll see you in two weeks. Have fun you two," he says, winking at me before leaving the room.

I wait for the door to shut before turning my attention to Jenna. She's trying to ignore me, but it won't work.

"Did you hear him?"

"Yes, he says you need an appointment in two weeks."

"Jenna," I whine.

"Jimmy." She stands up and walks over to me. "I'll be waiting in the car."

Before I can react she's out of the door and I'm left with a raging hard-on and a visit to the receptionist to get another appointment.

WHEN I GET into the car I don't say anything. I slide, for the first time in months, into the driver's seat. Jenna's looks out the window. There's a smile on her face. Yeah, she knows what's coming. I start the car and adjust the volume on the radio. Lyrics waft through the speakers, easing the tension that I'm feeling. I haven't had this feeling since I was a teenager.

My palms sweat against the steering wheel. I'm trying my hardest not to look over at Jenna until I get to our destination. It's fucking tough though. I want to touch her now. I want to hold her hand, but I'm afraid that if I let go I'll swerve off the road.

Why am I nervous? It's something I can't figure out. It's

not like we haven't been together before. Looking at her belly is evidence enough. But it's been months since we've *been together* and I've been out of commission.

Turning down a deserted road, I drive into the woods. I've driven out here a few times to clear my head and try to find the courage to ask Jenna out. Thing is, I didn't need courage, I just needed knowledge and it was Liam who supplied that to me one night in the studio. Parking the car, I turn off the engine. I plug my phone into the aux port and pick one of the many playlists I have for Jenna.

"How are we going to do this?"

I look at my wife whose eyes are wandering. "I think we've mastered the art of having sex, sweet lips."

Jenna shakes her head. "I'm big, Jimmy. It's not like I can lie down."

I wish she'd listen to me when I tell her that I think she's beautiful. That she's the most gorgeous woman I've ever seen. I get out of the car and walk to her side, opening the door and holding out my hand for her. She tries to walk away from me, but I stop her. I spin her around and pin her against the car.

I bury my nose in her hair as my hands move up her sides. My fingers dance under her shirt, inching their way to her full tits.

"I don't think you're fat. I think you're sexy as fuck and my dick wants to be buried in you."

Jenna throws her head back when my fingers squeeze her nipples. I latch onto her neck, biting her gently. My cock aches, begging for release. I know I won't last. I'm not expecting much. Pulling my hands away from her chest, I find the waistband of her shorts and slide them down her leg, taking her knickers with them.

"Step out," I request. She steps out of her shorts, never turning to look at me. I place them on the hood of the car. I drop my shorts, and my cock springs against the swell of her arse. She moans when I touch her, confirming what I already know—she wants this.

My leg pushes against hers, widening her stance.

"Put your foot on the tyre." Never have I been so thankful for her small car. I'm going to buy her a new one before the baby is born but we might need to keep this one for some little excursions.

She does as I ask, allowing me plenty of space to step forward. I exhale loudly the second my dick comes in contact with her. She bends, arching her back. Begging me to fill her. I meet her request with no hesitation.

Gripping her hips, I steady her and begin to move in and out, slowly. I need to last. I need to experience this as if it was our first time. With each thrust, she gets louder. My name falls from her lips in the most sensual way. It spurs me to increase my speed, and as much as I want to prolong it, I can't.

I slam into her as my hand snakes under her shirt. Pulling down her bra, I palm her breast. She pushes into me, rocking her hips. I'm so close, but I want her with me. I want to feel her clench as I pump into her. My fingers rub on her swollen clit. It's hard and ready to explode.

"Oh fuck, Jenna. Oh fuck, fuck fuck," I say with each thrust.

"I ... I'm ..."

"Fuck, sweet lips, I can feel you coming."

Jenna moans loudly. Her head is resting against the car. I bite down on her shoulder the moment I feel my body tense. Pumping into her faster, I pound my hips into hers.

My head rests against her back, my breathing laboured, but not out of control. "Fuck, Jenna, I needed that. God, I've missed you so much."

I've never craved sex the way I have these past few months. I guess what they say is true. Once you find your one, you know.

I sit up, moving as little as possible so not to disturb Jimmy. He still needs to sleep and heal. I'm ecstatic that his road to recovery is almost complete. Watching him with Xander yesterday filled me with such pride. To see him working so hard to achieve his goal is beyond rewarding. He knows the guilt I carry and is determined to prove to me that he's fine.

I'm sore right now, and with each movement the ache intensifies. I know I'm supposed to love this feeling after spending the night with my husband, but right now I just want to roll into the fetal position and lie on the bathroom floor.

The cold, hardwood floor makes me feel a little better. I must be coming down with the flu. I rest my hand against my forehead. I'm warmer than usual. I don't know how I'll handle being sick and this pregnant. I'm almost unbearable now. A cold on top of this will just make me a raging bitch. Each step I take down the stairs hurts.

"Morning, darling," Brigette says over her cup of coffee. She went back to London briefly before coming to Beaumont. She's going to help with the baby when she gets here. I think it's important for her and little one to bond, especially since she lives so far away. I asked Jimmy if he thinks his mom will move here and he said no because it was too close to his dad even though his dad is in Los Angeles ... playing house with Jimmy's ex.

"Morning," I say, leaning up against the kitchen counter. I look out into the backyard and smile. Nick, bless his heart, built little one a playhouse to match our house. Our house. I still can't get over saying that. It has everything I never knew I wanted. It's a two-story colonial with a big fenced-in yard and the necessary privacy we need. As soon as I saw the dark slate blue paint and white shutters I was in love. I didn't care what the inside looked like because just standing outside, I had my dream home.

"Are you okay?" Brigette asks, coming to stand next to me.

I shake my head and lean down to rest my head on the counter. "Everything aches and I think I have a fever."

"Let me check." I allow this because she's become my second mom even though we've just met. I'd give anything to have my mom here and she will be soon, but right now I'm happy that Brigette is with us. "You do feel a little warm. Why don't you go and lie down?"

"Jimmy's sleeping and I don't want to disturb him."

"The sofa will suffice." She starts to guide me to the couch, but my stomach isn't having any of it. I cover my mouth and run off to the bathroom. Brigette follows and holds my hair back as I expel last night's dinner into the Porcelain God.

I heave again and feel a warm trickle run down my legs. "Shit, I just pissed myself," I say through tears. Today is not going to be a great day for me.

"Does your back hurt?"

I nod. "Everything hurts."

After helping me stand, Brigette offers me a washcloth and a glass of water. "Honey, you're in labour. Sit down and I'll go and wake up Jimmy and get you a change of clothes."

"It's not time."

"Apparently little one says it is. You'll be fine. Now sit, I'll be right back."

I do as she says, except the moment I touch the seat a warm geyser rushes out between my legs, soaking the floor mat along with my yoga pants.

"Jimmy," I scream for him. I can hear him coming down the stairs too fast. I close my eyes when I hear a loud thunk followed by a string of curse words. I stand only to be met with an excruciating pain across my stomach. "Oh holy shit," I say as I bend over.

"Jenna," he says as he comes running into the bathroom. "Did you piss yourself, sweet lips?"

I roll my eyes and am about to give him a dirty look when I see how red and swollen his eye is. "Jimmy, your eye?"

"What's wrong with it?" He stands in front of the mirror and fixes his hair. "Oh yeah, it looks like I'll have a nice shiner." He leans forward, examining himself.

"Jimmy," I whine as another contraction rolls over me.

He turns and looks at me. "Oh shit, I forgot."

Great!

He pulls me into his arms. I lean on him, hobbling like I've broken every bone in my body. "Let's get you to the hospital."

"I need to change first."

"Jenna, don't be vain, you're fine. Besides, they'll give you a gown."

"I'm not being ... ahhhhhh, holy fuck." Leaning against the wall, I work on my breathing technique.

"What the hell, Jenna?"

"Oh God, Jimmy, I'm in freaking labor. Where's your mom?"

"Right here, darling. Come on, let's go and get you changed. Jimmy, by the door is Jenna's hospital bag. Take it to the car and bring the car around so we can leave."

"Um ..."

"Now, Jimmy, or Jenna will be delivering little one on your floor."

"Okay, Mum, but you'll stay with Jenna?"

"Yes, now go."

The back and forth with them is dizzying. I lean on Brigette for support as she walks me back to the bathroom. She leans me against the counter while she picks up the soaked floor mat.

"I'll take care of that later. Now let's get you changed."

That awkward moment when your mother-in-law is seeing your lady bits and you don't care. I don't even care that she's running a warm wash cloth up my legs. I want to be clean before having this baby.

"Thank you."

"For what, darling?"

"For being here and accepting me."

Brigette stands before me. "You make my son happy. That's something I haven't seen in a very long time. I should be the one thanking you."

I try to smile in return, but another contraction washes over me. This one is harder and longer. "I think we should go."

"I agree." Brigette washes up before dressing me quickly. She holds my arm as we walk to the door. Jimmy's pacing in the yard with a cigarette hanging out of his mouth.

"Jimmy!" the both of us yell. He looks at us, shocked.

"What the hell are you doing?"

"Waiting for you," he exclaims.

"Why are you smoking?" I demand.

He pulls it away from his lips and looks at it. "It's not lit, innit?"

I brow beat him until he sets it down. "You're going to kill yourself."

"I wasn't going to light it. Come on, sweet lips, let's go have a baby." Instead of walking to the car, Jimmy picks me up and carries me. He shouldn't be doing this, but I feel so much better being in his arms. He sets me in the car and even puts on my seatbelt. Brigette climbs in the back as Jimmy gets behind the wheel.

"I need to call my mom."

"Already taken care of, I called her when I was getting your clothes. She'll be on the next flight out," Brigette says. She starts rubbing my shoulders, easing away some of the tension building. Closing my eyes, I try to relax and breathe through my contractions.

"We're here," Jimmy says, slamming the car into park.

"Take her in, Jimmy, and I'll park the car."

Before I know what's happening my door is open and I'm in his arms. "Put me down, you're going to hurt yourself."

"Bollocks, I don't want the baby to fall out."

Only my husband would think that.

"Hi, Mrs. Davis, ready to have your baby, I see."

"Yep, she's like a burst pipe, she's leaking so much," Jimmy blurts out.

"That's normal. Follow me."

Still in Jimmy's arms, we walk down the hall into a room that is decorated in passion pink. Jimmy groans and I want to bleach my eyes. Who, in their right mind, decorates like this? Do they think all women are the same and just want to stare at pink flowers while pushing out a watermelon?

"This room looks like a bottle of Pepto threw up."

Turning to face me, the nurse smiles. Jimmy sets me down on the bed and stares at my feet. "You're not wearing any shoes."

I look down, he's right. "Imagine that. Guess I would've known had I walked to the car."

The nurse laughs. "Put this on and get comfortable. I'll be back."

Famous last words.

***

"OH MY GOD it hurts so much," I whine to anyone who'll listen. I'm uncomfortable and tired. I've been walking up and down the hall dozens of times. I've sat in every position ever created. I've rocked on a ball through my contractions ... and nothing.

Nothing is making them go away.

"It's almost over, babe."

"How the hell do you know, Jimmy? Do you have some magic spidey sense telling you that the baby is almost here?"

"No, I just thought —"

"Stop thinking."

"Okay."

"Okay? Nothing is okay. I'm in pain and your daughter is stretching me as far as the Grand Canyon. How is this okay?"

Jimmy closes his eyes and rests his head next to mine. I want to push him away, but he gives me the coveted ice chips that are like crack. I know he's holding them hostage and waiting for me to say nice things to him, but that's not going to happen. I'm angry with him right now.

"I love you, Jimmy."

"Love you, too, sweet lips."

My body tightens as a contraction works its way through my abdomen. "It hurts," I whine. Tears, or maybe just sweat, roll down my face.

"I'm sorry."

"You should be. It's your demon sperm that did this to me."

"Jenna—"

"Don't Jenna me. I let you stick that thing in me and now look at me."

"You're having a baby," he says as if he's trying to sweeten me up.

"Babies aren't this evil." I try to turn away from him, but he holds onto me. It should piss me off, but it doesn't.

"I need to go to the bathroom," I say as the pressure increases.

"I'll call the doctor." Jimmy stands but I pull him back to me.

"You can't leave me," I cry out.

"I'm not going to, don't worry." Reaching over, he presses the call button. The door bangs open, causing me to jump.

"How are you feeling, Jenna?" the nurse asks.

"I need to go to the bathroom."

"Let me have a look." *Say what?* The nurse lifts my blanket and puts my feet into the stir-ups. How in the hell is she going to check and see if I have to go to the bathroom? Is there some monitor I'm not aware of? "Looks like we're ready to start pushing."

What's this we shit? Is she pushing, too?

The nurse leaves me with my legs wide open on this joke of a bed only to return with the doctor. He sits down and smiles.

Creepy.

"Jimmy, do you remember what they taught you in Lamaze?"

"Yeah, I do."

"Well, it's time. Okay, Jenna, on the count of three I want you to push."

"How the hell do I do that?"

"I thought you said you had to go to the bathroom?" he asks.

"I do, but you won't let me up," I beg.

"Jenna, it's your body's way of telling you it's time to push. Push out your little girl so you can meet her."

Easier said than done in my opinion, but it's clear no one cares what I think.

Jimmy helps me sit up. He holds my hand as I bear down.

"It burns."

"Again, Jenna."

I do this again and again. Over and over. Each one is more taxing than the one before. Jimmy feeds me ice chips in between the contractions and pushing. He also wipes my forehead for me and moves my hair away from my face. He's doting when all I want to do right now is punch him in the junk. I never want to do this again.

"I can't do this anymore," I say, out of breath.

"Yes, you can, sweet lips. Just one more time."

"Oh, what do you know? You're never touching me again with that evil penis of yours. It's bad news."

"Okay."

"Okay? What, am I not sexy enough to have sex with now? Is it my fault my vagina is going to be as wide as the Atlantic?"

"With proper exercises you can decrease the stretching," the nurse by my head says.

Jimmy and I both look at her. He shakes his head and mutters, "Not cool."

"Jimmy, it hurts."

"I know. I'm sorry."

"Okay, Jenna, she's almost here. Take a look," the doctor says.

Jimmy and the nurse lean me forward and I can see the

top of her head. She has dark hair—it's slimy now but I bet it's beautiful.

"Look, that's our baby."

"She's going to be gorgeous like her mum," he says, kissing me on the lips. "One more push, sweet lips, and you'll get to hold her."

I nod and bear down again. I scream, hoping that the exertion will move her along. I cry when the pressure releases and fall back against my bed. Jimmy stands there looking at the doctor as he's handed a pair of scissors. Wailing starts immediately and while I should be concerned that he's cut our child, I'm not. I'm falling in love with someone I haven't even seen yet.

Little one is set on my chest while the nursing staff and doctors finish up with me. Jimmy sits down beside us. He takes my hand in his and brings it to his lips.

"I'm afraid to touch her," I say.

"I know, me too. We might break her."

Little one opens her eyes briefly before closing them again.

"You should hold her," the nurse says.

I run my finger down her nose and over her cheek. She reacts by moving her head to where my finger is going. I try not to giggle, but I can't help it.

"She's fucking beautiful, Jenna. Thank you so much." Jimmy stands and kisses me before kissing little one.

"She is, isn't she?"

The nurse takes her from us to run all the necessary tests to make sure she's okay. To me, she looks perfect, but I'm her mom; I'm going to be biased.

I hold Jimmy against my chest, my tears wetting his hair. "I'm sorry for being so mean."

He shakes his head and pulls away. His eyes are filled with tears, and one is definitely bruised, giving him the bad boy vibe. "I love you so much, Jenna. As long as you never tell me to leave you, I don't care what you say to me."

43

JIMMY

I'm left in the "Pepto" room (as Jenna calls it) with just a few nurses, while another one takes Jenna to the bathroom. I watch them as they weigh and measure little one, whose arms are waving around like crazy. She looks like a little boxer and has a set of windpipes that can go on for days. I'm not sure how on earth I'm going to get used to this crying. It just means I'll have to find a way to appease her. To make her happy because hearing her scream her little lungs off like this makes me want to take her in my arms and hold her tightly so I can take away her worries. Worries that she shouldn't have because her daddy is going to make everything better.

Daddy.

Daddy.

The word falls off my tongue like it's a foreign word. Even though I've said it many times when Jenna was pregnant it didn't have the meaning that it has now. I'm her daddy. I'm going to be the person she'll go to until some bloke comes along and tries to take my place. I'm responsible for this little creature and will be until she tells me that she's old enough to take care of herself. I can never see that happening. I'm going to make sure she always needs her daddy.

Jenna comes out of the bathroom looking as beautiful as ever. Her smile lights up her face and makes her eyes sparkle. She just accomplished a feat so glorious I'm not sure I can love her anymore. She brought my daughter—our daughter—into this world and has made our family complete.

The nurse guides her to the bed, and helps her get comfortable. How Jenna can walk after giving birth astounds me—she is frikking amazing. After what I just witnessed her body go through, I'd be bloody knackered. I'd probably want to curl up in a ball and beg for my mum to come in and make it all go away. I can admit I'm chicken shit when it comes to pain. That thought alone makes me grateful that I don't remember being shot. I've experienced enough of the horror story from Liam and Harrison to know it was a fucking nightmare. I'm perfectly fine remaining ignorant and not remembering all the pain I was in.

I don't know what to do. Go to Jenna or continue to watch the nurses fuss over little one? They're gushing—as they should be—at how beautiful she is. She looks like Jenna, but with dark hair. Not gonna lie, I was hoping she'd have dark red hair, a mixture of mine and Jenna's, but I'll take her just the way she is because she's ours.

Little one is wrapped up in a blanket and carried to Jenna. The nurse bypasses me as if I'm not even in the room. I get that she's the mother, but what am I? Do women really just consider the man the "demon sperm donor" and nothing else?

I follow the nurse like a lost puppy dog as she hands little one to Jenna. She's sitting up, smiling. When I look at her, I see nothing but pure elation. It dawns on me that she was going to have little one whether I was in the picture or not. I should feel good about that, but a part of me wonders where I'd be right now if I wasn't here. Nowhere, that's where. I'd be lost and still trudging through mud trying to find a purpose in life. I'd be half the man I am now and knowing that, I wouldn't change what I've got now for anything.

Jenna looks at me after little one is placed in her arms. The nurse leaves the room, giving us time to bond with our daughter. Jenna pats the side of her bed, beckoning me to sit next to her. I can't deny her. I'll never be able to deny her of anything she wants from me. I climb onto the bed slowly and with caution. I know she's sore, but she's not showing any signs of being in pain. It's easy for me to remember how gentle she was with me when I was in a bed like this. Her touch was as light as a feather and she left me begging for more. I wanted to hold her then and I want to hold her now.

My arm rests on her shoulder, allowing my fingers to touch the top of little one's head. She's wearing an offensive pink hat—the sure-fire sign that she's a girl—because all babies look the same; except my daughter is beauty personi-fied. Jenna runs her finger along little one's cheek and she raises it in a little smile.

Jenna reaches up to her shoulder and unsnaps her gown. Her glorious boob appears magically, and while I shouldn't be turned on, I am. I know I'm going to hell thinking that my wife, who has just given birth, is ready for sex, but I can't help it. I watch in awe as she brings little one to her chest to feed her. We learned about this in Lamaze class and if I hadn't just witnessed this moment I wouldn't believe it. Little one knows exactly what to do.

"Amazing," I say quietly.

"She is, isn't she?"

"Her mum is, too." I kiss Jenna on the forehead as she feeds our daughter. Every so often she runs her finger over little one's cheek, causing her to start sucking again.

"Does it hurt?"

"A little. The nurse said my nipples wouldn't be used to the sucking."

"Bollocks, I suck on them all the time."

Jenna rolls her eyes. "It's different."

"Want me to suck on the other one to get it ready?"

Jenna gives me a dirty look, but I burst out laughing. "No, Jimmy. You have to be patient."

"How patient?" I'm afraid to know the answer.

"At least six weeks."

"Six weeks? But I just got you back yesterday."

She shakes her head and pulls little one away from one of my favourite parts of her body.

"How do you know she's finished?"

Jenna shrugs. "My milk's not in yet, so right now she's just getting my antibodies to help her fight any infections."

"And that's enough?"

"It is for right now."

"Amazing."

JENNA and I agreed that I'd take little one out to the waiting room for everyone to meet her. She's tired, which is understandable, and doesn't want any company right now. Jenna places our daughter in my arms. A surge of warmth spreads through my body as I hold her to my chest. I wish her eyes would open so I could see her and she could see us. I know she's going to be the most loved little girl ever. All in due time I suppose.

"I love you, wifey. I'll be back soon." I kiss her on the lips before taking our baby out of the room. I don't want to be gone too long, but I know the importance of the group waiting to see her. They're my family.

As soon as I open the door, the two grandmothers meet me. How Jenna's mum got here so quickly is beyond me, but she'll be happy to know she's here.

"Say hi to your nana and grandma," I whisper into little one's ear. She doesn't react, but the mums do. They both cover their mouths and allow the happy tears to flow freely.

"Oh, Jimmy, she's so beautiful," my mum exclaims.

I nod. "You should see her mum, she's the most gorgeous woman in the world."

Mrs. Hardy steps forward. "Can I?"

As much as I want to say no, I can't. Her baby just had a baby and I can't begin to imagine what she's going through. I place little one in her arms and watch in amazement as the woman who gave me Jenna coo's over our daughter.

"She's so perfect."

Again, I'm not about to disagree with her on that one.

The mums take turns holding and gushing over the baby. I stand back and watch, wishing Jenna were witnessing this. But she wants to get some rest and I understand that more than anyone.

Finally, after a long, torturous five minutes, they hand her back to me. The moment she's in my arms, I'm both elated and calm. My heart is racing but in a good way. I'm breathing easily now and don't feel like I'm going to struggle anytime soon. Did I need little one to make me feel this way?

I walk into the waiting room and am met with a sea of eager faces. Josie and Katelyn are the first to stand up, but they keep their distance. Liam and Harrison stand behind their significant others and it dawns on me that I'm the only one who has witnessed their child being born. I can't even begin to imagine what's going through their minds right now.

I hold my arms up so they can see my daughter. The women, of course, gasp.

"I'd like to introduce Eden Davis, who made her way into the world at 11:59 a.m. weighing six pounds and eight ounces."

"Eden?" my mum says.

I nod. "Yeah, her name is Eden, or little one. I'm pretty sure she'll answer to both."

"Such a pretty name for a pretty baby."

"Thanks, Mum."

No one asks to hold her and for that I'm grateful. I have a feeling I'm going to be one of those parents who worry about germs and whether or not you've washed your hands or have a cold. I'm a dad now; these things are important. I have to protect her at all costs.

"Jenna is a little tired and has asked that you come back

later at dinnertime. She wants to have a nap for a bit. I can tell you, however, that she almost certainly hates me, even though I know that she loves me really. She says I'm not allowed to touch her again and I have demon sperm."

"I can attest to that," Katelyn says. "I hated Mason for the last trimester of my pregnancy. He was so happy we were having twins, though, and he'd carry them around like footballs."

"I remember that," Josie says. "When I was delivering Noah, I cursed Liam something fierce and prayed his dick would fall off."

"Hey?"

"What?" she says, looking at him. "I was young and in pain. Your son was a beast with his broad shoulders."

"Are you saying you don't want another one?" Liam asks Josie. The expression on his face is priceless while he waits for her to answer. She drags out her response, making his pained expression even more comical.

"No, I'm not saying that at all," Josie says, shrugging her shoulders as if having a baby is no big deal. Or maybe she's telling Liam he's no big deal. Either way, his face is full of determination.

"Good, let's go home and try for a while until we can see Jenna."

Liam pretty much drags Josie away. He stops and pats me on the shoulder as he walks by. "Little Eden, you have such a big family with lots of cousins who'll protect you from everything. Good luck ever finding a boyfriend."

I didn't have a big family growing up, but knowing that she does fills my heart with pride and love.

"She's precious, Jimmy."

"Thanks, Katelyn."

"We'll be back, JD. Go be with your wife and daughter. I wasn't there when Quinn was born, but the second he entered my life, I never wanted to let him out of my sight."

I nod. "I know. I almost had a panic attack when the grandmas were holding her. I'm not even sure how I'm going to give her back to Jenna."

"You'll find a way to share," Katelyn says, kissing me on my cheek.

The grandmothers kiss Eden and then me, promising to return with clothes and proper food in a few hours.

When I walk back into Jenna's room, she's asleep. I move quietly and sit in the rocking chair with Eden in my arms.

"Mummy's sleeping little one, so it's just you and me."

She makes this little squeaking sound and moves her head. It's going to be another sound that I need to record on my phone.

I place her on my chest and start rocking. Her head rests in the crook of my neck, which is her mum's favourite place. The warmth from her fills me, and as much as I don't want to, I can't help the tears as they fall. There was a chance that I could've missed this if it hadn't been for Liam being upset. If I weren't trying to find a way to talk to Jenna, I wouldn't have been in Beaumont that night. Everything that's good in my life right now is because of Liam. He's the glue keeping us together.

Little one squeaks again, and even though it's quiet, I don't want her to wake Jenna. I do what I've been doing since I found out I was going to be a dad. I sing to her.

After we set sail, there's gonna be storms
Just don't lose faith in me cause I'll keep us on course
Remember this day, it's written in the stars
We're on our way to forever, girl it's not that far
I've never felt like this before
I see our ship comin' from the shore
And that horizon in your eyes
Is like Tobacco Sunburst

"Someday, little one, you'll write songs or play the guitar. Maybe you'll be a novelist or a painter. As long as you're happy I'll do whatever I can help you succeed."

44

JENNA

The sound of Jimmy's voice wakes me. It's a pleasant sound, one that I love to listen to. I open my eyes slightly, but what I see needs all my attention. I move as quietly as I can so I can watch the scene in front of me.

Jimmy holds our daughter snug against this chest, rocking her back and forth. His eyes are closed, but he's singing to her. His head rests on hers in the sweetest of embraces. I wish I had my phone to take a picture because this is a moment I want to capture forever.

"What are you doing?" His voice startles me. He grins, which turns my insides to goo. He was sexy before, but seeing him hold our daughter puts him on a whole other level. I wink at him, causing him to shake his head.

"I heard you singing."

"Did I wake you?" he asks so quietly. Our life has changed now and we didn't even make an attempt to do so. With the arrival of Eden, we just know everything is different.

"We're having a girl."

"I know," I say, holding his hand against my stomach. "You with a daughter ... scary," I add, shaking my head. Jimmy kisses my nose then my lips.

"I'll be scared shitless, but I'm going to love every minute of it. I want to be a part of this, Jenna. I know I screwed up staying in L.A. for so long. My dad ... No, I don't want him to ruin our day. We're having a daughter, a daughter who needs a name by the way."

"I have a feeling naming her will be hard."

"Why?"

I shrug. "Name association."

Jimmy laughs even though I don't think it's funny. I don't want to pick my daughter's name and have it be the same as some bimbo he hooked up with. And I hope he doesn't tell me that he doesn't know most of their names. That wouldn't make me feel any better because honestly some things are better left unknown.

"Eden," he blurts out.

"Excuse me?"

Jimmy shrugs. "Eden, and let me tell you why," he says, pulling me over to the couch. We sit down and he turns to face me, holding my hand in his. "When I first met you, I knew you were off limits. The way Liam spoke about you was a warning sign. But everything about you made me curious. It was a little hair flip or the way your forehead smushes together when you're thinking. But the breaking point was the wedding and everything leading up to that moment. Watching you that night was complete torture. Having you, making you mine for those sacred moments, was my undoing. To me, you're my forbidden fruit. I can't get enough of *you, Jenna, and I think Eden represents what we created together."*

"Okay," I say, wiping tears away with the back of my hand. "I like Eden Davis. It sounds perfect." *Jimmy kisses me, holding my face in his hands.*

He leans down and pulls my shirt up over my belly. His lips press into my skin. "Eden Davis. That's your name, little one, and we can't wait to meet you."

Jimmy moves with caution as he carries Eden over to me. I move aside, still sore, but feeling better. He climbs on the bed, putting her on my chest. She stretches her neck and makes the most beautiful sound ever.

"I love that sound," Jimmy says, echoing my thoughts.

"Me too." I pull her close and rest my head on his shoulder.

"Let me take a photo." Jimmy pulls out his phone and holds it out in front of us. I turn Eden around and hold her between us. He presses the button and pulls the phone closer to us so we can see our first family photo.

"She's perfect."

"You both are. I can't even begin to explain how happy I am right now, Jenna." Jimmy kisses Eden on the forehead before kissing me. "You've changed my life and it's definitely for the better."

I lean into Jimmy and relish this moment. He has no idea how much he's changed my life and I don't know if I'll ever find the words to tell him.

"Surprise!" my mom and Brigette yell in unison.

"Hi, Mom," I say when she steps forward. She comes around to the side of the bed and pulls me into a hug. I refuse to move, not ready to let go of Eden yet.

"I'm so proud of you, sweetheart. She's absolutely gorgeous."

"Thank you." My voice breaks. Her approval means so much to me. After everything I've been through I know she never thought she'd see this day. But it's here and she's a grandma. Mom wipes her tears and steps away, allowing Brigette a moment with us.

"I want both the grandmas to have a photo taken with you and Eden," Jimmy says as he leaves my side.

"Jimmy, I look like crap," I whine.

"Nonsense, Jenna. You're a new mom. There's nothing more beautiful about that," my mom says.

"I agree," Jimmy says as his mom and mine each take a spot next to Eden and me. Each mom places a hand on Eden as I hold her up for Jimmy to take a picture.

"Say cheese, my favourite ladies."

I smile big enough that my cheeks hurt. I know how much this picture will mean to Jimmy and to me.

AFTER ONE NIGHT in the hospital I'm ready to go home. My bag is packed thanks to my mom. Eden is dressed, thanks to her dad, and ready to make her public debut. I was worried about the press, but thankfully none of the nurses called anyone so we'll be able to introduce Eden when we're ready.

Jimmy, of course, says she's ready now. I swear we should've had a boy. He has her dressed in a 4225 West baby outfit, custom made, and her dark hair is spiked ... with a pink ribbon. I gave him props for the ribbon.

I sit down in the wheelchair, holding Eden in her car seat on my lap. Harrison gave Jimmy an hour's long lesson on how to install the base in the back of the car. Jimmy says he has it mastered. This, I'm going to have to trust him on. The moms have already taken the copious amounts of flowers and gifts we received home. Everyone will be there for Eden's homecoming, and as much as I'd love to sleep, it won't happen at least for the next few hours.

He wheels us out, saying good-bye to the nursing staff as we pass. I think in the day and half that we've been here, he's charmed each and every one of them. Typical Jimmy.

The sliding glass doors open. I cover my eyes from the penetrating sun. I make sure Eden's blanket is over her carrier to block the sunlight. The last thing I want is a sick baby so soon. The car is all ready, having been brought around by valet. Valet in a hospital, who knew?

Jimmy takes Eden from me and places her in the backseat. He helps me from the wheelchair and guides me to the back. I told him that I want to be close to her. I want to watch her take her first car ride. I want to be the first person that she sees when she opens her eyes.

He drives away and though I would have expected him to drive like an eighty-year-old man, I was sadly mistaken. Jimmy's Jimmy, and not everything will change overnight.

The trees in front of our house are decorated with pink ribbons and balloons. The cars belonging to our friends line the street. My heart beats with anticipation of Eden making her grand appearance. I can't imagine all new babies do this, but Eden just isn't any baby, she's Jimmy's and he does things to the tenth degree.

Jimmy pulls into our driveway and shuts off the car. He

runs around the front to the backdoor, pulling it open. He helps me out before leaning in and unhooking Eden's car seat. Holding the carrier in one hand, he grasps my hand in his other. I kick the car door closed with my foot and smile at my family as we walk toward our party.

"Well, isn't this special."

My blood turns cold at the sound of Damien's voice. I don't dare turn around and face him because if I do, he'll be real. I eye Jimmy and Eden and the backyard wondering how they can escape. Damien wants me, not them.

"Turn around, Jenna."

I close my eyes and let the tears fall. My life is over. I'll never see her first birthday. I'll never see her dress for prom or watch her walk across the stage for graduation. I won't be there when she has her first boyfriend and her first heartbreak. I squeeze Jimmy's hand tightly.

"Don't," he says, quietly.

"I have to." I turn slowly and face the man who made it possible for me to stand here today. Yes, he was my husband, but he took his vows to the extreme and beat me. If he hadn't done that, I wouldn't be here right now.

"Is that your baby? Humph, at least you're not as fat now."

I wish I could say no, but it's obvious. I still have a pouch and my daughter is being held by her father right now.

"You know, I thought I killed that man you've been allowing to violate your body, but I guess I didn't do a good enough job."

I face Damien, waiting for him to deliver my punishment.

"What do you want, Damien?"

"You. I told you that I wanted you back, but you didn't believe me. You went and married this piece of shit and allowed him to do things to you. Things that you said you'd only do with me. You let him taint your body and now you've bore him a bastard."

Closing my eyes, I pray for help to arrive. He's going to hurt my family, not me. He's going to take away Jimmy and Eden, leaving me broken and empty.

"Say good-bye, Jenna."

"You're not taking her anywhere," Jimmy yells. I hope his voice carries loud enough into the house. We need help.

"She'll come willingly. I won't have to force her," Damien says calmly.

"Jenna doesn't love you."

"Of course she does. Don't you, Jenna?"

I don't answer, he knows. He knows I don't love him. If I did, I would've stayed and taken the beatings.

"*Don't you?*" He pulls out his gun and points it at Jimmy. He marches closer, just a few feet from us. Eden starts to cry, but we can't do anything to help her.

"Damien, please stop." I let go of Jimmy's hand and step in front of him. He stops me. "Just stop. I'll come with you, but you have to let them go in the house. The baby, she needs to eat and you don't want her to starve."

"I don't care about that bastard child. Put her on the ground."

"*No!*" Jimmy yells.

"*Put her the fuck down before I shoot her!*"

"*No!*" I scream, and step in front of Eden as Damien points his gun at her. The gun fires and all time stops.

45

JIMMY

I sit on the floor, playing with Eden. Her hair is an odd color, but it's completely unique to her personality. It's still dark, but with natural red highlights. It's definitely a combination of Jenna and me. I still like to put it in a Mohawk with a bow, just for a bit of fun. It drives Jenna nuts, but she never changes it. Little one is rolling over now. She thinks it's fun, until she gets stuck and can't get back to where she was. She screams. I say she's saying daddy, but Jenna assures me she's just making noises to get my attention. The minute her little yelp is out of her mouth, I'm always there to help her. Eden knows that I'll never leave her.

It's been two months since the shooting that changed our lives. I felt guilty at first, but now there's a sense of relief knowing that Jenna's ex won't be able to harm my family ever again. When the gun went off I didn't know what to do. I froze and so did Jenna. I was afraid to put Eden down, but I had to find out where Jenna had been hit. When she looked at me with tears in her eyes, I thought for sure that I had lost her. But the telltale sound of someone hitting their head hard caught our attention. Everything was in slow motion as we turned and saw Paul Baker standing in front of us with his gun pointed at where Damien was standing.

That day my eyes moved so slowly until they landed upon Damien on the ground, eyes closed and blood dripping from his mouth. I knew instantly that he was dead. What I didn't know was how Jenna was going to react. He was her first love and people don't forget that.

The back door opens. The sound of keys being thrown onto the kitchen-top echo through the house—it's a bad sign.

"Mummy's home," I say to Eden whose legs shake wildly. She loves her mum and gets most of her attention these days, but I'm okay with it. Eden's hard to compete with, but I guess that's what happens when you have a baby. Jenna dotes on her, and so do I.

"Hi, wifey," I say loud enough for her to hear me.

"Hi." I look up at the sound of her voice. She's leaning against the doorframe and has a piece of paper hanging from her fingers.

"What's that?" I nod to the paper.

She holds it up, as if she's going to read it. "A letter from Damien's parents."

I sit up suddenly and put Eden in her vibrating chair and place her tiny fingers around her favourite monkey to keep her occupied. I stand up, walk over to Jenna, and pull her into my arms.

"Do you want to me to read it?"

She shakes her head. "I thought we could read it together. Anything they have to say they need to say to the both of us."

"Okay." I lead her over to the sofa. I sit down first, and pull her onto my lap. Resting my head on her shoulder, I wait. Jenna clears her throat, but before she can start Eden lets it known that she's missing out on cuddle time.

Jenna gets up and takes her out of her seat. She hands Eden to me and thankfully resumes her spot on my lap. This is another moment that I want to capture, sans the letter that has my wife so upset, so I can remember it forever.

"Dearest Jenna,

When Damien brought you home for the first time we knew that he had met his destruction, we just didn't realize we'd lose our son in the process. The way Damien looked at you, the way he spoke about you, and the way he moved around you, you owned his heart. We were so happy when you married and couldn't wait for you to start a family.

It broke our heart when he confessed that he had hit you and continued to do so because it gave him a release that he couldn't explain. We offered to get him help, but he wouldn't admit that what he was doing was wrong. He said that you'd forgiven him after each episode only for him to find that he needed to do it again to keep you close to him.

We don't know where he learned to be abusive, but it wasn't in our home when we raised him. Society? Friends? We'll never know. What we do know is that when you left him, you took his heart with you. He looked in every possible place until he saw a woman that looked just like you. He said he needed to go and find you, to bring you home.

Damien told us that your first meeting didn't go as planned, but that he was going to make you fall in love with him again. We're just sorry that he'll never have the opportunity to love again, unlike you.

I hope this letter finds you well and that you're moving on. We're trying, but being a mother now, you know parents should never have to bury their children. But we have and we must live with the knowledge that we could've prevented all of this from happening.

"They didn't sign it. I guess that's their way of not getting closure or something." Jenna leans her head on my shoulder. Her fingers play with Eden's. "I don't even know why they wrote me. The tone ... they're blaming me."

"You know it's not your fault, right?"

"I know."

"People like that can't accept the responsibility that they failed as parents. He hit you, shot me with intent to kill, and was going to shoot our daughter. I'm happy Paul was invited to Eden's homecoming because if he hadn't been there at that moment ... I don't even want to think about it."

Jenna folds the letter and puts it on the cushion. I'm going to shred that stupid piece of crappy paper the minute I get up from holding my girls, but until then I'm going to keep them in my arms, grateful that I have them.

I almost lost them, too many times to mention. When I look at Jenna and Eden, I see my forever. She's the one I'm going to grow old with. She's the one who is going to laugh at me when my Mohawk won't stand up any longer or when Eden brings home a rock star boyfriend. Jenna's the one that is going to be by my side when I walk my daughter down the aisle and we'll be together when we become grandparents. We'll have matching rocking chairs on our front porch and we'll sip tea—even though I hate it—out of silly little teacups with our little fingers in the air because that will make her laugh.

Who knew that finding my forever would be so easy? I just needed my best mate to get married so I could hook-up with the bridesmaid. That's me in a nutshell, innit?

Want more of the Beaumont Series? Take a trip back to the beginning, before Liam Westbury became Liam Page in Finding My Way. Looking for a holiday romance or two, check out The Dating Series.

Stay up to date by joining Heidi's reader group on Facebook or sign up for her newsletter.

ACKNOWLEDGMENTS

First and foremost: I have to thank the fans because without you The Beaumont Series isn't possible. Your continued support and encouragement means the world to me.

And to Yvette: who once again has slaved tirelessly over my rambling to make it sound nice and pretty. You brought Jimmy to life and for that I can never thank you enough.

Now to my AMAZING Street Team: I gave you an impossible challenge when I handed you Finding My Forever and you all nailed it, each and every one of you. You're more than a street team; you're best friends, family, sounding boards and confidants. I can't imagine not having you part of not only this series, but others as well. Everything you tell me I take to heart.

Sarah when you sent me the cover Finding My Forever, I yelled YES, loudly! I love staring at this cover.

Ellie at Love N. Books: how do I begin to thank you? I probably can't in all honesty. You pushed me to make a decision that I'll forever be in debt to you for. You probably don't hear this enough, but you were right – haha! Any author who gets to work with you in the future should consider themselves lucky. Without your constant "trust me" my cover wouldn't be as fabulous as it is.

Brandyn Farrell: thank you for putting a "face" to Jimmy. To say you fit him perfectly is an understatement. The only thing missing is a British accent. Can you master that before a signing?

Eric Heatherly: How you can supply the perfect song is beyond me, but I love it. Thank you for being on this journey with me and providing my guys with the music that they needed to complete their stories.

To my family: Thank you for your continued support. Thank you for encouraging my crazy ideas and for helping create new ones.

To my girls: You're both so creative and your imaginations are wild. I can't wait to see what you do. You both have your own amazing stories ready to be written and I can't wait to help guide you through the process.

ABOUT HEIDI MCLAUGHLIN

Heidi McLaughlin is a New York Times, Wall Street Journal, and USA Today Bestselling author of The Beaumont Series, The Boys of Summer, and The Archers.

Originally, from the Pacific Northwest, she now lives in picturesque Vermont, with her husband, two daughters, and their three dogs.

In 2012, Heidi turned her passion for reading into a full-fledged literary career, writing over twenty novels, including the acclaimed Forever My Girl.

Heidi's first novel, Forever My Girl, has been adapted into a motion picture with LD Entertainment and Roadside Attractions, starring Alex Roe and Jessica Rothe, and opened in theaters on January 19, 2018.

Don't miss more books by Heidi McLaughlin! Sign up for her newsletter, or join the fun in her fan group!

Connect with Heidi!
www.heidimclaughlin.com

ALSO BY HEIDI MCLAUGHLIN

THE BEAUMONT SERIES

Forever My Girl

My Everything #1.5

My Unexpected Forever

Finding My Forever

Finding My Way

12 Days of Forever #4.5

My Kind of Forever

Forever Our Boys #5.5

The Beaumont Boxed Set - #1

THE BEAUMONT SERIES: NEXT GENERATION

Holding Onto Forever

My Unexpected Love

Chasing My Forever

Peyton & Noah

Fighting For Our Forever

CAPE HARBOR SERIES

After All

Until Then

THE ARCHER BROTHERS

Here with Me

Choose Me

Save Me

LOST IN YOU SERIES

Lost in You

Lost in Us

THE BOYS OF SUMMER

Third Base

Home Run

Grand Slam

Hawk

THE REALITY DUET

Blind Reality

Twisted Reality

SOCIETY X

Dark Room

Viewing Room

Play Room

THE DATING SERIES

A Date for Midnight

A Date with an Admirer

A Date for Good Luck

A Date for the Hunt

A Date for the Derby

A Date to Play Fore

THE CLUTCH SERIES

Roman

STANDALONE NOVELS

Stripped Bare

Blow

Sexcation

Santa's Secret

SNEAK PEEK

Love Quarrel Stirs Violence among High School Teachers. I can just picture the headlines if I were to lose control and hit that hussy square in the jaw.

But there she goes looking all superior, and I feel the urge to rip out her dark brown extensions and shove them straight down her throat. As tempting as it may be, I know for the sake of my career, I can't just haul off and knock someone out—and especially not over a guy. What kind of example would I be setting in a hallway full of hormonal adolescent students? So I guess I can understand why dating someone at work is not encouraged, especially when I want to punch that man-stealing whore. If she wasn't such a floozy, maybe I could move on. Maybe I wouldn't want him back so badly if he had left me for someone less sleazy. Not this waif in six-inch stilettos, acrylic nails, smothered in every possible product from the MAC counter. But this is who—or what—he chose. And yes, I still want him so bad it hurts.

A group of chatty kids snap me out of my frenzy.

"Check her out. I'd like to tap that ass," a squirrely freshman boy says, raising eyebrows at the previously mentioned man-stealing whore, my colleague—a science teacher—walking down the hall as if it were an America's Next Top Model runway. If she were in my class, I'd send her out for dress code violations on a daily basis. There's no doubt she heard him too, and liked it. If only I was a student again, I'd be tempted to stick glue in her body lotion during gym. That would wipe the smile off her face.

"I know right, if she were homework, I'd do her every night," his friend replies. They slap hands wildly in agreement. Great. Not only do half the male teachers here want her, the students are even drooling over this hoochie.

"Gross," one of the girls in the huddle says, smacking Boy #2 in the chest.

Another young lady chimes in, "Dude, she's a teacher. That's so wrong."

"So," Boy #1 retorts. "I'm sure teachers like to get it on." He pumps his hips back and forth, reminding me of Peewee from the old Porky's movies. Sucking back the urge to gag, I have to stop myself from going over to them and smacking him in the back of the head. Little pervert.

"Eww. They're so old. That's just nasty on so many levels." Girl #2 shudders at the thought. Now, I want to smack her.

"Yeah, it's like admitting our parents have sex. There's no way teachers do it," Girl #1 adds. Okay, I'm about to do a whole heck of a lot of smacking. These children are going to need ice packs when I'm done with them for all their stupid talk. We're teachers, not nuns and priests. No vow of celibacy here.

"Thanks," he pauses, staring her down. "You totally killed it." Boy #2 stalks off into class. The others follow, snickering.

Brats!

The bell rings. A few stragglers rush through the door just as I'm about to close it, and I have the overwhelming desire to change my welcome back spiel.

Good morning losers! Just an FYI. Teachers do have sex. Just like we eat, shit, and sleep every day. We also have to go to the grocery store so don't be in shock when you see me at Albertson's and I have a box of Tampax in my cart. I also have to buy clothes, so you might also see me at the mall and if you even make a face when I hit the dressing room with a year's supply of Spanx, I may be forced to mark your papers with a big fat bleeding F for the rest of the year. So, yes, teachers have sex! And it's not gross and it's not like your parents doing it either. But for crying out loud, gentlemen, don't go blind fantasizing about that skank you saw in the hall. She doesn't have sex. She just fucks—excuse my language.

Damn it. Listening to student chatter before class has totally thrown me for a loop. I'm totally off my first-day-of-school game. My students are looking up at me like little puppies wanting table food, and I don't have any scraps. I can't think of shit to say.

The ridiculous conversation between a bunch of sex-crazed teenagers should really have little affect on me. I wouldn't be bothered if those skinny little boys were talking about anyone else. But no..., they're poppin' chubs over Ms.

McGallian. And, while teachers do have sex, and Ms. McGallian is having plenty, I for one, am not. I'm not even fucking for Christ's sake. Oh shit, I just said Christ and fuck in the same sentence. Scratch that. I just said shit, Christ, and fuck in the same sentence. Twice.

One more thing ... we fucking cuss too, bitches.

While I wait for my Lean Cuisine to cool down enough to not cause first degree burns in my mouth, I notice my lunch isn't the only thing sizzling. The anger boils in my gut, and I wish it wasn't. I honestly wish I didn't care so much.

"Come on, Shel. It's the first day back and you're already showing your fangs. You look like you wanna rip off her head, shred her to pieces, and burn her hoochified remains," my bestie tells me, hand on her hip in disapproval.

Lowering my head at her, I try my hardest to give her the look. "Mel, the Twilight references are getting old. Besides, you're thirty-two. Can you please move beyond YA books and fantasize about guys who are legal?" I ask my best friend of twenty-two years.

"Edward is legal. He's over a hundred years old." Melissa, who I've called Mel since the fourth grade, tosses her lunch on the table and sits next to me. "And I'm married. I dream about every man I see, or read about. Thank God for fantasies or I'd never get the chance to be manhandled by so many beautiful men."

Allowing a grin to form, I have to try to stop full-blown laughter so I won't encourage her antics. "Yeah well, you're a slut in your fantasies."

She takes a huge bite of her sandwich and says, with grape jelly oozing out the side of her mouth, "I guess that makes me a fantastic slut." She winks at me and I can't help but laugh. She always manages to make me feel better. "Oh shit, here we go, Shel. Be cool."

"What?" I ask, watching Mel tense up and take a deep breath.

"He's here."

He's here?

And by he, she means my ex-boyfriend. My ex-love-ofmylife. My ex-almostthefatherofmychildren. My ex-happilyeverafter. My ex-fiancé. My ex who left me for that Kim Kardashian butt double, Ms. McGallian. He'd argue he didn't leave me for the curvy brunette with the million dollar highlights, big boobs, and scary acrylic nails. Of course he didn't. I mean, they started dating less than a month after he called it quits. Yet, I'm supposed to believe she had nothing to do with it. She's had practically every single man, a few of them married, on this damn campus and she couldn't let my guy escape her claws. No. She dug right in and he didn't even try to run from little Ms. Fake-Everything-From-Head-To-Toe.

I don't see him, but I'm sure he sees Mel's sneer. She's practically stabbing a dagger through his chest with her eyes. Maybe she could will his pecker to fall off. That seems like a fair punishment for dumping my ass after ten plus years.

But, that was last year. Summer vacation should've been enough time for me to lick my wounds and get over the bastard, but one look at him and my heart turns to mush all over again. His thick black hair is getting long and wavy, and I want to go over there and grab a handful of it. He must have gone shopping. I've never seen that shirt before. It actually has bling on it. She probably bought it for him. The Chase I know would never wear a shirt with wings on it. But, whatever. The Chase I know would have never dumped the woman he was engaged to either.

"Stop with the eyes already," Mel whispers, kicking me under the table.

"Ow. What the hell?"

She glares down at me, big Betty Boop brown eyes, with unnaturally long lashes, bulging from their sockets. Her eyes are the only things big about my best friend. She's this petite little thing: barely five feet tall, having stopped growing in the sixth grade. "Don't even look at him with those sad, pathetic eyes. It's been four months. Don't let him see you like this. Don't let her." Too bad her mouth isn't small and gentle like her frame. Her brash, sassy talk more than makes up for her elfin size.

I can't help glancing over at their table again. My eyes meet the tramp's and I'm certain I see a smirk on her face. Give me five seconds alone with this bitch. She'll be declawed in three, and with the other two, I'll punch her in each tit just for fun. I know I shouldn't take it all out on her, but Mel has Chase taken care of. Right about now, his balls are being hacked off with an ax in her mind.

Four months is clearly not long enough to get over someone you've been with half your life, I want to tell Mel. But I don't. My shin still stings from her swift kick and rubbing it like crazy is keeping me from looking in the happy couple's direction, again. I must look like an idiot massaging up and down my leg, but it beats the alternative.

Repeatedly seeing Ms. McGallian and my ex together will make this first day of school the worst in my career. Although, I'm pretty sure this entire year is going to kill me.

I may need to rethink my profession. Or maybe consider a transfer, at the very least. When people break up and go their separate ways, the dumpee is bound to get over the dumper after days and days apart. There's just one huge problem here: the dumpee and the dumper will be seeing each other five days a week, along with the ho bag who is now shacking up with the dumper. Now, the dumpee is feeling even dumpier.

"I'm gonna start eating in my classroom." It seems impossible to handle another day like this one, where I have to concentrate on not letting my eyes wander.

Mel shoots me another irritated look. "Don't you dare. You are not going to let them force you to hide out in your room all year. They should be the ones who hide in shame. But that bitch wants to rub it in your face." She's right. She always is. I shouldn't let her get to me.

"FYI... if I can hear this conversation on the other side of the room, so can they," a voice whispers in my ear. I look up and I'm eye to eye with Matty. He gives me a sympathetic look, squeezes my shoulder, and walks away.

"Dang, that guy wants you so bad," Mel says quietly, fluttering her brows at me.

"Mr. Fuller is a good friend. It's not like that," I remind her.

"Well as I've heard on many Lifetime Movie Originals, 'the best way to get over a man is to get under another one.' I doubt Matt Fuller will mind being on top if you know what I mean."

"You're scandalous."

Get under another one? Is she crazy? I guess if I ever did manage to get under another man, Matty would be high on my list of choices, if only we didn't work together. Whose list wouldn't he be on? The man is delicious with his bright blue eyes that twinkle every time he smiles, and his well-built physique and bronze skin. Every inch of his six-foot body is beautiful, inside and out. If I had to choose between him and Chase based solely on looks, Matty would beat him every day of the week. Chase is great looking and uber sexy. Women check Chase out all the time. But Matty, he's absolutely gorgeous and there's not an arrogant cell in his entire body. Now, there's the major difference between the two men.

And one more thing while I'm thinking about over and under, top and bottom.

If and when I decide to 'get over' my sexy, cheating ex, I will most definitely be on top.

Weeks later, I'm eating my Trader Joe's Pasadena Salad in my classroom. Alone. Mel refuses to eat with me. She's so damn stubborn. I know she wants to, but she keeps telling me, "It's the principality." Principality—that's not even a word. Not in the way she's using it. And she's an English teacher. Go figure.

The door opens slowly as I stuff my mouth with a forkful of lettuce, almonds, and chicken. I almost choke when I see who it is. In fact, I knew who it was the moment I caught a whiff of the air wafting in with him. Chase has been wearing Eternity for Men since we were in high school. I'm surprised Ms. Blingyshirts hasn't changed his scent too. At any rate, his timing couldn't be worse. My mouth is overflowing and I can barely chew. Time plays in slow motion as he makes his way to my desk. How anyone can look so sexy just merely walking is beyond me. There are no words to describe it. I blink hard and fast to snap myself out of his trance. Spitting back a wad of half-chewed salad in its container, I sneer, "What the hell do you want?"

Like my strategy? In an effort to not break down and cry hysterically every time I'm alone with this asshole, I have to be mean. I can't bring myself to be civil because every time I do, I end up asking him what went wrong and how I can fix it. As if I'm the one who needs fixing. Okay, maybe the fact that my innards are blubbering fools right now is evidence of that, but I can't let him get to me. So instead, I just act like a bitch. It's the only way to survive this stupid-ass breakup.

I'm snarling at him, yet he smiles.

If my heels weren't digging in the floor, I'd slide off my seat leaving snail trails behind. This man can make me ache down there with just an effing smile. It's a wonder how he can still do that with our long history together. For most people, doesn't that sort of thing fizzle out after a few years?

He doesn't say anything right away, so I utter again, "Well. What is it?"

He ignores my question and says as nonchalant as can be, "Hey, hon, how you been?"

Hon? Really? Un-frickin'-believable.

Raising my right brow, I give him the most disapproving

look I can muster. "Just great, Dear," I sneer with a snap of my neck.

"I haven't seen you during lunch in a while," his voice softens.

"It's too crowded in the staff lounge." Translation: I don't want to see you and your nasty ass girlfriend.

"Aw, come on. You should come down." Translation: making you feel like shit is so much more fun in public.

"I've got a lot of grading to do." Looking down at my desk, I notice just one small stack of papers. Shit. That's what I get for having nothing better to do than grade papers night after night.

He sits on my nearly empty desk. "Well, I hear everybody misses you." He plumps out his bottom lip in a pout. I think my heart just stopped. Is he trying to kill me? Could he be prosecuted for murder? Cause of death: broken heart. Murder weapon: words laced with bullshit. It's me who should be thrown in jail for eating up every one of those words. But, I can't help myself.

Okay, Shel, relax. Keep it cool. Back to bitch mode.

I summon the courage to shout at him, "Shut the hell up and get the fuck out of my room. And don't come back unless it's about work. Even then, don't bother. Just send me an email."

"Shel Belle, don't be that way. I still wanna be friends." Oh no he didn't just pull out the friend card. He needs to shove that crap back from wherever he yanked it from. He's so full of shit, no wonder his skin is so tan.

"Friends, my ass. We've been friends since the second grade, since I kissed you on the cheek on Space Mountain when you were so scared you wanted to cry. I should have just let you piss your pants and never talked to you again and I wouldn't be in this mess." I glare at him with as much pissiness as I can exude. "Fuck friends. I have enough friends. I don't need any more. And I sure as hell don't need you. So get to steppin', Chase." Tears threaten to bubble over the edge of my eyelids but I will them back. I swear to God, if I cry in his presence, I'll kick my own ass.

Chase's chocolate brown eyes glare at me, his nose flares, and I can see the muscles in his jaw twitch, but I don't say another word and my tears don't fall. But his do. He gets up and walks out my door. Before it slams, my heart fails me and tears start streaming down my heated face like a flash flood.

He has no right getting teary-eyed on me. He did this. I didn't break up with him. He can't toss me aside, put me in the junk drawer and come find me when he needs me.

I can't still be his friend. It doesn't work like that. How can we possibly be buddies? Am I supposed to chat with him about the good old days, or go out to dinner with him and what's her face? I don't know how we can go from long-term relationship to friends with everything just peachy. That's bullshit.

The bell rings. Son of a mother lover. I grab for the box of tissues near my computer and blot my already puffy eyes. There's no way I can camouflage this. I just hope my class doesn't say anything. I'll probably cry more.

"Ms. Gelson, are you okay?" Meg, my student aide, asks.

Trying to muffle my sniffling noises, I force myself to respond. "Oh, I'm fine honey. Nothing some chocolate and a little makeup can't fix." I open the bottom drawer to my desk to reveal a rather large bag of Dove dark chocolates. Too bad I can't rig a keg of beer in my desk. Or maybe squeeze a twelve pack in my mini-fridge. I wish. For some reason, I don't think chocolate is going to cure this one.

"I saw Mr. Marino leaving and he looked like crap. Don't worry. It's not gonna last, ya know. My best friend, Keesha, is his aide this year and she says she's rallying for you. She wants him to dump that big assed beeyotch soon. She's so fake with her caked-on makeup and hooker heels. She reminds me of my ex-best friend. You have class, something Ms. McG doesn't. Marino will figure it out." I look at her all wide-eyed, and she says, "Oh, sorry. I shouldn't have said that. I forget you're my teacher."

I can remember comforting her when she was a freshman and found out her best friend was doing the deed with her boyfriend. Can you imagine having to deal with that level of drama when you're fourteen? I wish I could tell her it gets better. But what I want to do is hug her, and say thank you. I knew there was a reason I liked her. I should buy her lunch.

My students fill their desks and immediately get started on the bell-ringer—the assignment I posted on the board. I sense the whispers, but I don't look up. I take attendance, all the while thinking about Chase. I wonder if Ms. McGallian knows about his little lunchtime visit. I doubt she's included in the masses of people who miss me at lunch. If she doesn't know he stopped by, she will by the end of the period. If there's anything I know about my school and my students, it's that information spreads like the plague. Right now, Meg is on her cell texting, and I'd bet a hundred bucks she's telling her friends. I wish I could see Ms. Fiancé-Stealer's face when she finds out her man left my room all weepy.

Let the games begin, bitches!

Against The Wall is the first book in the Against The Wall series. The ebook version is free at all book retailer sites. Visit Julie's website for links.